Client-Server Web Apps with JavaScript and Java

Casimir Saternos

Beijing · Cambridge · Farnham · Köln · Sebastopol · Tokyo

Client-Server Web Apps with JavaScript and Java

by Casimir Saternos

Copyright © 2014 EzGraphs, LLC. All rights reserved.

Printed in the United States of America.

Published by O'Reilly Media, Inc., 1005 Gravenstein Highway North, Sebastopol, CA 95472.

O'Reilly books may be purchased for educational, business, or sales promotional use. Online editions are also available for most titles (*http://my.safaribooksonline.com*). For more information, contact our corporate/institutional sales department: 800-998-9938 or *corporate@oreilly.com*.

Editors: Simon St. Laurent and Allyson MacDonald	**Indexer:** Judith McConville
Production Editor: Kristen Brown	**Cover Designer:** Karen Montgomery
Copyeditor: Gillian McGarvey	**Interior Designer:** David Futato
Proofreader: Amanda Kersey	**Illustrator:** Rebecca Demarest

April 2014:   First Edition

Revision History for the First Edition:

2014-03-27:   First release

See *http://oreilly.com/catalog/errata.csp?isbn=9781449369330* for release details.

Nutshell Handbook, the Nutshell Handbook logo, and the O'Reilly logo are registered trademarks of O'Reilly Media, Inc. *Client-Server Web Apps with JavaScript and Java*, the image of a large Indian civet, and related trade dress are trademarks of O'Reilly Media, Inc.

Many of the designations used by manufacturers and sellers to distinguish their products are claimed as trademarks. Where those designations appear in this book, and O'Reilly Media, Inc. was aware of a trademark claim, the designations have been printed in caps or initial caps.

While every precaution has been taken in the preparation of this book, the publisher and author assume no responsibility for errors or omissions, or for damages resulting from the use of the information contained herein.

ISBN: 978-1-449-36933-0

[LSI]

Table of Contents

Preface

There are only two hard things in Computer
Science: cache invalidation and naming things.

—Phil Karlton

While cache invalidation is not a difficulty encountered when writing a book, choosing a suitable title is. The title of this book is intended to represent a broad area of changes in web development that have resulted in a new approach to designing web applications.

Of course, many aspects of web development can be considered new. Developers scramble to keep up with enhancements to desktop browsers, new mobile device clients, evolving programming languages, the availability of faster processors, and an increasingly discerning audience of users with growing expectations about usability and interactivity. These changes require developers to continually innovate when coming up with solutions for their specific projects. But many of these solutions have broader implications and are not isolated to any particular project.

Therefore, I chose "client-server" as the term which in many ways captures the changes to web development that have occurred in response to these innovations. Other descriptions of modern development practices currently in vogue don't adequately represent the problem domain. Web application development is associated with desktop browsers, but excludes the increasingly relevant area of mobile applications.

The terms Single Page Application and Single Page Interface have been used to distinguish modern web applications from earlier static websites. These terms correctly identify modern sites as far more dynamic and interactive than their predecessors.

However, many modern dynamic applications are made up of multiple pages rather than a single page. The focus in these terms is on the page, the client portion of an application. They make no specific statement about corresponding server-side development. There are JavaScript frameworks that are also associated with highly dynamic pages (such as Angular, Ember, and Backbone), but these are also concerned with the client tier. I wanted the title of this book to encompass more than front-end innovations and to recognize the corresponding server-side design and web service messaging.

The method of communication captured by the popular acronym *REST (Representational State Transfer)* does suggest the web service messaging style. But the definition of REST as specified by its author Roy Fielding is very limiting. On his blog, Fielding lists specific restrictions (*http://bit.ly/1g7Min9*) to REST that are commonly violated in so-called RESTful APIs. And some even question whether a JSON API can be truly RESTful (*http://bit.ly/1lDCAuh*) due to the fact that it does not satisfy all of the constraints associated with the style of architecture. There is a continuum (*http://bit.ly/1fh2AGt*) by which REST services can be described; so that an API can be described as RESTful only to the degree that it adheres to the constraints. REST does include client-server as one of its constraints, and the verb and URL naming conventions are certainly applicable.

So a JavaScript client consuming messages from a pragmatic "RESTful" API is a significant part of the method of development. What about the server component?

Java Enterprise Edition (JEE) includes the JAX-RS API (*http://bit.ly/1bXOKei*), which uses Java's flavor of REST (which is not inherently strict) and is demonstrable using the Jersey reference implementation. But limiting to *JAX-RS web application development* ignores frameworks and alternate JVM language solutions that are available and particularly appealing for quick prototypes.

And so crystallizing the intentions of a book in a simple, catchy title is not an easy task. Fortunately, James Ward (*http://www.jamesward.com*) did a presentation at OSCON 2012 in which he described the development of "Client-Server Web Applications with HTML5 and Java." He listed the benefits of a method of web application development that is increasingly popular, a method that I have been involved with in recent years on various projects. And the phrase "client-server" is the key to understanding what this method is. It captures the fundamental architectural changes that include aspects of the terms listed above, but represents the distinct partitioning between the client and server and considers each of the roles significant.

A client-server architecture of web applications requires a shift (in some cases seismic) in the way programmers work. This book was written to enable developers to deal with this revolution. Specifically, it is intended to provide a proper perspective in building the latest incarnation of modern web applications.

Who Is This Book For?

This book is written for web application developers who are are familiar with the Java programming language, as well as HTML, JavaScript, and CSS. It is geared toward those who "learn by doing" and prefer to see and create specific examples of new technologies and techniques integrated with standard tools. If you want a better understanding of recent developments in JavaScript and how the language and its development process compare with those of Java, this book is for you.

A bit of a balancing act is evident as you read this book. On the one hand, the most important thing you can take away is a sense of the "big picture"—the influences and trends causing a shift in the technologies in use. On the other hand, technologies are often best understood by seeing specific examples. If you are interested in an overview of how these technologies actually fit together, you will benefit from this book.

My goal in writing this is to help you to make informed decisions. Good decisions result in the right technologies being used on new projects. They allow you to avoid pitfalls caused by mixing incompatible technologies or having the wrong expectations about the implications of a given decision. They help you to step into projects in process and better support existing code. In short, informed decisions will make you a more productive programmer. They help you make effective use of your time in researching areas of specific interest in your work now and in the future.

How This Book Is Organized

Chapter 1 provides a general overview of the client-server web application architecture. It discusses the history of web development and provides a justification for the paradigm shift in development. This leads into the next three chapters that will describe the tools used in the development process.

Chapter 2 describes JavaScript and the tools used in JavaScript development.

Chapter 3 introduces web API design, REST, and the tools used when developing RESTful applications over HTTP.

Chapter 4 pertains to Java and other software that's used in the remainder of this book.

The next section of the book discusses higher-level constructs (such as client libraries and application servers) and how these provide separation and allow for rapid development.

Chapter 5 describes major client-side JavaScript frameworks.

Chapter 6 addresses Java API servers and services.

Chapter 7 discusses rapid development practices.

Chapter 8 delves into API design in greater depth.

With an understanding of libraries and a process for speedy development of prototypes, the next several chapters apply these to specific projects using various JVM languages and frameworks. The next two chapters use lightweight web servers and microframeworks instead of traditional Java web application packaging and servers.

Chapter 9 provides an overview of a project using jQuery and Jython.

Chapter 10 documents the development of a project using JRuby and Angular.

The final chapters detail projects using traditional Java web application servers and libraries.

Chapter 11 looks at the range of packaging and deployment options available in the Java ecosystem.

Chapter 12 explores virtualization and innovations emerging from the management of large server environments.

Chapter 13 draws attention to testing and documentation.

Chapter 14 wraps up with some final thoughts on responding to the tumultuous changes to Internet-related technologies and software development.

Appendix A describes how to explore and manipulate Java classes interactively.

Conventions Used in This Book

The following typographical conventions are used in this book:

Italic
> Indicates new terms, URLs, filenames, and file extensions.

`Constant width`
> Used for program listings, as well as within paragraphs to refer to variables, method names, and other code elements, as well as the contents of files.

`Constant width bold`
> Highlights new code in an example.

`Constant width italic`
> Shows text that should be replaced with user-supplied values.

 This element signifies a tip, suggestion, or general note.

 This element indicates a warning or caution.

Code Examples

Projects and code examples in this book are hosted on *https://github.com/java-javascript/client-server-web-apps*. You can view them online or download a *.zip* file for local use. The assets are organized by chapter.

The code examples provided in this book are geared toward illustrating specific functionality rather than addressing all concerns of a fully functional application. Differences include:

- Production systems include greater refinement of selected data types, validation rules, exception handing routines, and logging mechanisms.

- Most production systems will include one or more backend datastores. To limit the scope of discussion, databases are not accessed in most of the examples.

- The modern web application includes a large amount of infrastructure geared toward mobile device access and browser compatibility. Again, unless these are the specific topic of discussion, responsive (*http://bit.ly/1hcCHOX*) design is eschewed for a more minimal design.

- The practice of some degree of unobtrusive JavaScript (*http://bit.ly/1guPBTM*) to separate CSS and JavaScript from HTML is a generally accepted best practice. In the examples in this book, they are frequently commingled because all aspects of a given application can be immediately apprised by viewing a single file.

- Unit tests and testing examples are only included when they are directly related to the topic under discussion. Production systems would include far greater test coverage and extensive testing in general.

That said, this book is intended to help you get your job done. In general, you may use the code in this book in your programs and documentation. You do not need to contact us for permission unless you are reproducing a significant portion of the code. For example, writing a program that uses several sections of code from this book does not require permission. Selling or distributing a CD-ROM of examples from O'Reilly books does require permission. Answering a question by citing this book and quoting example code does not require permission. Incorporating a significant amount of example code from this book into your product's documentation does require permission.

We appreciate, but do not require, attribution. An attribution usually includes the title, author, publisher, and ISBN. For example: "*Client-Server Web Apps with JavaScript and Java*" by Casimir Saternos (O'Reilly). Copyright 2014 EzGraphs, LLC., 978-1-449-36933-0."

If you feel your use of code examples falls outside fair use or the permission given here, feel free to contact us at *permissions@oreilly.com*.

Long Command Formats

Code displayed inline will be adjusted to be readable in this context. One convention used is that of backslashes to allow newlines in operating system commands. So for instance, the following commands are equivalent and would execute the same way in a bash session. (Bash is a standard operating system shell that you see when accessing a Linux server or Mac OS X at the command line.)

```
ls -l *someVeryLongName*
...
ls -l \
*someVeryLongName*
```

The same convention also appears in other settings where OS commands are used, such as Dockerfiles.

Similarly, JSON strings, being valid JavaScript, can be broken up to fit on multiple lines:

```
o={"name": "really long string here and includes many words"}

// The following, as expected, evaluates to true.
JSON.stringify(o)=='{"name":"really long string here and includes many words"}'

// The same string broken into multiple lines is equivalent.
// So the following statement also evaluates to true.
JSON.stringify(o)=='{"name":' +
                   '"some really long ' +
                   'JSON string is here' +
                   ' and includes many, many words"}'
```

Safari® Books Online

 Safari Books Online is an on-demand digital library that delivers expert content in both book and video form from the world's leading authors in technology and business.

Technology professionals, software developers, web designers, and business and creative professionals use Safari Books Online as their primary resource for research, problem solving, learning, and certification training.

Safari Books Online offers a range of product mixes and pricing programs for organizations, government agencies, and individuals. Subscribers have access to thousands of books, training videos, and prepublication manuscripts in one fully searchable database from publishers like O'Reilly Media, Prentice Hall Professional, Addison-Wesley Professional, Microsoft Press, Sams, Que, Peachpit Press, Focal Press, Cisco Press, John Wiley & Sons, Syngress, Morgan Kaufmann, IBM Redbooks, Packt, Adobe Press, FT Press, Apress, Manning, New Riders, McGraw-Hill, Jones & Bartlett, Course Technology, and dozens more. For more information about Safari Books Online, please visit us online.

How to Contact Us

Every example in this book has been tested, but occasionally you may encounter problems. Mistakes and oversights can occur and we will gratefully receive details of any that you find, as well as any suggestions you would like to make for future editions. Please address comments and questions concerning this book to the publisher:

O'Reilly Media, Inc.
1005 Gravenstein Highway North
Sebastopol, CA 95472
800-998-9938 (in the United States or Canada)
707-829-0515 (international or local)
707-829-0104 (fax)

We have a web page for this book, where we list errata, examples, and any additional information. You can access this page at *http://oreil.ly/client-server-web-apps-js*.

To comment or ask technical questions about this book, send email to *bookquestions@oreilly.com*.

For more information about our books, courses, conferences, and news, see our website at *http://www.oreilly.com*.

Find us on Facebook: *http://facebook.com/oreilly*

Follow us on Twitter: *http://twitter.com/oreillymedia*

Watch us on YouTube: *http://www.youtube.com/oreillymedia*

Acknowledgments

Thank you to the following people:

- Meg, Ally, Simon, and the gang at O'Reilly for the opportunity to write this book.
- My brother Neal Saternos and Dr. James Femister for the early suggestions from days gone by that I might be able to do the "programming thing."
- Michael Bellomo, Don Deasey, and Scott Miller for their time and expertise as technical reviewers.
- Charles Leo Saternos for taking a break from Lua game development to do some fine image and design work.
- Caleb Lewis Saternos for inspiration in perserverence (early morning run anyone?) and editorial work.
- David Amidon for the first opportunity to work as a software developer and Doug Pelletier for first the opportunity to develop Java web apps.

- All the folks that headed up the projects that inspired this book, including managers Wayne Hefner, Tony Powell, Dave Berry, Jay Colson, and Pat Doran, and chief software architects Eric Fedok and Michael Bellomo.

- Geoffrey Grosenbach from PluralSight (*http://pluralsight.com/training*), Nat Dunn from Webucator (*http://www.webucator.com*), Caroline Kvitka (and others from Oracle and *Java Magazine*) for technical writing opportunities over the past several years that led to the current one.

- My parents Leo and Clara Saternos for bringing me up in a loving household that included a Radio Shack Color Computer when having a PC at home was still a novelty and my sister Lori for reminders of important things that have nothing to do with programming.

My love and thanks to my wonderful wife Christina and children Clara Jean, Charles Leo, Caleb Lewis, and Charlotte Olivia for the consistent love, support, patience, and inspiration while this project was underway.

Finally, J.S. Bach serves as a creative inspiration on many levels. Not the least of which is the dedication that would appear at the beginning of his works—and so I say with him, Soli Deo Gloria (*http://bit.ly/1fZijLH*).

Change Begets Change

*The entrepreneur always searches for a change,
responds to it, and exploits it as an opportunity.*

—Peter Drucker

What kinds of changes encourage developers to adopt a client-server approach? Shifts in user behavior, technology, and software development process are the significant forces that have driven developers to change their patterns of design. Each of these factors, in a unique and significant way, makes established patterns obsolete. Together they have encouraged related innovations and a convergence in practice despite the absence of enforcement or mandated standardization.

Web users have changed. In the early days of the Web, users were satisfied with static pages and primitive user interfaces. The modern web user has come to expect a high-performance, interactive, well-designed, dynamic experience. These higher expectations were met with an explosion in new technologies and expansion of web browser capabilities. Today's web developer needs to use tools and a development approach that are aligned with the modern web scene.

Technology has changed. Browsers and JavaScript engines are faster. Workstations and laptops are far more powerful, to say nothing of the plethora of mobile devices now being used to surf the Web. Web service APIs are the expectation for a modern web application rather than a rare additional feature. Cloud computing is revolutionizing the deployment and operation of web applications.

Software development has changed. The now popular "Agile Manifesto" values:

- Individuals and interactions over processes and tools
- Working software over comprehensive documentation
- Customer collaboration over contract negotiation
- Responding to change over following a plan

It is now possible to quickly spin up web applications that prove—at least on a small scale—the viability of a given technology. There is tremendous value to prototyping. As Fred Brooks, author of *The Mythical Man Month* (Addison-Wesley Professional), famously stated: "Plan to throw one away; you will, anyhow." A prototype can allow for early customer or end user interaction that helps solidify requirements early in the process. It is no longer an insurmountable task to write a functional web application in a matter of minutes.

Web Users

Modern web application users have well-defined expectations about how they will be able to interact with a web application:

- Web applications will be available across *multiple platforms.*
- They will provide a *consistent experience across devices.*
- They will respond with *little or no latency.*

The Gartner group (*http://gtnr.it/1omcPRg*) claims that in 2014, the personal cloud will replace the PC at the center of users' digital lives. There are many implications for web app development. Users are more technologically savvy and have high expectations for site responsiveness. They are less passive than in previous years and instead are interactive and engaged. Websites need to be designed in a way that suggests no limitations in the ability of a browser to mimic native application experience.

Users expect an application to be exposed in various ways and available in different situations. Responsive design and support for multiple browsers, platforms, and devices are the new norm. The use of JavaScript libraries and frameworks is essential to support the wide variety of target clients.

The *New York Times* recently reported on the impatience of web users (*http://nyti.ms/1esukXm*). Among its findings: a company's website will be visited less often than that of a close competitor if it is slower by more than 250 milliseconds. Performance needs to be a key consideration in web application development.

Technology

Java web application developers are typically familiar with server-side dynamic content. J2EE and JSP have been refined into JEE and JSF. Projects such as Spring provide additional capabilities geared toward server-side development. This mode of development made a great deal of sense in the early days of the Web, when web pages were relatively static, servers were relatively fast, JavaScript engines were slow, and there were few libraries and techniques to address browser incompatibilities.

By way of contrast, a modern client-server approach involves a server largely responsible for providing access to resources (typically communicated as messages in XML or JSON) in response to client requests. In the old server-driven approach, the browser requested an entire page and it was generated (along with relevant data) for rendering in the browser. In the client-server approach, the server initially serves pages with little data. The pages make asynchronous requests to the server as the user interacts with it and the server simply responds to these events with messages that cause the current page to be updated.

Initial web development efforts consisted of the creation of static HTML sites. Later, these sites were augmented with dynamic content using server-side processing (CGI, Java Servlets). Subsequently, more structured language integration emerged using server-side templating (ASP, PHP, JSP) and MVC frameworks. More recent technologies continue in the same tradition and provide additional abstractions of one sort or another.

Based upon a desire to shield developers from design concerns and the underlying architecture of the Web, component-based frameworks have emerged. Tag libraries were an early innovation, and now a component-based approach has been widely adopted in several popular frameworks:

- Java Server Faces (JSF), an XML-based templating system and component framework with centralized configurable navigation.
- The Google Web Toolkit is another component framework that leverages the abilities of Java programmers by letting them focus on Java coding with little need to directly modify HTML, CSS, or JavaScript.

Each of these frameworks has its place and has been used successfully in production systems. But like many solutions that try to hide underlying complexities, their usage is problematic in situations where you need greater control (such as the ability to integrate large amounts of JavaScript) or you do not conform to the framework assumptions (for instance, availability of server sessions). This is because these solutions attempt to hide the fundamental architecture of the Web, which uses an HTTP request-response protocol following the client-server computing model.

Browser innovations also led to a shift of responsibility from the server to the client. In the late 1990s, Microsoft developed the underlying technologies that led to Ajax (a term coined on February 18, 2005 by Jesse James Garrett). *Ajax* is an acronym for "asynchronous JavaScript and XML," but is more generally applied to various technologies used to communicate with the server within the context of a given web page. This allowed small messages to be sent, which made better use of bandwidth when designing JavaScript-based web applications. Browser performance has increased significantly due to processor improvements and optimizations to JavaScript engines, so it has made sense to offload more work from the server to the browser. User interface responsiveness has evolved to a new level of sophistication.

Mobile device browsers have also provided an additional incentive to further isolate client-side code from the server. In some cases, a well-designed application leveraging responsive design principles can be created. If this is not an option, a single consistent API available for all device clients is very appealing.

Roy Fielding's doctoral dissertation in 2000 led Java EE 6 to new APIs that deviated from the previous component-based trajectory. JAX-RS (Java API for RESTful Web Services) and Jersey (a "production quality reference implementation") are designed to create applications reflecting a client-server architecture with RESTful communications.

Software Development

In the past, setting up a new Java project was a rather monumental task. A vast array of configuration options made it tedious and error-prone. Very little was automated, as the assumption was that each project would have unique characteristics that developers would want to account for to meet their specific requirements.

Later influences led to innovations that made setting up a project much simpler. "Convention over configuration" was an influential mantra of the Ruby on Rails community. Maven (*http://bit.ly/MLOLbU*) and other Java projects also chose sensible defaults and target easy setup for a subset of popular use cases.

The availability of scripting languages on the JVM makes it possible to speed development by bypassing the somewhat rigorous type checking of Java. Languages like Groovy, Python (Jython), and Ruby are loosely typed and constructed in a manner that requires less code to accomplish equivalent functionality. So-called microframeworks like Sinatra or Play provide minimal *Domain Specific Languages* (DSLs) to quickly write web applications and services. And so today, it is a trivial task to set up a minimal set of web services in a development environment.

The failure of enough large-scale waterfall-style software projects has also made it clear that there are many advantages to producing a small-scale version of the final product. A prototype (or prototypes) of the final product can serve many purposes:

- Verify technical foundation of the project
- Create constructs that bridge disparate technologies to be used together
- Allow end user interaction to clarify intended usage and user interface design
- Allow system designers to clarify the interfaces and data structures to be passed between systems
- Allow programmers to work on different parts of the application in parallel

Prototypes have numerous benefits:

- They are a specific, tangible asset representing the final system to be designed. As such, they incorporate information that is otherwise stored in design documents, diagrams, and other artifacts (and frequently in more informal locations like email and people's memories of water-cooler conversations).
- Prototypes are concrete implementations. As such, they present the requirements in a much more tangible form. This can lead to a better understanding of the extent and quality of the requirements gathered, and can suggest areas where there is need of clarification.
- Prototypes can immediately expose potential points of failure that are not apparent before attempting a specific implementation.
- The preceding benefits can lead to better estimates and scheduling due to a more comprehensive understanding of what is intended.

Prototyping can be leveraged extensively in client-server web application development because of the clear and unambiguous separation between the client and server. Prototypes of the server can be provided to the client developers (and vice versa) while development proceeds in parallel. Or if development is not proceeding in parallel, server-side calls can be quickly stubbed out so that client-side code can be developed.

What Has Not Changed

The fundamental nature of the Web (a client-server architecture transmitted over HTTP) has not changed.

New technology does not change everything. High-level programming languages have not removed the need to understand operating system specifics. Object-relational mapping frameworks have not removed the need to understand relational databases and SQL. In like manner, there have been consistent attempts to ignore the underlying architecture of the Web in an effort to emulate the experience of desktop applications.

Medium Specificity

Medium specificity is a term that appears in aesthetics and modern art criticism but which can be applied to technology as well. It indicates the "appropriateness" of a given artistic subject to be presented by a given medium. The idea has been around for centuries. Gotthold Ephraim Lessing states in his Lacoon:

> [B]odies, with their visible properties, are the legitimate subjects of painting. [A]ctions are [therefore] the legitimate subjects of poetry.
>
> — *The Limits of Poetry and Painting*

Its application in modern art is usually to challenge traditional limits that appeared in the arts. Technology is a creative activity, but our primary concern is working systems, not abstract beauty. The idea of medium specificity is important in that, *if you ignore the underlying nature of a platform, the resulting system will never perform in an optimal manner or will not work at all.* This has become painfully obvious in many areas of technology. The goal of this book is to promote web application design strategies that are aligned with the way the Web itself is designed. Such applications operate well because they work within the Web's fundamental constraints rather than ignoring them.

The Nature of the Web

The essence of the Web has not changed. It is still made up of servers that serve HTML documents to clients via the HTTP protocol. See Figure 1-1.

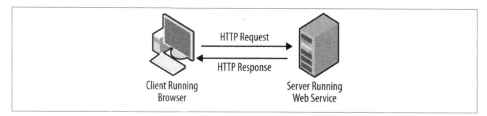

Figure 1-1. HTTP request and response

A client-server web architecture more closely maps to the underlying architecture of the Web itself. Although not technically protocol-specific, REST was developed based upon and in conjunction with HTTP. REST essentially defines constraints on the usage of HTTP. It seeks to describe a well-designed web application: a reliable application that performs well, scales, has a simple elegant design, and can be easily modified (Figure 1-2).

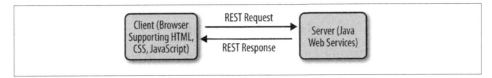

Figure 1-2. REST request and response

In fact, to more accurately emphasize the challenges in the modern web environment, we need to consider multiple devices and cloud deployments. See Figure 1-3.

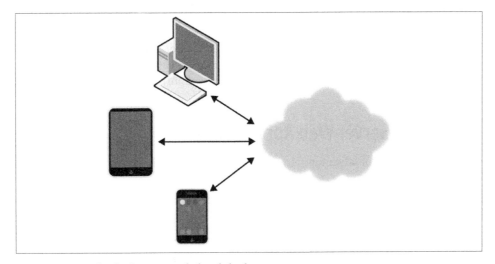

Figure 1-3. Multiple devices and cloud deployments

The specific area of "medium specificity" that has been ignored in web development in general (and in component frameworks in particular) is the stateless, client-server nature of the Web itself.

Server-Driven Web Development Considered Harmful

Just because a given feature is available does not mean that it should be used. In many cases, a server-driven, component-based approach to web development should be replaced with a client-server one. Server-driven approaches obscure the nature of the Web itself, which is a client-server technology built on the HTTP protocol. Ignoring or obscuring the fundamental underlying architecture of the Web makes development, debugging, and support of software systems more difficult. The intention, to make the Web somehow simpler or easier to understand, breaks down rather quickly in any nontrivial system where there needs to be a clear understanding what functionality is available and how the system actually works.

Considered Harmful

In 1968, Edsger W. Dijkstra published a letter entitled "Go To Statement Considered Harmful." Besides being of interest because it made a considerable impact on reducing the use of the goto statement in structured programming, it introduced the phrase "considered harmful" into hacker culture. Tom Christiansen argued against programming in csh (*http://bit.ly/1lEk8S9*). Douglas Crawford published a blog post entitled "with Statement Considered Harmful" (*http://bit.ly/1kCBW1U*). The phrase has appeared in many other settings as well, and despite the amusingly self-referential "'Considered Harmful' Essays Considered Harmful" (*http://bit.ly/1lEk4C1*) by Eric A. Meyer, the phrase continues to appear.

Although "Considered Harmful" attention articles are not always of equal merit, the theme arises out of a valid recognition that just because a language feature or technical solution is available, does not mean it is a great general purpose, long-term solution.

Why Client-Server Web Applications?

There are a number of advantages to a client-server approach to web development.

Code Organization/Software Architecture

There are clear advantages to being able to decouple logical sections of code and promote higher cohesion both in the original construction and ongoing support of any system. The clear separation between client and server tiers makes for manageable, modular sections of code. In addition, data and display markup can be more clearly separated. The data can be delivered in JSON rather than inline. This is consistent with the modern JavaScript notion of *unobtrusive JavaScript* where a page's behavior, structure, and presentation are separated.

Flexibility and code reuse are a logical outcome of good code organization. There is flexibility at many stages in the application life cycle when sections of code can be developed in relative isolation (APIs can be exposed, mobile device clients created, new versions of sections of the application tested and released independently). Code reuse is more likely when there are clear components. At minimum, the same RESTful APIs can be used to serve data to a wide variety of browsers and mobile devices.

Component approaches tend to introduce brittle coupling and are less adaptable. There is no way to plug in a different frontend easily.

Flexibility of Design/Use of Open Source APIs

Component-based approaches include tightly integrated server-side code that requires specific JavaScript technology. They also generate HTML and CSS that limits the options available from a design and behavior perspective. A distinct client running JavaScript can take advantage of the latest libraries that ease browser compatibility, standardize DOM manipulation, and provide complex widgets.

Prototyping

Prototyping works well with client-server web applications due to the clear separation between tiers. As previously mentioned, prototypes can test and verify initial ideals. They help clarify vague notions and facilitate clear communication regarding requirements. They can inspire and generate new ideas as people interact with something more concrete than a long text description or a series of pictures. Bad ideas and inconsistencies can be quickly recognized and eliminated. Used correctly, prototypes can save time, money, and resources and result in a better final product.

Developer Productivity

Besides the ability to prototype either the client portion or the server component (or both), work can be split clearly, and development can progress in parallel. The separation allows sections of code to be built in isolation. This prevents the problem in component approaches where a server build is required every time a page is changed during development. Development tasks require less time and effort, changes are less complex, and troubleshooting is simplified.

This is especially evident when a need arises to replace, upgrade, or relocate server-side code. Such changes can be done independently, without affecting the client. The only limitation is that the original interface, specifically the URL and message data structure, must remain available.

Application Performance

User experience is greatly impacted by the perceived performance of a page in the browser. Faster JavaScript engines allow the client to perform computationally intensive operations so server workload can be effectively offloaded to the client. Ajax requires relatively small amounts of data to be retrieved when needed so full page reloads can occur infrequently and less data is sent in the intervening requests. Users perceive a snappier, more immediate response as they interact with an application.

There are many benefits to stateless design that ease the lives of developers and support staff. Resources dedicated to session management can be freed up. This simplifies load-balancing and configuration that would otherwise be required. Servers can be easily added to accommodate increased load allowing for *horizontal scalability*. This replaces the unwieldy process of hardware upgrades traditionally used to increase throughput and performance.

The benefits even extend to the simplification of the overall architecture of a system. For instance, problems related to maintaining state are extremely challenging in a cloud-based environment. When using traditional stateful sessions, it is challenging to efficiently persist data so that it is readily available across multiple requests within a user's session. If data is stored on a backend server, subsequent requests directed to different servers will not have access to it. Possible solutions include:

- Use an application server that supports clustering and failover. Weblogic uses the concept of managed servers, for instance. These solutions require additional management and vary in each application server implementation.

- Use session affinity or *sticky sessions*. In this scenario, all requests within a user session are sent to the same backend server. This does not provide automatic failover.

- Utilize a separate centralized data store. Typically this involves persisting data in a database. This option may not provide the best performance.

- Store the data on the client side. This avoids the performance problems associated with storing session data in a database as well as the failover issues with sticky sessions. This is because any backend server can handle each client's request.

The move toward avoiding server-side state management is becoming more prevalent. Even a framework like JSF, which is designed for the traditional server-side management of user sessions, is adding features to allow for stateless functionality.

There are a few inherent challenges with creating client-server applications. It is necessary to embrace JavaScript as a first-class development language in its own right. This means learning the language in some depth, utilizing available libraries, and adopting mature development techniques. Areas of application architecture that were previously generally accepted require a different design, such as standard practices regarding session management. There is no carefully defined standard for client-server web applications. Certain parts of JEE, such as JAX-RS, provide some clarification; others such as JSF do not apply.

Beyond the initial learning (and unlearning) curve, a client-server approach for building web applications is extremely effective and stable. The clear separation of responsibilities between client and server allow for easy modification extension to a code base. A recognition of the essential nature of the Web reduces problems that result from attempting to obscure its design. The capacity for horizontal scalability far exceeds what is possible using other patterns of design.

Conclusion

New challenges and developments afford new opportunities. A client-server web application design is a natural response that recognizes and accounts for the changes to the Web and web development. And it does so in a way that recognizes what has not changed, and so can allow for development of stable, enduring solutions that are well-positioned for future enhancements.

## CHAPTER 2

JavaScript and JavaScript Tools

*JavaScript is most despised because it isn't SOME OTHER LANGUAGE.
If you are good in SOME OTHER LANGUAGE and you have to program
in an environment that only supports JavaScript, then you are forced to
use JavaScript, and that is annoying. Most people in that situation don't
even bother to learn JavaScript first, and then they are surprised when
JavaScript turns out to have significant differences from the SOME
OTHER LANGUAGE they would rather be using, and that
those differences matter.*

—Douglas Crockford

Thus Douglas Crockford summarizes JavaScript as the language that many use but few learn. His book goes on to identify parts of the language that are legitimately useful and powerful and points out others that are truly problematic and best avoided. If you are a programmer required to extensively use JavaScript, it simply makes sense to take the time and energy to study it thoroughly. Crockford's approach makes the programmer's learning task more manageable by effectively ignoring large parts of the language and focusing on a powerful and concise subset.

In addition to learning JavaScript itself (later standardized under the name ECMA-Script), you need to invest time learning about the specific programming environment. While other languages run on underlying operating systems, relational databases, or host applications, JavaScript was designed originally to run in a browser. The ECMA-Script Language Specification (*http://bit.ly/1m9b0IQ*) explicitly states this.

> ECMAScript was originally designed to be a Web scripting language, providing a mechanism to enliven Web pages in browsers and to perform server computation as part of a Web-based client-server architecture.
>
> — ECMAScript Language Specification

The core JavaScript language needs to be understood in relation to two distinct APIs: the *Browser Object Model* (BOM) and the *Document Object Model* (DOM). The BOM consists of a window and its child objects: navigator, history, screen, location, and document. The document object is the root node of the DOM, a hierarchical tree representation of the contents of the page itself. Some of the complaints about JavaScript are actually due to issues with BOM or DOM implementations. Development of JavaScript in a web browser cannot be done effectively without a thorough understanding of these APIs.

The remainder of this chapter will introduce the main topics that need to be understood in a browser JavaScript development. It will not be exhaustive or comprehensive, but will highlight the necessary starting points and categories that you need to understand in order to develop an in-depth understanding of the language.

Learning JavaScript

The Java language has been widely adopted in educational settings. Developer certifications have been available for a number of years. There is therefore a well-understood, standardized, general, common body of knowledge associated with Java. Java is often learned first in the classroom, and professionals obtain certification after a fairly defined program of self-study. The same cannot be said of JavaScript, but there are a number of good books on JavaScript:

- *JavaScript: The Good Parts* (O'Reilly), by Douglas Crockford, has been mentioned already. It has become fashionable in some circles to take issue with Crockford at various points, but that is because he is a recognized authority who has helped shape the thinking of many JavaScript developers. In some cases, he provides arguably overly strict "rules of thumb," but you will do yourself a great disservice if you don't understand the subset of the language he considers "the good parts" and the parts he avoids.

- *Secrets of the JavaScript Ninja* (Manning Publications) is by John Resig and Bear Bibeault. John Resig is the author of jQuery and as such has a broad understanding of practical challenges related to browser compatibility and DOM implementations.

- Several books are closer to standard language reference texts, including *JavaScript: The Definitive Guide* (O'Reilly) and *Professional JavaScript for Web Development* by Nicholas C. Zakas (Wrox Press). These are more comprehensive (and less opinionated) than the previous two books. They may not be the type of book you would read end to end, but they are invaluable for delving into specific topics.

This section will not attempt to replicate all that you can learn from these and other books, but will provide starting points for you to evaluate your own knowledge of JavaScript. Additional books and resources will be referenced throughout the chapter that you can consult if you encounter terms or concepts you want to research further.

Conscious Competence

A crucial step in the learning process is to be aware of what you know relative to what can be known. There is a documented cognitive bias known as the Dunning–Kruger effect (*http://bit.ly/1aL7dbt*). It describes a tendency for unskilled individuals to mistakenly rate their ability as much higher than average. Because of the confusion related to JavaScript and the frequency with which it is dismissed as a "toy language," the goal of this section (related to the "conscious competence" learning model (*http://bit.ly/MLPda0*)) is to raise awareness of what there is to learn.

JavaScript History

The history of JavaScript is well documented, originating with Brendan Eich writing the initial version in 10 days in 1995 (*http://bit.ly/1dIR7hF*). But it is instructive to consider JavaScript in light of earlier computer science history, especially in relation to Lisp, the second-oldest high-level programming language in existence. Lisp was invented by John McCarthy in 1958 (one year after Fortran) as a practical mathematical notation for computer programs. Scheme is one of the two main dialects of Lisp. Strangely enough, Scheme plays a significant part in JavaScript's history despite being a stark contrast in language design. Figure 2-1 illustrates some of the significant programming languages that influenced the design of JavaScript.

The simple, minimalist design philosophy of Scheme is not at all evident in JavaScript. Its relative verbosity is based in influences from other languages cited in the JavaScript 1.1 Specification (*http://bit.ly/1aVTmmX*):

> JavaScript borrows most of its syntax from Java, but also inherits from Awk and Perl, with some indirect influence from Self in its object prototype system.
>
> — JavaScript 1.1 Specification

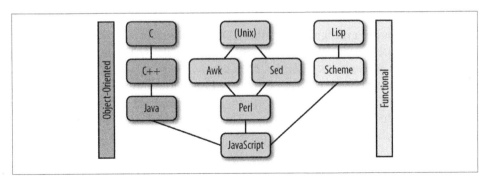

Figure 2-1. JavaScript syntax influences

This is quite a contrast to Scheme, which does not have several different languages informing its syntax. Perl directly influenced parts of JavaScript, such as regular expressions support. Perhaps the Perl motto TMTOWTDI ("there's more than one way to do it") (*http://bit.ly/1bNrmwX*) influenced JavaScript in a broader way as well. At least it can be said that the converse, "there's only one way to do it" (popular among the Python community) does not apply. Consider the variations available to create and initialize an array:

```
var colors1 = [];
colors1[0]  = "red";
colors1[1]  = "orange";

var colors2 = ["yellow", "green", "blue"];

var colors3 = new Array(2);
colors3[0]  = "indigo";
colors3[1]  = "violet";

var colors4 = new Array();
colors4[0]  = "black";
colors4[1]  = "white";
```

Therefore, it might appear that any connection between JavaScript (with its many influences and syntactical variations) and Scheme (a minimalistic dialect of Lisp) seems unlikely. As it turns out, JavaScript's heritage does include close connections with and direct influences from Scheme (*http://brendaneich.com/tag/history*):

> As I've often said, and as others at Netscape can confirm, I was recruited to Netscape with the promise of "doing Scheme in the browser."
>
> — Brendan Eich

This is also reflected in the ECMAScript Language Specification (*http://bit.ly/1m9b0IQ*):

> Some of the facilities of ECMAScript are similar to those used in other programming languages; in particular Java, Self, and Scheme.
>
> — ECMAScript Language Specification

The influence has been recognized by others. Douglas Crockford wrote the "The Little JavaScripter" (*http://bit.ly/NDmRzU*) based on the classic by Daniel Paul Friedman called *The Little Schemer* (*http://bit.ly/1bNrxZ5*) (MIT Press), which illustrates commonalities between Scheme and JavaScript. The Lisp community itself (as represented by the European Lisp Symposium (*http://www.european-lisp-symposium.org*)) describes ECMAScript as a "dialect of Lisp." There are undeniable similarities between JavaScript and Scheme that are due to the intentions of its creator.

A Functional Language

Java developers tend to approach programming problems from an object-oriented perspective. Although JavaScript can support object-oriented programming of a sort, it is generally not the most productive way to approach problems. It is far more productive to leverage JavaScript's functional capabilities. An understanding of what this means and its implications clarifies the nature and power of the language.

The primary trait of JavaScript that makes it like Scheme, as it relates to both its origin and syntax, is that is in a *functional language*. Functional language here is used to indicate a language that supports functional programming (*http://bit.ly/1eUS2QP*) and first-class functions (*http://bit.ly/1nuHp81*). This fundamental concept of JavaScript provides an orientation about other aspects of the language. Adoption of functional programming entails a significant paradigm shift for many programmers, especially those grounded in a language like Java that does not (yet) directly support it.[1]

Scope

Scope, the portion of a program in which a variable is visible and operative is a rather slippery subject as implemented in JavaScript. Like many other languages, a function is used to enclose a set of statements. This allows functions to be reused and limits the visibility of information to a well-understood modular unit. There are three execution contexts defined in the ECMAScript Language Specification (*http://bit.ly/1m9b0IQ*): global, eval, and function. JavaScript has function-level scope rather than block-level scope like other C-like languages. Blocks such as those used by if statements and other language constructs do *not* create a new scope.

One danger in JavaScript is that a method or variable might be *hoisted* or moved to top of scope where it is defined. Since a function declaration is already available at the moment of the scope's execution, the function appears to be *hoisted* to the top of the context. A rule of thumb to avoid the issue is to use a single var statement at the top scope to declare all variables that will be needed within that scope:

```
//this is not like an instance variable in java...
var x = 'set';

var y = function () {

// WHAT YOU DON'T SEE -> var x; is effectively "hoisted" to this line!
```

---

1. Functional programming has been available for some time on the JVM via scripting language support in several languages, including the *Rhino* JavaScript implementation. Lambda expressions for the Java programming language are slated for Java 8 and will add closures and related features to the language. Java 8 will also add support for a new JavaScript implementation known as *Nashorn*. So based on the features being added to the language, JavaScript development in general and functional programming in particular will be areas that Java developers will be expected to understand to a greater degree in coming years.

```
    if (!x) {  // You might expect the variable to be
               // populated at this point...it is not
               // though, so this block executes
        var x = 'hoisted';
    }

    alert(x);
}

//... and this call causes an alert to display "hoisted"
y();
```

The hoisting example includes a few other features that do not exist in Java:

- In JavaScript, `null`, `undefined`, and a few other values evaluate to `false`.

- The `if` conditional expression is `!x`. The exclamation point is a NOT logical operator. Therefore, if x is undefined (or null), this expression `if (!x)` evaluates to `true`. If x had contained a value such as a number or a string at this point, it would have evaluated to `false`, which is what a developer from another language is likely to expect.

- The `var` keyword is used to define a local variable. Variables declared without it are global. This definition results in the variable being associated with the scope of the function.

- A function is being created and assigned to a variable named y. This is particularly strange to Java programmers who deal with methods that only exist attached to a class or object instance. This syntax calls attention to the functional nature of JavaScript.

First-Class Functions

Simply having scope-limiting functions available in a language does not make it a "functional" language in any strict sense. A functional language supports first-class functions. According to the Structure and Interpretation of Computer Programs (*http://bit.ly/MLQA8I*), first-class functions can be named as variables, passed in and returned as results of functions, and included in data structures. The following (contrived) example illustrates these features as well as another characteristic that some researchers cite as a requirement for functional languages: support for anonymous functions:

```
//
// The following example can be run in a
// modern browser at the JavaScript console
//

// Assigning a function to a variable
```

```
var happy = function(){
    return ':)';
}

var sad = function(){
    return ':(';
}

// A function that will be used to receive a
// function as an argument and return it as well.
var mood = function(aFunction){
        return aFunction
}

// Functions added to data structures, arrays:
list = [happy, sad]

//...JavaScript objects
response = {fine: happy, underTheWeather: sad}


// A function can be passed in as an argument,
// returned as a result of a function call
// and assigned to a variable
var iAmFeeling = mood(happy);
console.log(iAmFeeling());

// Try it again
var iAmFeeling = mood(sad);
console.log(iAmFeeling());

// A function can also be included in data structures;
// in this case, a JavaScript object.

console.log(response.fine());

// - or if you prefer an array...
console.log(list[0]());

// Finally, an immediate, anonymous function.
console.log(function(){
        return ";)";
}());
```

So as is apparent from this example, functions are fundamental units in JavaScript and are in fact "first-class." They can stand alone and are not required to be included in an object or other construct. They can appear anywhere an expression can. The property that distinguishes a function from other types of JavaScript objects is the fact that it can be invoked. Terse, compact code can be written because functions are first class and primary modular units of execution. The fact that scope is related to functions has implications for JavaScript idioms that are unfamiliar to many new JavaScript developers.

Is JavaScript Really Functional?

Some question whether JavaScript qualifies as a functional language. After all, functional programming is supposed to mimic mathematical functions, which are free of side effects. Anyone who worked with JavaScript has dealt with its notorious global context, and most likely encountered side-effect-laden functions when wrangling the DOM. This hardly qualifies as referential transparency. On the contrary, much JavaScript programming involves an acute awareness of the surrounding environment. Besides, variables are, well, *variable*. Purely functional languages utilize immutable variables (which provide various benefits such as ease in implementing concurrent operations).

In addition, JavaScript does have objects and prototypical inheritance. It could arguably be classified as object oriented or at least multiparadigm.

What is beyond argument is that JavaScript does indeed include functional constructs and supports first-class functions. So you can choose a definition for "functional language" (since there does not appear to be an authoritative definition) and make up your mind whether JavaScript qualifies in a theoretical sense for this designation. The reason for using it in this book is that it aligns JavaScript with languages and techniques that highlight the features and best qualities of the language. For a much more in-depth look at the language from this perspective, see *Functional JavaScript* by Michael Fogus (O'Reilly) which introduces a wide range of functional techniques implemented in JavaScript, many using the excellent underscore.js library (*http://underscorejs.org*).

Function Declarations and Expressions

A JavaScript function literal consists of four parts:

- The function operator
- An optional name
- Open and close parentheses (optionally containing one or more parameter names)
- Open and close brackets (optionally containing one or more statements)

A valid minimal JavaScript *function declaration* statement is as follows:

```
function(){}
```

A function can also be given a name, which leads to a style that looks a bit more like traditional C-language family syntax:

```
function myFunctionName(){}
```

If a function does not have a name, it is said to be anonymous. An *anonymous function* can be used in an expression and assigned to a variable. Some authors prefer this syntax to declaring a named function because it makes it clear that a variable contains a function value:

```
var x = function () {}
```

It is also possible to assign a named function to a variable:

```
var x = function y() {}
```

The practical use of this named function expression is that while the function is available from the outside through the variable x, it is also available from inside the function itself (in a recursive call) as y.

Functions can be attached to objects and then are referred to as *methods*. A method is implicitly passed the object that called it. It can access and manipulate data that is contained within the object. The object is referred to using the this keyword as illustrated here:

```
var obj = {};  // Create a new JavaScript object
obj.myVar = 'data associated with an object'
obj.myFunc= function(){return 'I can access ' + this.myVar;}  // this: the object
console.log(obj.myFunc())
```

A function can be defined inside of another function, where it also can access variables of the function that encloses it. A *closure* occurs when a function returns an inner function. The returned object includes the function itself as well as its environment when it was created:

```
function outer() {
  var val = "I am in outer space";
  function inner() {
    return val;
  }
  return inner;
}

var alien = outer();
console.log(alien());
```

An *immediate function* is a way to limit code to a local functions scope so as to avoid polluting the global scope:

```
(function() {console.log('in an immediate function')}());
```

Function Invocations

There are four ways to call a function:

- As a function
- As a method
- As a constructor
- Using call() or apply() methods

The chosen method affects what the this keyword references. In the first option (as a function), this references the global context when not in strict mode. In strict mode, undefined or the value assigned in the execution context is returned. The second two (method and constructor) are specific to an object-oriented approach. A method invocation involves a call to a function that is attached to an object. A call to a constructor causes a new object to be created. Unlike the first three options, the call and apply methods allow you to explicitly set the context when you invoke them on a function.

This and That

A JavaScript convention that can be a bit baffling at first glance is:

```
var that = this
```

This usage is obvious once you understand the way this works in JavaScript. Because this can vary based on context (scope), some developers alias it to that as a way to retain access to the original value of this.

Function Arguments

As previously mentioned, each function can receive arguments through named parameters in the function signature. There is a special variable named arguments that can hold any and all variables passed to a function whether they are named or not. The following examples demonstrate how to add three numbers using a standard function call and also using a function's apply and call methods:

```
function add(){
    var sum=0;
    for (i=0; i< arguments.length; i++){
        sum+=arguments[i];
    }
    return sum;
}

console.log(add(1,2,3));
```

```
console.log(add.apply(null, [2,3,4]));
console.log(add.call(null,3,4,5));
```

Objects

In Java, an object is created as an instance of a defined class. In JavaScript, an object is simply a collection of properties. JavaScript objects do inherit (from a prototype object) and so object-oriented design principles are applicable. But the differences from Java's classical approach are significant. JavaScript allows for the creation of classes (*http://bit.ly/1jyuCo1*), but it is not useful to think about them in the same way as you would in Java (where classes are required and fundamental).

Classical and prototypical inheritance differentiates Java and JavaScript and results in confusion due to their differences. Other features of JavaScript can be highlighted by contrasting it with Java.

JavaScript for Java Developers

Most developers realize that JavaScript syntax superficially resembles that of Java or other C-based language (for loops, conditional statements, and so on). But when full Java applications are viewed, the differences become immediately evident. The following are well-known basic Java programs that illustrate differences in JavaScript code and development practices.

HelloWorld.java

```
/**
 * HelloWorld
 */
class HelloWorld{

        public static void main (String args[]){
                System.out.println("Hello World!");
        }

}
```

To see the venerable Hello World example program in action at the command line, you need to:

1. Create a source file named *HelloWorld.java*.

2. Compile the Java code into a class file (using the Java Compiler via the `javac` command).

3. Execute the resulting class file (using the Java interpreter via the `java` command).

If you use an integrated development environment like Eclipse or IntelliJ, these steps are represented by corresponding menu options. Simply enough, the program prints out the string literal "Hello World!" when executed. But this simple program serves to highlight a number of significant differences between Java and JavaScript.

The following is the comparable JavaScript program that produces the same output:

```
console.log('Hello World')
```

Program execution

First of all, JavaScript is an interpreted language. No compilation is necessary. The execution environment for JavaScript immediately comes into question. If you have node (*http://nodejs.org*) installed, you can run this at the node prompt:

```
> console.log("Hello World")

Hello World
```

This code can be executed at a browser console. In Chrome, select View → Developer → JavaScript Console (see Figure 2-2).

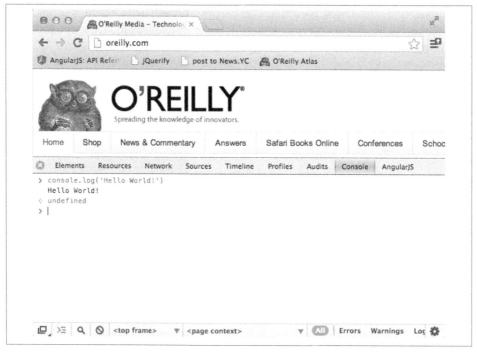

Figure 2-2. Chrome JavaScript console

In Firefox, select Tools → Web Developer → Web Console (see Figure 2-3).

Figure 2-3. Firefox JavaScript console

Other modern browsers have comparable menu options that provide the same functionality.

Host Objects

Technically, there is no built-in I/O functionality in JavaScript (although the runtime environment—in this case, the browser—does provide it). This is in accordance with the ECMA standard (*http://bit.ly/1nuHFE7*):

> ECMAScript as defined here is not intended to be computationally self-sufficient; indeed, there are no provisions in this specification for input of external data or output of computed results. Instead, it is expected that the computational environment of an ECMAScript program will provide not only the objects and other facilities described in this specification but also certain environment-specific *host* objects, whose description and behavior are beyond the scope of this specification except to indicate that they may provide certain properties that can be accessed and certain functions that can be called from an ECMAScript program.

The implications of this not being defined are more than a mere curiosity, not the least of which that *console.log* is not available in certain versions of Microsoft's Internet Explorer and consequently, unexpected errors can occur. Many of the challenges and problems associated with the JavaScript programming language are actually the fault of the execution environment (which is often a web browser). The DOM is a cross-platform, *language-independent* means of referencing and manipulating HTML elements. It also is not part of the JavaScript language itself.

Back to the the Hello World example itself: you might have noticed that single quotes were used instead of double quotes and that there was no trailing semicolon. JavaScript syntax is forgiving (or ambiguous, if you prefer). There have been a number of innovations to reduce confusion in this area. A "strict" mode (*http://mzl.la/MLQL42*) was added to the language itself. Utilities like Douglas Crockford's JSLint (*http://www.jslint.com*) were created to enforce the use of the "good parts" of the JavaScript language. See his book (*http://amzn.to/1kCC1Ts*) on the subject for more in-depth coverage. Suffice it to say, JavaScript has a number of leniencies that can result in an undisciplined developer or team causing some difficult-to-debug problems. It is well worth the time to learn the language well enough to adopt conventions and practices that avoid these problems.

File system organization

The file and directory structure of a Java project are directly linked to the structure of the code. A source file generally contains a single (public) class with the same name as the file. The file exists in a directory that reflects the package name associated with the class. (There are a few other rules and exceptions related to inner classes, access modifiers, and other constructs, but it is clear that file and directory structures will follow similar general structures across Java projects). At times, these restrictions can be an inconvenience (especially in small applications). As a project grows, it provides an clear indication of the general scope and organization of the code base. A glance at the file system makes it immediately evident when a project is becoming disorganized without ever opening a file.

JavaScript enforces no such restrictions. There is no necessary connection between file or directory structures. And so, you need to give particular attention to the organization of your code as a project grows, and will likely need to invest time in refactoring it if a larger development team is involved. Alex MacCaw explains this well in *JavaScript Web Applications* (O'Reilly):

The secret to making large JavaScript applications is to not make large JavaScript applications. Instead you should decouple your application into a series of fairly independent components. The mistake developers often make is creating applications with a lot of interdependency, with huge linear JavaScript files generating a slew of HTML tags. These sorts of applications are difficult to maintain and extend, and so they should be avoided at all costs.

— Alex MacCaw

Other aspects of code organization need to be considered as well. Besides naming files and intelligently including code in the proper file, dependencies between files require that they be loaded in a specific order. And when JavaScript is being served from a web server, efficiencies can be gained by loading a given file when it is actually needed (rather than causing a browser to hang while all of the files are downloaded). Performance gains can be accomplished utilizing the *Asynchronous Module Definition* (AMD) API (*http:// bit.ly/Yp9ozD*), supported by libraries like RequireJS (*http://bit.ly/1grnHZZ*). This API allows module definition that lets the module and its dependencies be loaded asynchronously.

HelloWorld.java (with Variables)

The typical next step in demonstrating a Hello World application is to make it greet a specified party by the name specified in a variable:

```
/**
 * HelloWorld2
 */
class HelloWorld2 {

    public static void main (String args[]) {
        String name;
        System.out.println("Hello " + name);
    }

}
```

This code will not compile:

```
HelloWorld2.java:5: variable name might not have been initialized
```

```
var name;
console.log('Hello ' + name);
```

This code will run in JavaScript, which leads to another source of confusion: too many *bottom values* that evaluate to `false`. The way that they are evaluated that can be confusing and difficult to remember:

```
// All evaluate to false
console.log(false    ? 'true' : 'false');
console.log(0        ? 'true' : 'false');
console.log(NaN      ? 'true' : 'false');
```

```
console.log(''        ? 'true' : 'false');
console.log(null      ? 'true' : 'false');
console.log(undefined ? 'true' : 'false');
```

All other values evaluate to `true`:

```
// All Evaluate to true
console.log('0'      ? 'true' : 'false');
console.log('false'  ? 'true' : 'false');
console.log([]       ? 'true' : 'false');
console.log({}       ? 'true' : 'false');
```

So after we initialize the variable in Java, the program compiles and runs:

```
/**
 * HelloWorld2
 */
class HelloWorld2{

    public static void main (String args[]){
        String name = "Java";
        System.out.println("Hello " + name);
        }


}
```

Likewise, if we assign a value to our variable in JavaScript, we see the result printed out as expected:

```
var name='JavaScript';
console.log('Hello ' + name)
```

The `var` keyword is not required, and if you are in the global scope, it will not produce any difference in behavior. If called within a function, then `var` will create a local variable. So in general, variables should be declared within a function and declared with the `var` keyword to prevent pollution of the global namespace.

The Java example required that the type of the variable be declared. JavaScript is loosely typed and has no such requirement. The `typeof` operator (*http://mzl.la/1m9ezPe*) can be used to illustrate the most common types. See Table 2-1 for examples.

Table 2-1. JavaScript typeof operator examples

Type	Result	Example
Undefined	"undefined"	typeof undefined
Null	"object"	typeof null
Boolean	"boolean"	typeof true
Number	"number"	typeof 123
String	"string"	typeof "hello"
Function object	"function"	typeof function(){}

Development Best Practices

JavaScript has its own set of unique challenges and characteristics that demand a unique development process. Although we can shoehorn a lot of JavaScript development into familiar Java processes, it is much more fitting to use specialized tools and procedures that are uniquely fitted to it.

Coding Style and Conventions

Much of the book is concerned with the loose coupling of client and server tiers. *Unobtrusive JavaScript* is the practice that establishes loose coupling of UI layers within the client application:

- HTML defines the data structure of the page.
- CSS applies design styles to the data structure.
- JavaScript provides interactive functionality for the page.

Otherwise stated:

- Avoid JavaScript in CSS.
- Avoid CSS in JavaScript.
- Avoid JavaScript in HTML.
- Avoid HTML in JavaScript.

Browsers for Development

The browser is a piece of software so ubiquitous that many web users don't even know that it is distinct from the underlying operating system. The browser is not only the environment in which an end user views a web page, *the browser is an IDE*. Browsers now include integrated debuggers, code formatters, profilers, and a plethora of other tools (some available as plug-ins or add-ons) that can be used during the development process.

Firefox (along with Firebug (*http://getfirebug.com*) and other developer add-ons and extensions) has been popular for development for some time. Chrome has bundled developer tools and has gained popularity more recently.

Chrome Tips

It is worthwhile to investigate the developer tools available on your browser and the command-line options that can influence the behavior of the browser. These generally bypass certain security constraints or performance optimizations for the sake of developer access and increased productivity. For instance, in Chrome:

- There are certain settings such as clearing the browser cache (*http://bit.ly/1j5JW80*) that can prevent confusion when swapping out changes.
- Command-line syntax varies between browser versions and operating systems. For example, Chrome can be run on OS X by running:

```
/Applications/Google\ Chrome.app/Contents/MacOS/Google\ Chrome
```

Running at the command line allows you to include flags that alter browser behavior. If you are including files using Ajax (for example using AngularJS), `--allow-file-access-from-files` allows for development outside of a web server. And if you are using JSONP referencing your local machine (localhost) `--disable-web-security` is required.

There are a number of other somewhat hidden features in Chrome. Enter `chrome://chrome-urls/` in the URL bar to get a listing of URLs that can be entered to access screens to configure or monitor activity. To whet your appetite, try out `chrome://flags/` which reveals a list of experimental features available to the current version of the browser.

Another implication of browsers as the JavaScript environment are the emergence of online collaborative JavaScript development sites like JSFiddle (*http://jsfiddle.net*) and jsbin (*http://jsbin.com*). These sites allow you to create example applications that replicate bugs, and communicate in rather exact terms with others about specific language questions. There is little reason to struggle with snippets of out-of-context code in JavaScript. It is the norm to provide specific examples and to code up small demonstrations when asking questions or demonstrating techniques online.

Integrated Development Environments

WebStorm (*http://bit.ly/jb-webstorm*) is a particularly good IDE that is fast and lightweight and includes debuggers, a great project view, powerful shortcuts, extensibility via plug-ins and a host of other features. While not strictly necessary, WebStorm captures a lot of best practices through the use of wizards, shortcuts, and code completion.

Unit Testing

There are a number of unit testing frameworks (*http://bit.ly/1gvnROC*) that have been developed for JavaScript. Jasmine (*http://pivotal.github.io/jasmine*) is a Behavior-Driven Development (*http://bit.ly/1dkUNKU*) framework with no dependencies and a simple syntax that will be used in this book.

Java unit tests can be executed each time a project is built by the build tool or script. JavaScript can use a node module (Karma (*https://github.com/karma-runner/karma*), which was formerly known as Testacular) to execute unit tests on a variety of different browsers *each time a source code file is changed and saved!* This is really worth noting. If you are disciplined about your creation of unit tests, the ability to run them all each time a source file is saved can result in early identification of otherwise obscure bugs. This is especially valuable when working with languages like JavaScript that do not use a compiler to perform initial code validation. Frequent, effective unit tests serve as a sort of pseudo-compiler. They provide immediate feedback regarding the quality of the code and catch certain bugs as soon as they are introduced.

Documentation

There are a few different automatic documentation generation options in JavaScript. Jsdoc (*https://github.com/jsdoc3/jsdoc*) is similar to Javadoc in its markup and output. Dox (*https://github.com/visionmedia/dox*) is a node module for document generation.

Literate programming (*http://bit.ly/1bYqPvs*) (introduced by Donald Knuth in the 1970s) strives to enable programmers to develop programs in the order demanded by the logic and flow of their thoughts. Docco (*http://jashkenas.github.io/docco*) is a node module that incorporates comments presented in parallel to source code in a form much like the text of an essay. Although Docco does not directly validate or enforce code conventions, its presence and use can encourage thoughtful commenting and structuring of code instead of knee-jerk copy-and-paste exercises.

Project

This project is a small object hierarchy in JavaScript and includes tests and documentation. All files can be found on GitHub (*http://bit.ly/1cxb2R7*).

`Animal.js` is at the root of our object hierarchy:

```
// Animal is the top of the object hierarchy
function Animal() {}

// Define a speak function that have specific implementations in subclasses
Animal.prototype.speak = function() {
    return "Animal is speaking.";
};
```

It has two subclasses, `Cat.js`:

```javascript
// Define the Cat
function Cat() {
    Animal.call(this);
}

// Set the object's prototype
Cat.prototype = new Animal();

// Name the constructor in a manner to suit the class
Cat.prototype.constructor = Cat;

// Create a class-specific implementation
Cat.prototype.speak = function(){
    return "meow";
}
```

and `Dog.js`:

```javascript
// Define the Dog class
function Dog() {
    Animal.call(this); // Call the parent constructor
}

// Dog inherits from Animal
Dog.prototype = new Animal();

// Update the constructor to match the new class
Dog.prototype.constructor = Dog;

// Replace the speak method
Dog.prototype.speak = function(){
    return "woof";
}
```

The latest version of Jasmine is available on GitHub (*https://github.com/pivotal/jasmine*):

```
curl -L \
https://github.com/downloads/pivotal/jasmine/jasmine-standalone-1.3.1.zip \
-o jasmine.zip
```

A test specification that includes a test for each of the classes defined in the preceding code is run by Jasmine:

```javascript
// Animal Test using beforeEach
describe("Animal", function() {

    beforeEach(function() {
        animal = new Animal();

    });
```

```
    it("should be able to speak", function() {
        expect(animal.speak()).toEqual("Animal is speaking.");
    });
});

// Dog inherits from Animal and overrides the speak method.
// A function scoped variable is used for testing.
describe("Dog", function() {

    it("should be able to speak", function() {
        var dog = new Dog();
        expect(dog.speak()).toEqual("woof");
    });

});

// A bit more terse: a cat that inherits from Animal.
// Object constructor called in the same line as the speak method.
describe("Cat", function() {

    it("should be able to speak", function() {
        expect((new Cat()).speak()).toEqual("meow");
    });

});
```

The simplest way to see this in action is to open *SpecRunner.html* in a browser, as shown in Figure 2-4.

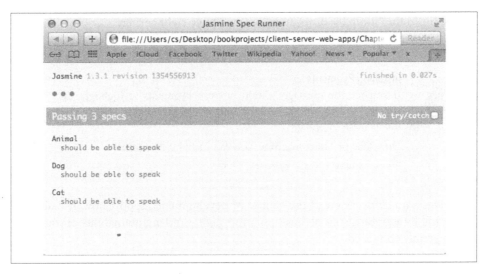

Figure 2-4. Jasmine run example

To run the tests each time a file is changed, you will need an installation of *node.js* (*http://nodejs.org*). You can verify your installation by checking the version of node installed:

```
node --version
v0.8.15
```

You should also have node package manager installed:

```
npm --version
1.1.66
```

With these installed, you can install Karma:

```
npm install karma
```

Once installed, you can view the help:

```
karma --help
```

The project configuration file was initially created using the init option. This created a file named *karma.conf.js* that can then be edited to reference applicable JavaScript files and run in installed browsers. Once configured, tests can be run every time a file changes by using the start option.

Use npm to install the docco module used to generate documentation:

```
npm install docco
```

Run the docco command to create HTML documentation in the docs directory. Figure 2-5 shows one of the generated files. The comments are on the left, and syntax-highlighted code is on the right. You can access documentation for other files by choosing the file in the "Jump to" drop-down on the upper-right corner:

```
docco app/*.js
```

 Installing Pygments

If you see the message "Could not use Pygments to highlight the source," this is referring to a Python syntax highlighter called Pygments (*http://pygments.org*).

On a Mac or Linux machine, you can install it by running:

```
sudo easy_install pygments
```

This gives a quick overview of the caliber of development support now available for JavaScript. By adopting a few of these tools, the quality and maintainability of your code will be greatly enhanced.

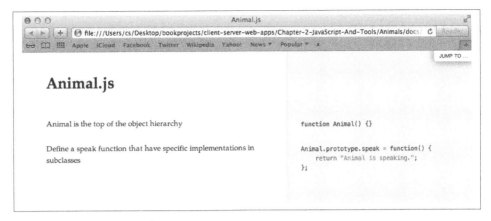

Figure 2-5. Docco screenshot

This chapter really only scratched the surface of this sophisticated and ubiquitous language. Other books delve deeper into the subjects introduced here. For instance, *Java-Script Web Applications* by Alex McCaw (O'Reilly) demonstrates the use of certain established patterns (Model-View-Controller) and techniques related to building larger-scale JavaScript applications. *Maintainable JavaScript* by Nicholas C. Zakas (O'Reilly) helps deal with the undeniable challenge of establishing practices and standards that promote a maintainable and extensible codebase. And of course many resources are available online, through sites like the Mozilla Developer Network (*http://mzl.la/ 1bYrbCl*) and StackOverflow (*http://bit.ly/1lEqJMh*).

JavaScript is most certainly not Java. It is a language all its own with a burgeoning ecosystem of projects to support its development. A knowledge of the language itself and the development tools available will provide you with a good foundation as you explore the many frameworks and libraries that will be subsequently introduced.

## CHAPTER 3

REST and JSON

Good fences make good neighbors.

—Robert Frost

Whenever a technology is introduced, there is an instantaneous response about what it does *not* do. This response can be puzzling to those who have already learned to operate within its limits. Fences can be viewed in a negative sense, as barriers that restrict or prevent movement. In the positive sense, in the quote by Robert Frost, they provide a clear, visible demarcation of a boundary and indicate the purpose, use, and dangers of a given space. In a similar manner, constraints on a software system impose limitations in the interest of providing better functionality, efficiency, and clarity of roles. Good constraints are specified not simply to block or restrict, but for the purpose of achieving a positive goal. REST is an architectural style characterized by a set of constraints that represent how the Web (or other similar construct) should work. These constraints, though limiting, promote the design of systems that are well suited to the nature of the Web itself.

Descriptions of REST are often articulated from a substantially different starting point: REST as a *web services protocol*. It is true that REST can be understood when compared with SOAP or other messaging services. In relation to SOAP, it is considered a minimalistic protocol, lacking extensive definitions and additional constructs required in SOAP implementations. It is characterized as relying directly upon underlying features of HTTP, including request methods, URI addressing, and response codes. REST can also be compared with *Remote Procedure Call* (RPC)-style APIs, which use URLs to indicate actions, whereas REST uses URLs to access resources. In this regard, REST is noun-oriented while RPC is verb-oriented.

Why REST over SOAP?

Involved debates have taken place over the virtues of REST over SOAP, or vice versa. Although SOAP does provide a formal contract and is suitable as a sophisticated RPC architecture, it introduces additional overhead and complexity without providing substantial advantages for most web application development. SOAP remains in heavy use as an RPC platform due to nontechnical considerations such as the fact that it is firmly entrenched in existing large-scale legacy applications.

SOAP messages are large, require extensive processing, and are expressed in verbose XML envelopes. This makes the protocol unattractive for client-server-style web applications, which can so easily process JSON using JavaScript.

Many developers initially encounter REST as a web services protocol characterized by pretty URLs and free-form, lightweight messages. While this perspective has great practical value, it is important to understand REST as it was articulated by its author Roy Fielding.

What Is REST?

Fielding states (*http://bit.ly/1iPSLU1*) that the "Representational State Transfer (REST) architectural style...[was] developed to represent the model for how the modern Web should work." Although technically protocol-agnostic, it was developed in conjunction with HTTP. And because of this association, a few of the salient features of HTTP should be kept in mind.

Resources

A *web resource* is simply something available on the Web. The definition of a web resource has expanded over time. It originally referred to a static addressable document or file. It was later given a more abstract definition and now encompasses every entity that can be identified, named, addressed, or handled on the Web. Some examples of resources are a traditional HTML web page, a document, an audio file, and an image file. Resources can refer to things that you might not find in your typical digital library as well, such as a hardware device, a person, or a collection of other resources.

REST uses web addresses (URIs) to access and manipulate resources using verbs (HTTP request methods).

Verbs (HTTP Request Methods)

HTTP 1.1 defines a set of verbs (or *request methods*) that indicate an action taken on a resource. Of those available, the ones of greatest signficance using a RESTful approach are GET, POST, PUT, and DELETE. One way of thinking about these verbs is by comparing them with commands used to manipulate data in a database.

In a database, a data entity is typically referred to as a record. In REST, the corresponding entity is the resource. The HTTP verbs (POST/GET/PUT/DELETE) roughly correspond to traditional CRUD (create/read/update/delete) operations in a database or *object-relational management* (ORM) system. A REST architecture stipulates that resources on the Web are retrieved or changed in much the same way that SQL or similar query language is used to access or modify records in a database. A full listing of HTTP 1.1 options related to REST can be found in Appendix B.

HTTP verb	Action to take on a resource	Analogous database operation
POST	Create (or append)	insert
GET	Retrieve	select
PUT	Update (or create)	update
DELETE	Delete	delete

Other HTTP Methods

Several other HTTP methods are useful but don't correspond to traditional CRUD database operations. The HEAD method is identical to GET except that the response does not include a response body. This is applicable when using REST-related technologies that take advantage of HTTP Headers. Cross-Origin Resource Sharing (CORS) returns JSON otherwise forbidden due to browser's same origin security policy and manages its negotiations with servers through HTTP headers. Certain methods of specifying links for documents use headers as the location to store links. So at times when the salient information resides in the response header rather than the body, it makes sense to use a HEAD call rather than incurring additional overhead of returning the response body through a standard GET.

The HTTP OPTIONS method can be used to retrieve a listing of HTTP request methods available for a resource. This has implications not only for debugging and support but also for creating systems with a uniform interface of links available through a single entry point embodying a self-describing system. In conjunction with such *links*, which represent the access points for all resources in a system, a proper implementation of HTTP OPTIONS would return a comprehensive list of *methods* available for each resource available through a link.

Uniform Resource Identifiers

In a networked system there needs to be some sort of handle or address that allows a resource to be acted upon. *Uniform Resource Identifier* (URI) is the general term for a string of characters used to accomplish this. A URI can be further differentiated as either a *Uniform Resource Name* (URN) that represents the name of a resource or a *Uniform Resource Locator* (URL) that represents the address of a resource.

Most URL schemes base their URL syntax on this general format:

```
<scheme>://<user>:<password>@<host>:<port>/<path>;<parameters>?<query
key/value pairs>#<fragment identifier>
```

See *HTTP: The Definitive Guide* (O'Reilly) for more details about URIs and HTTP in general.

In REST, resources are specifically identified as path elements. Slashes within the URL are used to delimit resources and express their relationship in a hierarchical manner. REST URLs are demonstrated in examples and explained in greater detail in Chapter 8.

In web-based APIs, URL names used to identify resources and specify their relationship to others typically adhere to some additional conventions. These are not required by REST, but are stylistic concerns that promote readability and consistency of URLs. For the most part, URLs should be lowercase, use hyphens but no underscores, and include trailing slashes. An individual resource is referred to using a singular noun. A collection of resources is identified using a plural noun. File extensions are discouraged but tend to show up when an API supports multiple formats such as XML *and* JSON. A more suitable alternative is to use "Accept" and "Content-Type" headers to control the format. The *REST API Design Rulebook* by Mark Masse (O'Reilly) includes the conventions listed above and many others, but in practice, there is a fair amount of latitude in the structure and format of URLs.

Hyphens Instead of Underscores?

It should be emphasized that all of the URL naming conventions mentioned above are *not* etched in stone. Many popular APIs, including Twitter (*http://bit.ly/1a1kZ9i*) and Dropbox (*http://bit.ly/1aZh2He*), use underscores. There are other considerations such as search engine optimization that had caused this to be considered a bad practice in the past (underscored elements were concatenated together in Google's search indexes, while hyphenated strings were broken into separate words). Though there are differences of opinion in these details, there is clear agreement that URLs should be as short as possible, readable, clear, and consistent across an API.

REST Constraints

REST is defined (*http://bit.ly/1hdbEmt*) as a specific software architectural style characterized by a group of selected constraints. Benefical system properties and sound engineering principles are evident in a system designed to conform to these constraints.

Client–Server

A client-server architecture provides an immediate separation of concerns. It makes the best use of the processing power available in modern clients—once only available to high-end computers. The server side is simplified due to the shift of many responsibilities to the client. Such a system tends to be easily scalable, and the separation between tiers allows for independent development of each.

Stateless

REST requires a stateless design. Session data is stored client-side. Each request made by the client must be "context-free" and self-contained. This means that a request will include the entire client state. This requires all data needed for the server to respond without doing additional outside retrieval of data related to application state. It is much easier to comprehend the intent of a given interaction since all data is available in each request. Fault tolerance and scalability are also improved because session data is not maintained server-side. Server resources are not consumed by the storage and retrieval processing otherwise required.

There are a number of challenges in designing systems that conform to REST's stateless nature. One is the additional network traffic caused by larger and more frequent requests. (These would be reduced through the use of server-side sessions in nonRESTful client-server applications that do maintain server-side state). Because each request includes all state-related data, there are bound to be certain data elements that are repeatedly sent. The fact that the server is not maintaining sessions means that the client has more responsibility and is therefore typically more complex (this is one reason for the increasing sophistication of JavaScript in modern RESTful applications). Browser storage mechanisms are of greater interest in such systems. And since REST systems typically support multiple client versions, considerable planning and effort is required for the client tier.

Even with these challenges, the benefits of statelessness are many, especially deployments involving several servers that receive requests distributed by a load balancer. If a server-based session is used, two basic options are available. One is to require the same server to respond to all requests for a given session. The other is to create a centralized session data store available to all servers. This centralized data store then needs to be accessed each time a request is made. This practice (sometimes called *session-affinity* or the use of sticky sessions) makes scaling much more difficult. Large-scale deployments typically roll out changes to servers over time. If server-side sessions are in use, there is a need to wait for old sessions to expire before migrating incoming requests to servers with the latest changes. This is a complex and difficult operational process. The entire situation is nonexistent if no state is stored server-side. In addition, standard browser functions like navigating to previous history or reloading the current page require no special handling when server-maintained sessions are eliminated.

The stateless design of REST is one of the most challenging aspects for many developers to comprehend. It requires some significant adjustments to typical web development practices. But the benefits are many, and the performance concerns due to the entire state being contained in each request are not insurmountable, especially when REST's next constraint is considered.

Cacheable

The performance issues associated with REST's stateless constraint can largely be compensated for via caching. REST requires that data be labeled to indicate whether or not it is cacheable. This allows a client application to reuse cacheable responses rather than making equivalent requests at a later point. Like caching in any system, this can provide quite a performance boost to the client application but also introduces the standard complexities associated with proper cache invalidation to avoid stale data. In the context of the Web, caches can be maintained client-side (in the browser), server-side, or in between (in a gateway or proxy server).

Uniform Interface

A uniform interface stipulates a common way to address resources that all RESTful applications use. Every REST system therefore has a common structure immediately evident to those familiar with the architecture. This severely restricts the ability to customize an interface for application-specific needs, but there is a great deal of flexibility within the constraint bounds. HTTP itself has been enhanced in each version to provide additional mechanisms available to RESTful design (the inclusion of new request methods, for instance). This particular constraint actually includes a number of other constraints that comprise it (see Table 3-1).

Table 3-1. Uniform interface constraints

Uniform interface constraint	Description
Identification of resources	Resources are addressable through URIs.
Manipulation of resources through representations	The resource is the thing represented. Its representation is what is sent in the request (e.g., the XML/JSON document).
Self-descriptive messages	Stateless requests that use HTTP verbs.
Hypermedia as the engine of application state	HATEOAS: Availability of links that dictate how the application state can be changed.

Layered

A layered design allows for network components to interact with each request en route. Each component does not have visibility beyond the layer with which it is communicating. This means that familiar network devices like firewalls and gateways can be in use, and caching or translation can be done by proxy servers.

Code on Demand

The ability to provide code on demand—through JavaScript or embedded browser applications—is allowed in REST but not required. This opens up a wide range of possibilities in how an application might be extended. The downside is a reduction in visibility otherwise inherent to RESTful systems (especially in the case of objects like Java Applets).

HTTP Response Codes

When developing REST APIs, standard HTTP status codes (shown in Appendix B) provide feedback to the client and report potential errors. The exact nature of a given response can be dependent upon the HTTP method in use.

What Is Success?

There is no widespread agreement on the use of HTTP codes in web APIs. In part, this is because the responses are not aligned with the HTTP verbs, but with five categories of occurences: general information, a successful request, redirect, error on the client side, or error on the server tier. In some cases, the applicable response code appropriate to a call is evident, but in others, it is dependent on the specific API call or the discretion or preferences of the API designer.

Take for instance a (nonspecific) success (200). This is recognized as the proper response to a succesful GET in most cases. In fact, in HTTP 1.1 (*http://bit.ly/1dkzBVq*), it is specifically listed in regards to GET and POST. The response depends on the HTTP request type, as indicated in Table 3-2.

Table 3-2. HTTP 1.1 success (200)

HTTP verb	Expected response content
GET	An entity corresponding to the requested resource
HEAD	The entity-header fields corresponding to the requested resource without any message-body
POST	An entity describing or containing the result of the action
TRACE	An entity containing the request message as received by the end server

And though some would also use an HTTP 200 in response to a PUT or DELETE, other codes might be used. A HTTP 201 (created) is used by some APIs in the case of a PUT or POST. A 204 (no content) might be used for a DELETE that returned no other response, but might also apply to other verbs (even a GET) if a request is successful but the server intentionally does not return content. If a web application is using basic authentication, the logoff can be accomplished by returning an HTTP 401 (not authorized) response code to the browser. So the definition of success depends on the context, and so the selection of a proper response code requires an understanding of the meaning of the codes and the nature of the request being made.

The first digit of each code specifies the classes of response. Since the bare minimum for a client is that it recognize the class of the response, there is expected flexibility and variance in the use of response codes (see Table 3-3).

Table 3-3. Classes of HTTP response codes

First digit	Meaning
1	Informational
2	Success
3	Redirection
4	Client Error
5	Server Error

Mozilla (*http://mzl.la/1eszuTv*), Yahoo Social APIs (*http://yhoo.it/MLRsKx*), and the *REST API Design Rulebook* include thoughtful presentations on the use of response codes. The similarities highlight the conventions and best practices that have emerged, and the differences demonstrate variance in design opinion and distinctions that are predicated on the particular nature of a given API.

JSON (JavaScript Object Notation)

Douglas Crockford is well known not for emphasizing every feature that JavaScript has, but for focusing on a subset. In essence, he sets constraints on language usage. Another application of his approach is his design of *JavaScript Object Notation* (JSON) as a data interchange format derived from JavaScript.

A variety of data interchange formats have been in use since the advent of modern computing. Besides binary and proprietary formats, some types attempted to incorporate some degree of human as well as machine readability. Fixed-width and delimited file formats were used initially (and still can be found in use today). The first XML working draft was produced in 1996. XML specifically sought to be both machine-readable and human-readable, but over time has been criticized as verbose and unnecessarily complex. In reaction, smaller languages that included aspects of XML such as hierarchical organization have been created (such as YAML). In 2002 Douglas Crockford acquired the *http://www.json.org* domain where he described JSON as:

- A data interchange format (a lightweight alternative to XML)
- A programming language model that is a subset of JavaScript
- A format that is is trivial to parse (in fact, in JavaScript you can simply call `eval()` on a JSON string to convert it into a JavaScript object, though this not a particularly safe option)

He also emphasized JSON's advantages over XML:

- Response sizes are smaller because begin and end tags and metadata require additional space in XML.
- JSON interoperability is better with web pages. It is a subset of JavaScript making client-side integration trivial.
- The previous two characteristics result in performance benefits and ease of integration in the context of Ajax calls.

JSON does have a few quirks worth noting:

- JSON is "almost valid" (*http://bit.ly/1dIU8OW*) JavaScript.
- There is no way to specify a comment in JSON.
- As previously mentioned, because it is a subset of JavaScript, it can be consumed by JavaScript `eval()`. However, the use of `eval()` is dangerous (*http://mzl.la/1iPTa8X*). It is often said that `"eval() is evil."`
- The "same origin policy" that is in force in most modern web browsers prevents JSON from being evaluated from a separate site. JSONP (sometimes also referred to as JSON-P or "JSON with padding") has been used to request data from a server in a different domain (via HTTP GET). A call to a function already defined in the caller's environment is used manipulate the JSON data. This function is the cause of the "padding" used in this approach. More recently, *Cross-Origin Resource Sharing* (CORS (*http://www.w3.org/TR/cors*)) has been developed as a more robust, secure alternative to JSONP. CORS uses HTTP headers to allow servers from specified domains to serve resources. It also requires specific server-side configuration for the service emitting the JSON to operate.

Comments in JSON

The fact that JSON does not allow comments is a bit surprising and has led to various workarounds. One is to add "comment" elements to JSON objects with comment content as a corresponding value. One possibility that should be avoided is creating two elements *with the same name* and assume that the parser will choose the last one. For example:

```
({"a":"This is a comment", "a":"CONTENT"})
```

Although this happens to work in a number of JSON parsers, it is a result of their implementation and not a part of the specification.

HATEOAS

JSON is a very simple and terse format. Unlike other formats that provide elaborate type systems for the data they represent, only a few data types are available in JSON. These data types—strings, numbers, booleans, objects, arrays, and null—are more than expressive and extensible enough for most applications. Because of JSON's popularity as a data interchange format used by RESTful APIs, you might expect a specific data type for hyperlinks, but no such type exists! This is especially problematic since REST includes a constraint called *Hypermedia as the Engine of Application State* (HATEOAS).

This constraint restricts a client to interactions through links that are included under the term "hypermedia." Therefore, a web API cannot possibly be classified as "RESTful" in a strict sense because there is no link data type in JSON or in JavaScript (upon which it is based).

XML-based REST APIs often use Atom Syndication Format (where links consist of a *rel*, *href*, *hreflang*, and *type*) or links in headers. Likewise, JSON extensions that provide for standardized linking within JSON documents have been developed:

- HAL (*http://stateless.co/hal_specification.html*)
- Siren (*https://github.com/kevinswiber/siren*)
- JSON-LD (*http://json-ld.org*)
- JSON Reference (*http://tools.ietf.org/html/draft-pbryan-zyp-json-ref-00*)
- Collection+JSON (*http://amundsen.com/media-types/collection/format*)
- JSON API (*http://jsonapi.org/about*) (extracted from the Ember JS REST Adapter (*http://emberjs.com*))

The W3C has a JSON-based Serialization for Linked Data (*http://bit.ly/1hdc1gZ*) posted on its site (at the time of this writing: W3C Recommendation 16 January 2014).

Many links conform to a similar category or relationship regardless of the entity represented. For example, in a collection, there is a convention of referencing the first, last, next, or previous member of the collection. A help, glossary, or about link appears and is relevant in many different contexts. Because of these commonalities, there have been efforts to standardize (*http://bit.ly/MdidHJ*) link relations (*http://bit.ly/1bYsgKc*) as well. An established set of link relations would make automatic generation of links much more specific and attainable.

It is worth being aware of the debate and work related to defining HATEOAS, but it is far from clear what the final outcome will be. The issues involved are complex, and there is no general consensus that a full implementation is required in every API design.

Hypermedia Linkability Continuum

A range of linkability possibilities exist in resources that appear on the Web. At one end of the spectrum are formats that require strict, well-defined links. At the other end are formats that forbid the use of links by definition.

Format	Description	Examples
1	Automatically generated standard links	Atom Publishing Protocol (APP)
2	Manually specified standard links	XHTML
3	Extension-format links	Links as an extension to an existing format (HAL (*http://bit.ly/hal-spec*))
4	Character links	Links as character strings
5	No links	Specified data interchange format forbids their use

REST as defined by Fielding requires proper use of a format of 1. Many web APIs that might be REST-inspired fall somewhere else on the scale.

REST and JSON

Certain implied values became evident as REST (as expressed in Fielding's dissertation) was interpreted and applied to real-world projects other than the Web itself. Fielding has expressed frustration at APIs termed RESTful that are not hypertext-driven (*http://bit.ly/1g7Min9*):

> REST is software design on the scale of decades: every detail is intended to promote software longevity and independent evolution. Many of the constraints are directly opposed to short-term efficiency. Unfortunately, people are fairly good at short-term design, and usually awful at long-term design. Most don't think they need to design past the current release. There are more than a few software methodologies that portray any long-term thinking as wrong-headed, ivory tower design (which it can be if it isn't motivated by real requirements).

Fielding's intention for REST to be a viable long-term solution is admirable. He promotes ideas that will remain relevant as long as the Web and its underlying technologies retain their fundamental structure. That said, HATEOAS and its relevance to JSON are not going to be investigated, demonstrated, or critiqued in depth. After the dust settles a bit, this book might be expanded and revised or accompanying content added to reflect an emerging consensus or convergence of opinion on the topic.

In general, Fielding's perspective is important because he is a seminal thinker and he invented REST. But many systems designed today are not intended (or billed) to exist for decades. His articulation of REST is excellent and should be understood as he has expressed it. But for better or for worse, the term REST has been adopted in a broader context, and has become a useful shorthand for identifying the architectual style of minimal web API design that is based largely on the underlying functionality of HTTP.

Pragmatic REST

Why have many APIs been designed in this "pragmatic" way? In part, it is because the HATEOAS principle places such a high bar for the client-side programmer. A programmer who, inadvertently or on purpose, hardcodes a URI path into an application may be in for a rude shock in the future, and the server-side API team may simply tell the client that they failed to follow the spec.

Although HATEOAS is a good theoretical approach to designing an API, it may not apply in practice. It is important to take into account the audiences of the API and their possible approaches to building apps against it and factor that into your design decisions. HATEOAS, in some cases, may not be the right choice.

— *APIs: A Strategy Guide (O'Reilly)*

It is fascinating that Fielding does recognize JavaScript (*http://bit.ly/1fZwMHA*) in his dissertation in relation to REST. He discusses the reasons for JavaScript's success on the Web as opposed to embedded Java "applets," which were not widely adopted as a client-side development technology. He points out that JavaScript fits the deployment model of the Web, is consistent with the principle of visibility evident with HTML, includes fewer additional security complications, involves less user-perceived latency, and does not require a separate, independent, monolithic download.

Typical JavaScript usage is consistent with the design principles of the Web. Its extensive use in the browser made JSON an attractive option for data interchange that could be easily produced and consumed.

Unfortunately, the very fact that JSON was specified as a subset of JavaScript rather than a hypermedia format means that there remains an impedance mismatch between JSON and strictly RESTful APIs. Although a browser running JavaScript is consistent with the design of the Web and the formal definition of REST, the use of JSON as a data interchange format is not.

Not everyone is interested in using the strict definition to classify whether a web API is RESTful or not. The fact that JSON web APIs are so popular and REST design is so influential has led to the development of a few different measures for classifying REST compatibility on a spectrum.

API Measures and Classification

The Richardson Maturity Model (*http://bit.ly/1fh2AGt*) introduced by Leonard Richardson in 2008 (*http://bit.ly/1hdcr70*) expresses a continuum by which services can be evaluated against the REST standard.

Level	Service	Description
Level 0	HTTP	HTTP as a transport system for remote interactions (remote procedure calls).
Level 1	Resources	Rather than making all requests to a singular service endpoint, reference specific individual resources.
Level 2	HTTP methods	Utilize HTTP verbs.

Jan Algermissen proposed a similar classification that describes APIs based upon adherence to REST constraints (Table 3-4).

Table 3-4. Classification of HTTP-based APIs adapted from Jan Algermissen (http://bit.ly/MdiqdW)

Name	Verbs	Generic media types	Specific media types	HATEOAS
WS-* web services (SOAP)	N	N	N	N
RPC URI-tunneling	Y	N	N	N
HTTP-based Type I	Y	Y	N	N
HTTP-based Type II	Y	Y	Y	N
REST	Y	Y	Y	Y

Both of these classification systems serve the admirable purpose of preserving Fielding's strict definition of REST while recognizing the compromises that have been made in implementing web APIs.

Functional Programming and REST

Functional programming and REST share a number of common traits. Both are declarative in nature and include very little description of control flow. Both have a similar view about controlling side effects, maintaining referential transparency, and operating in a stateless manner. So, as in the case with JavaScript, having a clear understanding of a functional paradigm is certainly helpful for effectively utilizing REST and recognizing its benefits.

The Web-Calculus Web

Beyond the pragmatic comparison of REST and functional programming, Tyler Close prevents a view of the Web as a lambda-calculus derivative (*http://bit.ly/1bpBS2Y*). Because functional programming languages are also based on lambda-calculus, the connection is even closer than mere appearances or benefits:

> Recognizing the primacy of the resource web in HTTP reveals that the WWW is a lambda-calculus derivative. A resource is a closure. The POST method is the "apply" operation. A web of resources is a web of closures. The key innovation of the WWW is the addition of introspection of the web of closures: the GET method...Understanding HTTP as a lambda-calculus derivative opens the possibility of using HTTP as a basis for distributed computation, not just distributed hypermedia.

In their book *Programming Scala* (O'Reilly), Wampler and Payne pointed out that in many cases, object-oriented systems did not deliver on the promise of widespread software component reuse. Instead, component models that have succeeded tend to be relatively simple. They conclude their chapter on functional programming by reiterating the relative simplicity of this approach:

> Components should interoperate by exchanging a few immutable data structures, e.g., lists and maps, that carry both data and *commands*. Such a component model would have the simplicity necessary for success and the richness required to perform real work. Notice how that sounds a lot like HTTP and REST.

Project

The following project involves the creation of a minimal API that responds to GET, POST, UPDATE, and DELETE requests and returns information about how the server interpreted the request to the client. This will be used to demonstrate various tools available when testing REST or other web APIs.

To set up the project:

1. Download the project (*http://bit.ly/1eQNr3y*) from GitHub.
2. Navigate to the *jruby-sinatra-rest* directory.
3. While connected to the Internet, build the project:

   ```
   $ mvn clean install
   ```

   This will download any Ruby or Java resources required for the project. It should end with:

```
[INFO] ------------------------------------------------------------------
[INFO] BUILD SUCCESSFUL
[INFO] ------------------------------------------------------------------
[INFO] Total time: 32 seconds
[INFO] Finished at: Tue Apr 30 12:59:15 EDT 2013
[INFO] Final Memory: 13M/1019M
[INFO] ------------------------------------------------------------------
```

4. Start the server:

```
$ mvn test -Pserver
```

Within a few seconds, you will see that the application server is running and ready to handle requests:

```
== Sinatra/1.3.1 has taken the stage on 4579 for development...
[2013-04-30 13:00:24] INFO  WEBrick::HTTPServer#start: pid=29937 port=4579
```

5. Navigate to the about page in a browser: *http://localhost:4579/about*.

You should see something like the following in response:

```
{
  "ruby.platform": "java",
  "ruby.version": "1.8.7",
  "java.millis": 1367342095907
}
```

This indicates that JRuby is available, required RubyGems (packages) are available, and Java (system) can be called successfully.

Now that the server is running, you can experiment with REST calls in a client of your choice. A few examples follow using Curl (*http://curl.haxx.se*). Curl is a command-line tool for transferring data that is accessible via URLs. It works for a wide variety of protocols beyond HTTP and is capable of performing a variety of tasks usually done in a web browser.

To get started, GET can be called with an arbitrary URL. It returns the response, which in the case of our server, is information about the request:

```
$ curl http://localhost:4579/about
{
        "ruby.platform": "java",
        "ruby.version": "1.8.7",
        "java.millis": 1367342095907
}
```

Curl has a huge number of options available to modify the behavior of the call and the information reported. One bit of information not readily available in a typical browser is HTTP header information. The -i (include the HTTP header) and -I (fetch the HTTP header only) can be used to display HTTP header information in the response:

```
$ curl -iI http://localhost:4579/about
```

The server is relatively simple. It is written in Ruby (and so runs via JRuby). It uses a microframework called Sinatra that is described (*http://bit.ly/1md4fG1*) as "a DSL for quickly creating web applications in Ruby with minimal effort." As such, it provides a great way of creating a server that exposes the underlying HTTP functionality without including a lot of additional code and constructs that might obscure its functionality.

The first few lines describe packages to be imported and some configuration options. Then, the "before" section defines what is, in essence, a before filter. In each case, the content type is set to JSON, the response is assigned some values from the incoming request, and the response status is set either to 200 or to the value passed in on the httpErrorCode request parameter. To see both the response from the server as well as the HTTP header, simply specify the -i option:

```
$ curl -i http://localhost:4579/?httpErrorCode=400
```

This example returns an HTTP 400 (Bad Request) error as specified in the parameter:

```
HTTP/1.1 400 Bad Request
Content-Type: application/json;charset=utf-8
Content-Length: 197
X-Content-Type-Options: nosniff
Server: WEBrick/1.3.1 (Ruby/1.8.7/2011-07-07)
Date: Tue, 30 Apr 2013 17:43:17 GMT
Connection: Keep-Alive
```

Examples that POST or PUT JSON are as follows:

```
$ curl -i -H "Accept: application/json" -X POST -d "['test',1,2]" \
http://localhost:4579

$ curl -i -H "Accept: application/json" -X PUT -d "{phone: 1-800-999-9999}" \
http://localhost:4579
```

And similarly, to DELETE:

```
$ curl -i -H "Accept: application/json" -X DELETE http://localhost:4579
```

The server processes arbitrary paths (matched using a wildcard), so you can pass arbitrary paths and query parameters to be reported back in the response:

```
curl -i -H "Accept: application/json" -X POST -d "['test',1,2]" \
http://localhost:4579/customer?filter=current
HTTP/1.1 200 OK
```

Several browser plug-ins can be used to test REST calls as well. Rather than introduce these, our application includes a minimal REST client using jQuery. The call just described using Curl appears as follows in Figure 3-1 when parameters are entered in *http://localhost:4579/testrest.html*.

In the Network tab of Chrome's Developer Tools, you can view header information and response codes as well. Figure 3-2 shows what would appear if the previous call is modified to return a 401.

Figure 3-1. Testing REST

This simple application also introduces how, in just a few lines of code, you can set up a web API with a minimal implementation to serve as a backend for client developers working in parallel with server developers implementing the complete set of server functionality. Here are the lines of code at a glance:

```
$ cd jruby-sinatra-rest/src/main
$ find scripts -name *.* | xargs cat | wc -l
141
```

This does not include jQuery and bootstrap being served from publicly hosted *Content Delivery Networks* (CDNs), but still indicates the possibilities available in only a few lines of code.

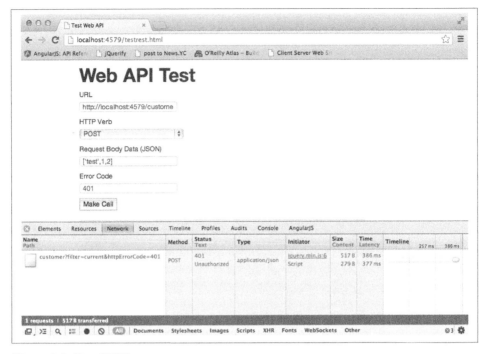

Figure 3-2. Test REST error

Other Web API Tools

Web APIs are not tied to a particular platform, so the tools used to debug them are more of a matter of developer preference and culture. Browsers and browser plug-ins are certainly useful, and as demonstrated, Curl is a flexible command-line option. Java-based web clients (*https://code.google.com/p/rest-client*), REST frameworks (*http://rest let.org*), and Eclipse IDE plug-ins (*http://www.ywebb.com*) appeal to the Java community, while Fiddler (*http://fiddler2.com/home*) is a popular choice among Microsoft aficionados.

Constraints Redux

The idea of a creative genius who throws off all external influences is largely mythological. This approach has absolutely no application in software development and little to do with most great work accomplished in the arts. Instead, it is far more profitable to identify the best set of constraints to apply in a creative activity. The *New York Times* described (*http://nyti.ms/1dIUUf0*) composer Igor Stravinsky as identifying constraints at the onset of music composition geared to "obtain precision of execution":

To Stravinsky, composing music was a process of solving musical problems: problems that he insisted on defining before he started to work.

Before writing "Apollon Musagete," for example, he wrote to Elizabeth Sprague Coolidge, who had commissioned the ballet, for the exact dimensions of the hall in which it would be performed, the number of seats in the hall, even the direction in which the orchestra would be facing.

"The more constraints one imposes, the more one frees one's self," he would say. "And the arbitrariness of the constraint serves only to obtain precision of execution."

— New York Times

The constraints that resulted in REST and JSON are anything but arbitrary, but they do promote precision of execution in the development of client-server web applications.

## CHAPTER 4

Java Tools

The original role of programming languages is that of a communication medium between a human and a computer. Today, the life span of software has increased, and programming teams have grown in size. As programmers need to communicate about software, computer code has also become an important human communication medium.

—Gilles Dubochet

In this quote, Gilles Dubochet introduces "distributed cognition" as he analyzes the role of programming languages for human communication. Programming languages are often studied in the abstract without considering a number of rather obvious contextual issues:

- Programming has never been a completely isolated activity. Many recent projects involve large, distributed teams.

- Computer languages are an important medium for human communication among programmers themselves.

- Programmers use literary terms to describe code quality. There is a stated or implied expectation that code be readable by peers.

- "Code comprehension" is improved with denser code for programmers who share common ground.

- Programmers cannot hold all system requirements of large systems in their own (human) memory.

- Human-readable documentation (when available) tends to get out of sync with the system described.

- Documentation does not always capture every edge case handled by a piece of software. Knowledge resides in the code itself.

This chapter points out the variety of languages that can be run on the Java platform. This allows the possibility of choosing the best language for a particular task or group of people. This chapter also describes Maven as a tool that promotes a variety of established best practices related to programming with groups of people.

Java Language

Although Java is a mature, stable, and well-known language, there are challenges with its usage in certain instances because of its design as a class-based, statically-typed, object-oriented language. It is helpful to acknowledge areas where there might be a mismatch between technologies and to consider alternatives up front that might alleviate the disjunction altogether.

Developers are familiar with the challenge of integrating an object-oriented language (like Java) with a relational database system in all but the most trivial of cases. Although some of the tension can be mitigated by altering usage practices, there is always a layer of mapping involved due to fundamental philosophical differences between the object-oriented and relational model.

This is not unique to Java; such a tension also exists between JSON and REST. REST requires links as defined in the HATEOAS *Uniform Interface* constraint. JSON, as a subset of the JavaScript language, has no such construct. Neither implementation is inherently wrong, but they have different origins that result in incongruities when they are integrated.

A similar tension exists between object-oriented systems and REST. In an object-oriented system, you take actions on an object itself. In REST, a resource is manipulated through its representation. This additional level of abstraction allows resources to be manipulated through a common interface not available by default in an object system.

Java developers have devised specific libraries that can be used to address most translation or integration activities related to interfacing with other technologies. In addition, a component of the Java platform itself that introduces the possibility of using an entirely different language is the *Java Virtual Machine* (or JVM).

Java Virtual Machine (JVM)

Java is translated into bytecode, which is then executed on the JVM (see Figure 4-1). Because Java was designed to be executable cross-platform, JVMs have been developed and refined for a wide range of operating systems, from high-powered servers to embedded device implementations.

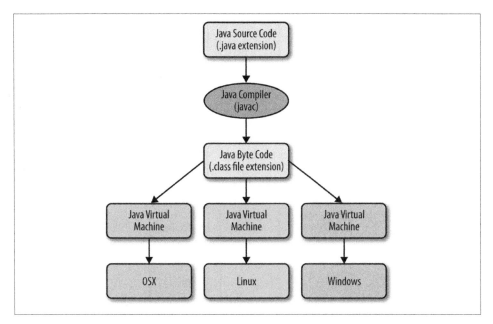

Figure 4-1. Java compilation process

The relative independence of the JVM from the Java language itself led to the development of other languages that can run on the JVM (*http://bit.ly/1mcN6MC*), including Ruby (JRuby, introduced in the previous chapter), Python (Jython), Groovy, Clojure, and JavaScript. The JVM, once seen only as the part of the language installation that enabled cross-platform development, now serves as an interface for other languages' implementations (see Figure 4-2).

JVM Scripting Interface and Static Typed Language Support

The languages shown in Figure 4-2 are used in the project later in this chapter and elsewhere in this book. They were selected among the many JVM languages supported because they are relatively well-known and are available through the scripting interface defined in JSR 223: Scripting for the Java Platform (*http://bit.ly/1nvTPwu*). The scripting interface provides a common mechanism for the integration of supported languages in a single project. Several of these languages are also affected by later work for JSR 292: Supporting Dynamically Typed Languages on the Java Platform (*http://bit.ly/1eShs38*) and so are now driving development and enhancements to aspects of the JVM itself.

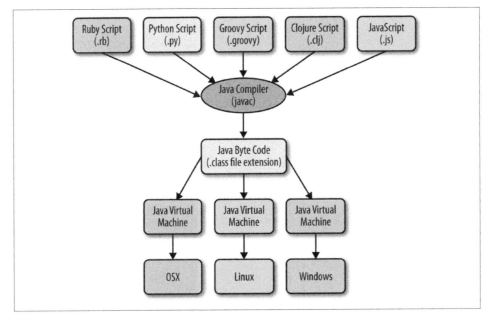

Figure 4-2. JVM language compilation process

The availability of relatively terse and powerful scripting languages provides an appealing alternative when creating APIs to run on the JVM. The project later in this chapter will demonstrate a variety of the server-side options for manipulating JSON in JVM languages.

Java Tools

Java is a mature language with many standard options for IDEs, including Eclipse (*http://www.eclipse.org*), NetBeans (*http://netbeans.org*), and IntelliJ (*http://www.jetbrains.com/idea*). These IDEs contain development tools and plug-ins that take the drudgery out of writing code, debugging, profiling, and a myriad of other programming chores. The IDE is front and center of the individual developer's work, and mastering is an indispensable skill for modern Java development. IDEs provide integration with other systems that are a significant part of team projects, version control, and build automation.

There are many different tools available for building projects (Apache Ant (*https://ant.apache.org*) is a long-time favorite in the Java community). Maven (*http://maven.apache.org/index.html*) goes significantly beyond defining a simple build process and also coordinates a range of widely accepted software development tasks. Gradle (*http://www.gradle.org*) is a relative newcomer based on Groovy. Both Ant and Maven are XML-based, while Gradle is a full-fledged *Domain Specific Language* (DSL).

Beyond a certain critical complexity, there needs to be additional infrastructure to help guide the development process. The specifics of such an infrastructure vary somewhat from project to project, but by following well-understood and established programming practices, it is possible to decrease ramp-up time and maintain control of a project with minimal impact on programmer productivity. Simply put, such an infrastructure allows a project team to scale in ways that would otherwise be impossible.

Build Tools

One of the most important decisions an architect or lead developer makes is what assets to initially include in a project. This decision impacts subsequent development when the project stabilizes but becomes more difficult to change. The choice of a build system has immense ramifications for later activities. There are a number of factors that go into this choice.

The flexibility provided by the syntax of a programming tool is a significant factor in its usefulness. Martin Fowler (*http://bit.ly/LX9Y1U*) has contrasted make (*https://www.gnu.org/software/make*) (which has its own custom syntax) with ant (*http://ant.apache.org*) (which uses an XML-based syntax) and rake (*http://rake.ruby forge.org*) (which uses the Ruby programming language) to call attention to the value of having a full-fledged programming language available to build scripts. A factor that has been of perhaps greater interest in recent years is the availablity of *dependency management* in a build tool. Without dependency management of some sort, a developer is in the unhappy situation of having to identify, locate, download, and install dependent modules and related resources (sometimes with limited documentation). The automatic management of specified versions of modules from online code repositories is immensely valuable to individual developers and benefits the general stability of a project. See Table 4-1.

Table 4-1. Comparison of build tools

	Custom DSL	XML DSL	Programming language	Dependency management
make (*https://www.gnu.org/software/make*)	Y	N	-	N
ant (*http://ant.apache.org*)	N	Y	-	N
rake (*http://rake.rubyforge.org*)	N	N	Ruby	N
maven (*http://maven.apache.org*)	N	Y	-	Y
gradle (*http://www.gradle.org*)	N	N	Groovy	Y
SBT (*http://www.scala-sbt.org*)	N	N	Scala	Y

This is a bit of a simplification because build tools are incredibly extensible. Dependency management add-ons and support for other programming languages can be added to expand the capabilities of those that do not provide these natively. For example, Ant supports dependency management using Ivy (*http://ant.apache.org/ivy*), and a Groovy-based version of the project named Gant (*http://gant.codehaus.org*) also exists.

The list is representative of widely used build tools but is not exhaustive. Since 1977, Make has influenced most other build tools to some degree (including Rake). Rake itself has inspired several Java-oriented projects (including Raven (*http://raven.rubyforge.org*) and Apache buildr (*http://bit.ly/1eWWluV*)).

Dependency management is indisputably an excellent feature for practically any project of any size. Having a full-fledged programming language provides a good deal of flexibility. Ruby has been a popular choice but has been superceded by Groovy in many cases because of Groovy's greater similarity to Java (as noted earlier, a valid Groovy file is generally a valid Java file). And so Gradle (*http://www.gradle.org*) is emerging as a popular choice that includes dependency management support of a full-fledged scripting language in a syntax that is succinct and immediately accessible to Java developers. Similarly, Scala users have *Scala Build Tool* (SBT) (*http://www.scala-sbt.org*), which is roughly analogous to Gradle (build tool for Groovy) in its design and purpose. A notable use of the tool outside of Scala is the Play Framework, which supports both Scala and Java.

Though there are many options, and flexibility is often advantageous, there are significant benefits to using a tool that is "opinionated" and effectively makes a number of up-front decisions based on best practices. This approach is best represented by Maven.

Is Less Flexibility Desirable?

Martin Fowler's article highlighted the flexibility of having a full-blown programming language available from within your build scripts. Benefits include less code duplication and no frustration from having to drop out of the DSL to do "interesting things." His focus was in the context of building his site (a largely solo endeavor). However, there are benefits to having *more* controls and conventions (and *less* flexibility) when groups of people are involved. Standard naming and a known sequence of build steps lessen confusion when developers join a project at various points after its inception (a common occurence in both large-scale distributed open source projects and corporations that shift programmers to different teams based on demand). When there is an idea to implement a somewhat unusual task in the context of a build, a system that makes it just a little bit more difficult can slow down an otherwise rash decision. It forces a development team to pause and ask, "Do we really need to do this?" and, "What exactly are we trying to accomplish?"

A system geared toward flexibility (like Gradle) is convenient for calling arbitrary tasks (as opposed to a simple standard build). For a relatively small, static team that communicates clearly, is not given to questionable architectural decisions, and enjoys the control available, such a system can be a real boost to productivity. In a larger group, standard conventions are often preferable, because you can check out and build a project

---

without first stopping to ask: "What is the proper command to build this system? We've got tasks to compile install, build, make, package…" Maven enforces standard conventions that save the time and communication overhead that are required to keep a more flexible system viable in a large group.

Maven (*http://maven.apache.org*) (the word in Yiddish means "accumulator of knowledge") organizes a project and defines its software development workflow. It is described as a "software project management and comprehension tool." It simplifies the build process and provides a uniform system for setting up a project (by allowing the specification of project dependencies in a declarative fashion). Its reporting and documentation features serve to produce and centralize all project-specific technical artifacts.

Maven has a number of notable characteristics:

- It promotes convention over configuration (while remaining extensible and customizable).
- It presents a common interface across projects.
- It provides a well-defined build life cycle.
- It defines a common project configuration through the *project object model* (*pom.xml*).

For more details on Maven, see *Maven: The Definitive Guide* (O'Reilly), which is also available free online (*http://bit.ly/1c1FTbN*).

Benefits of Maven

Maven's value is immediately evident even in minimal Java projects, as it allows JARs to be identified declaratively. As part of the build process, Maven locates these JARs in online repositories along with all dependencies and downloads them to their proper location in a local repository. It takes care of specifying the required CLASSPATH entries so all of the basic setup tasks that are needed to initially build a project are taken care of in a single command. This is sufficient enough to consider using Maven for even the simplest of projects, but its benefits don't end there.

As a project expands or is formalized, assets such as unit tests, generated documentation, and build reports can be run, assembled, and subsequently stored in standard locations. Having standard project structures and conventions makes it far easier to onboard new developers. This has advantages for a range of projects from those done in open source development to others in large organizations where developers are moved from project to project as staffing requirements change.

Well-structured projects are well-suited for sophisticated development and deployment options. Maven-built projects can be easily integrated into a *continuous integration* (CI) process (*http://bit.ly/1aYPrWp*). And with its references to the version control system, release management is done in a controlled and standardized manner using tags with incremental version numbers. In fact, if a system includes a robust set of tests run regularly on a CI server and the production environment includes sufficent monitoring and alerts, it is possible to shift from managing specific releases to *continuous deployment* (*http://oreil.ly/1jBA9tX*) of software on a much more frequent basis. The proper initial organization of a project provides immediate benefit to developers and saves effort all the way through to production deployment.

Functionality of Maven

Maven itself is fairly simple and provides little functionality out of the box. Through the use of plug-ins, it can execute a wide range of standard build tasks and can be extended to incorporate any others you can imagine. A few concrete examples:

- Standard unit testing via JUnit (*http://bit.ly/1lJ2exG*) and code coverage reports (*http://bit.ly/1aYPAZW*) are included as standard features when generating many new projects (from Maven project templates called *archetypes*).

- A project website (mvn site (*http://bit.ly/1aYPEJr*)) can be created to document the purpose and status of your project. A Maven site can be created using the default wiki-like format called *Almost Plain Text* (APT) or other supported option. This site provides a central location for project information, contacts, reports, and resources.

- An embedded application server can be run with minimal configuration using a simple command (`mvn jetty:run` (*http://bit.ly/1aYPDFg*)) for use during development. This server can also be run as part of the build itself to support unit tests. Other plug-ins are available to deploy web applications to your application server of choice.

- Although rooted in the Java development community, Maven plug-ins have been written to support development in other languages. JavaScript plug-ins (*http://bit.ly/1jaB4hI*) provide code organization and unit testing. Minification (*http://bit.ly/LXbReS*) and code quality tools (*http://bit.ly/1mcQVRU*) are also readily available.

Maven is often described as "opinionated software." Understood negatively, this suggests that it is difficult to adapt to certain types of projects. However, its opiniated character promotes a defined software development life cycle and best practices worth considering even when using another build system. It replaces reliance on individuals to remember and manually enact details of proper build processes and project management with standardized configuration that can be heavily augmented with a wide range of plug-ins. It promotes unified practices within a project or even across an organization. Rather than using a wide-open system that puts the onus on the developer to remember,

Maven's "opinions" can be leveraged so that the average developer does not even think about peripheral issues and will simply do the right thing because many wrong options require too much additional effort.

The assets initially included in a project profoundly impact subsequent development. This is true not only of the components that comprise the project itself, but also the choice of development tools and build system. The decision to include Maven or any other built tool has immense ramifications for later activities. The purpose for including Maven in the project presented later in this chapter is to demonstrate how simple it is to set up an absolutely minimal configuration and show its value for declarative management of modules. Once a project is already being built on Maven, it is relatively easy to integrate additional plug-ins and features.

Version Control

If you are reading this book, you likely do not need to be convinced of the value of using version control. Most development shops need to maintain control of their software assets and use version control systems to this end. If treated as a mere file-system backup, many of their greatest benefits are missed. These include viewing historic changes of code over time, comparing various versions, establishing defined releases of code (tags), creating branches to facilitate parallel development of integration of code, and creating patches.

Version control systems (VCS) are fundamental for enabling groups of developers to effectively work together on large-scale projects. They greatly ease conflict resolution that results when several developers need to change the same file. Support for existing projects is greatly eased through the use of VCS because there is an audit history of who changed what, and when. If useful comments are included on commit or there is integration with issue tracking systems, there is also an indication of why a given change was made.

Individual developers benefit from VCS because they can confidently experiment, knowing that they can revert to a previous "known-good" version as needed. If a project takes an extended period to complete, VCS history can make visible progress that has been made over time and provide helpful reminder of why changes were made.

Maven projects (*http://bit.ly/1dnCCEt*) manage source code using Git or Subversion.

Unit Testing

It is easy to incorporate unit tests into a project using Maven/Junit (for Java), node/Karma (for JavaScript) or other testing framework using virtually any other programming language. There are also Java frameworks that support other types of testing. JBehave (*http://jbehave.org*) can be used for *Behavior-Driven Development* (BDD) and is available through a Maven plug-in (*http://bit.ly/1opJvcO*). It is also possible to test using browser automation through the Selenium (*http://www.seleniumhq.org*) plug-in (*http://bit.ly/1g1teEL*).

One challenge encountered in ongoing unit testing is isolating code from dependence on external systems. This can be overcome by creating an object to replace or mimic real objects in a testing context. There are actually a number of different kinds of objects that can be used. Martin Fowler (*http://bit.ly/1gamvHM*) highlights dummies, fakes, stubs, and mocks. Testers vary as to how much mock objects should be used in testing, but projects like Mockito (*https://code.google.com/p/mockito*) and JMock (*http://jmock.org*) make it much easier to make tests that are otherwise difficult or impossible to create.

The applicability of a given testing approach varies based on the project, customer, development team, and available resources. Regardless of the choice, Maven makes the inclusion of a unit test framework (*http://bit.ly/1eSjd0b*) easy. And as pointed out earlier, a comprehensive set of tests makes possible a range of development and deployment options that are simply not feasible without this sort of validation and coverage.

JSON Java Libraries

There are a number of Java Libraries that can process (parse or generate) JSON. Because the fundamental structure in Java is a Java object, libraries written for JSON in Java tend to rely on mappings between JSON and Java objects and provide methods to serialize and deserialize objects from JSON. Jackson (*http://jackson.codehaus.org*) and Gson (*https://code.google.com/p/google-gson*) are two popular libraries that can convert Java objects into their JSON representation and vice versa.

Projects

These projects provide an absolutely minimal Maven pom to show its value for declarative management of modules. Once a project is already being built on Maven, it is relatively easy to integrate additional plug-ins and features.

Each project can be built using the following command from the root directory for the project:

```
mvn clean install
```

An Internet connection must be available to allow Maven to locate and download the modules required by each project. The first time you run this command for a project, it checks your local repository (which is in *<your OS user's home directory>/.m2/repository* by default). If the project does not exist there, it will find it in a Maven repository online and download it so that it is available for subsequent use. Running a `mvn clean` command results in resources in your project being removed but does *not* affect the modules have been downloaded to your local repository.

Java with JSON

The java_json (*http://bit.ly/1lJ3voq*) project demonstrates basic usage of Maven along with the Jackson and JSON Java APIs. The *pom.xml* needed to include both JSON and Jackson as dependencies in a project is as follows:

```xml
<?xml version="1.0" encoding="UTF-8"?>
<project xmlns="http://maven.apache.org/POM/4.0.0"
        xmlns:xsi="http://www.w3.org/2001/XMLSchema-instance"
        xsi:schemaLocation="http://maven.apache.org/POM/4.0.0
        http://maven.apache.org/xsd/maven-4.0.0.xsd">
    <modelVersion>4.0.0</modelVersion>

    <groupId>JSON_Java</groupId>
    <artifactId>JSON_Java</artifactId>
    <packaging>jar</packaging>
    <version>1.0</version>

    <dependencies>
        <dependency>
            <groupId>com.google.code.gson</groupId>
            <artifactId>gson</artifactId>
            <version>2.2.3</version>
            <scope>compile</scope>
        </dependency>
        <dependency>
            <groupId>org.codehaus.jackson</groupId>
            <artifactId>jackson-mapper-asl</artifactId>
            <version>1.9.12</version>
        </dependency>
    </dependencies>
    <build>
      <plugins>
            <plugin>
              <groupId>org.codehaus.mojo</groupId>
              <artifactId>exec-maven-plugin</artifactId>
              <version>1.2.1</version>
            </plugin>
      </plugins>
    </build>
</project>
```

This pom specifies the project's identity (or *coordinates*: groupId, artifactId, and version) and mode of packaging (JAR). Specific versions of Jackson and JSON are identified by version, and a plug-in that facilitates the execution of main methods is included. This is an extremely simple *pom.xml* that shows how easily Maven can be used to manage JAR dependencies. This should be less intimidating if you are a Maven beginner, and Maven pros can expand on what is provided to add unit tests, documentation, reports, and all of your favorite bells and whistles.

The Java code included is comprised of three classes. A *plain old Java object* (POJO) is defined which will be used for serializing and deserializing the JSON:

```java
package com.saternos.json;

public class MyPojo {
  private String thing1;
  private String thing2;

  public MyPojo(){
    System.out.println("*** Constructor MyPojo() called");
  }

  public String getThing1() {
    return thing1;
  }

  public void setThing1(String thing1) {
    this.thing1 = thing1;
  }

  public String getThing2() {
    return thing2;
  }

  public void setThing2(String thing2) {
    this.thing2 = thing2;
  }

  @Override
  public boolean equals(Object o) {
    if (this == o) return true;
    if (o == null || getClass() != o.getClass()) return false;

    MyPojo myPojo = (MyPojo) o;

    if (thing1 != null ? !thing1.equals(myPojo.thing1) : myPojo.thing1 != null)
        return false;
    if (thing2 != null ? !thing2.equals(myPojo.thing2) : myPojo.thing2 != null)
        return false;

    return true;
  }

  @Override
  public int hashCode() {
    int result = thing1 != null ? thing1.hashCode() : 0;
    result = 31 * result + (thing2 != null ? thing2.hashCode() : 0);
    return result;
  }
}
```

The code required to instantiate a POJO, export its JSON representation, and parse the JSON to create another POJO in the DemoJSON class is as follows:

```
MyPojo pojo = new MyPojo();
//... code to populate pojo can be found in the project source code

Gson gson = new Gson();
String json = gson.toJson(pojo);

MyPojo pojo2  = gson.fromJson(json, MyPojo.class);
```

DemoJackson follows the same pattern using object and method names particular to the Jackson API:

```
MyPojo pojo = new MyPojo();
//... code to populate pojo can be found in the project source code

ObjectMapper mapper = new ObjectMapper();
String json = mapper.writeValueAsString(pojo);

MyPojo pojo2  = mapper.readValue(json, MyPojo.class);
```

These Java classes can be executed using the following commands:

```
$ mvn exec:java -Dexec.mainClass=com.saternos.json.DemoJackson
```

```
$ mvn exec:java -Dexec.mainClass=com.saternos.json.DemoGSON
```

JVM Scripting Languages with JSON

The preceding Java-based examples convert JSON to Java objects, which makes sense for Java but not for other languages. JSON is based on a few simple data structures (JavaScript arrays and objects). These correspond to arrays (or lists) and hashes (or dictionaries, tables, or hash maps) in other languages. Many libraries make a simple translation between a JSON object and the appropriate native data structures.

The jvm_json (*http://bit.ly/1lJ3xN7*) project shows how a JSON document can be read and a field extracted and outputted using Clojure, JavaScript, Jython, and Groovy. Figure 4-3 provides a visual representation highlighting how the ScriptEngineManag er class is used to call the correct engine based on the file extension.

JVM JavaScript Engines

The examples in this book use the Rhino JavaScript engine developed by Mozilla (which gets its name from the O'Reilly book (*http://oreil.ly/JavaScript-TDG-5e*) on the subject). A new Java JavaScript engine dubbed Nashorn (*http://bit.ly/MfJfyq*) is being developed by Oracle Corporation and is scheduled for release with Java 8.

The *pom.xml* in this project includes the relevant dependencies for the programming languages being used. In addition, two plug-ins are configured:

1. The Exec Maven plug-in (*http://bit.ly/1kEDqZA*) allows Java classes and other executables to be run at the command line.

2. The Maven Shade plug-in (*http://bit.ly/1kEDuZk*) is one of a number of plug-ins available that can be used to package JARs. The Shade plug-in is unique in its ability to package projects in JARs that otherwise have issues with conflicting class names. This is a somewhat common occurence when working with modules that implement the Java scripting interface mentioned earlier.

The pom also includes references to repositories that contain referenced modules.

The main Java class (`Jvms.java`) opens a script file specified as an argument to the program and executes it using the appropriate scripting engine (based on the file extension).

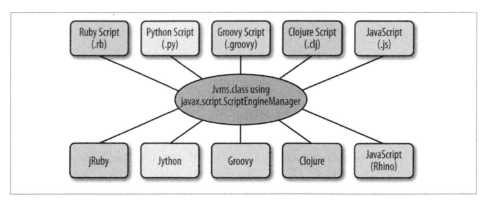

Figure 4-3. Script engine manager role

`Jvms.java` has a simple main method that iterates through the arguments passed to it at the command line. For each argument, the program tries to verify the existence of a file with that name. If one is not found, it appends *src/main/resources/scripts* as the path to the filename. This is the directory where the script files are stored. Note that exception handling and other details are omitted in the interest of presenting the aspects of the program relevant to the current discussion. In this case, if a file is not found, the exception is simply passed out of the main method (which is defined to throw `Excep tion`). The extension is identified to be the portion of the file name from the first dot to the end of the filename. Finally, a new `ScriptEngineManager` is instantiated, and a script engine is retrieved by extension. The `File` is read from the file system and evaluated by the script engine associated with the file extension:

```
public static void main( String[] args ) throws Exception
{
  for (String fileName: args){

    if (!fileName.trim().equals(""))
    {
      File file=new java.io.File(fileName);

      if (!file.exists())
        fileName ="src/main/resources/scripts/"+fileName;

      String ext = fileName.substring(
        fileName.indexOf(".") + 1,
        fileName.length()
      );

      new ScriptEngineManager().getEngineByExtension(ext).eval(
        new java.io.FileReader(fileName)
      );

    }
  }
}
```

The program can be executed from Maven, and one or more of the scripts can be passed in as arguments:

```
mvn -q \
exec:java -Dexec.args="testJson.clj testJson.js testJson.groovy testJson.py"
```

If you prefer, you can execute the JAR file directly without using Maven by using an included script:

```
jvms.sh testJson.clj testJson.js testJson.py testJson.groovy
```

The Python (Jython (*http://www.jython.org*)) example is terse and straightforward. The use of indentation in lieu of blocks with begin and end tokens makes it a great example that emphasizes the functionality in question in an almost pseudocode form without additional overhead or distractions. Python is a very regular language and has less ambiguities due to its consistency of design:

```
import json

print('*** JSON Jython ***')

for item in json.loads(open("data/test.json").read()):
    print item['title']
```

A library for processing JSON is imported, loaded from the file system, and the object is iterated through so each title will print. The Groovy example follows nearly the same pattern. Groovy (*http://groovy.codehaus.org*) is based heavily on Java (a valid Java file is usually a valid Groovy file as well). It introduces a number of idioms that are more compact and concise than pure Java. This makes it a popular language to introduce to Java developers who can fall back on their Java knowledge while they learn Groovy distinctives:

```
import groovy.json.JsonSlurper

println "*** JSON Groovy ***"

def json = new File("data/test.json").text

new JsonSlurper().parseText(json).each { println it.title }
```

The Clojure example follows the same basic pattern, although you might notice a certain plethora of parentheses. Clojure (*http://clojure.org*) is a dialect of LISP that is a stark contrast to the C-like syntax of the other examples:

```
(require '[clojure.data.json :as json])

(println "*** JSON Clojure ***")

(def recs (json/read-str (slurp "data/test.json")))

(doseq [x recs] (println (x "title")))
```

The JavaScript version is a bit different. There is no need to import (we are using eval() in this example just for illustration purposes). If you recall, JavaScript does not have built-in I/O functionality. So this example uses a bit of a hack to make a call to a static Java method to read in file (using Java) and convert the file contents (available from Java as a Java string) to a JavaScript string:

```
println('*** JSON Javascript ***')

// Call a Java static method to read and convert the file to a JavaScript string
var str = String(com.saternos.app.Jvms.readFile("data/test.json"));

var o = eval(str);

for (var i=0; i < o.length; i++){
    println(o[i].title);
}
```

Although this might be considered a less pure implementation, it demonstrates the ease of integration between languages on the JVM.

Conclusion

People learn a new programming language or supporting utility like Maven for many reasons. The most common one is that it is needed for a specific project. Many Ruby developers started using the language when developing Rails applications or while using Chef or Puppet for system administration. Scientists have gravitated toward Python due

---

to its specialized libraries relevant to their work as well as its disciplined design and high performance.

Studies suggest that natural languages shape thinking. This is highlighted in an article (*http://on.wsj.com/LXcKUX*) that appeared in the Wall Street Journal. The article describes how language can have a profound effect on how an individual sees and thinks about the world. The article states:

Some findings on how language can affect thinking.

- Russian speakers, who have more words for light and dark blues, are better able to visually discriminate shades of blue.

- Some indigenous tribes say north, south, east and west, rather than left and right, and as a consequence have great spatial orientation.

- The Piraha, whose language eschews number words in favor of terms like few and many, are not able to keep track of exact quantities.

- In one study, Spanish and Japanese speakers couldn't remember the agents of accidental events as adeptly as English speakers could. Why? In Spanish and Japanese, the agent of causality is dropped: "The vase broke itself," rather than "John broke the vase."

Languages that are particularly expressive in a given area make an individual more attuned to that area. The same is true of programming languages. In this view, learning a new programming language is not an end unto itself, and is not merely done to complete a specific project. It helps you see the world differently. It improves your ability to solve problems in general. Most programmers who learn Clojure (or other LISP dialect) do not do so because of a specific project. Their intention is to improve their ability to conceptualize and solve problems. LISP dialects are well known for being among the most simple, expressive, powerful, and flexible languages available (or perhaps even possible). But the same is true to a lesser extent when learning other programming languages. Each one has features and a community that can differ widely from others. But many of these differences are not absolute, and a programmer can grow by simply learning other languages and tools, even if they are not of immediate use.

This chapter presented several JVM languages and Maven from the viewpoint of how they affect development done in community with other developers. Certain languages might facilitate good communication among developers. They might serve to encapsulate requirements in a way that will make the system easier to reverse-engineer and support in the future. Maven can be used to structure project resources and development processes in a way that has been conducive to many successful projects involving teams of developers. Although reading a book is a relatively solitary activity, it is certain that a significant amount of your work as a programmer will be done with others. JVM languages and Maven provide suitable features for projects that require extensive interaction with other developers over extended periods of time.

## CHAPTER 5

Client-Side Frameworks

You know also that the beginning is the most
important part of any work...for that is the time at
which the character is being formed and the desired
impression is more readily taken.

—Plato

Overview

In the early days of the Web, starting a new web page involved opening a text editor and creating an HTML document from scratch. This approach still works for creating minimal examples for educational purposes or testing isolated bits of JavaScript functionality. However, this starting point is *not* the place from which most modern web applications originate. Instead, a viable project template includes a well-organized directory structure and some combination of a particular set of JavaScript libraries, CSS files, HTML, and other assets. The selection might vary from project to project, but in general should address concerns such as project consistency, cross-browser compatibility, sound design principles, software development practices (such as unit testing), and superior performance.

Historically, starter projects have been generated (by tools like Maven, utilizing archetypes) or specified during the creation of a new project in an IDE. Such projects were often tied to the tool that generated them. With no standard IDE or build tool for web development, starter projects have no such tie (though are integrated in tools and IDEs). They vary in complexity and purpose, but successful ones have a common characteristic of being simple to understand, set up, and deploy. They provide a basic infrastructure that reduces tedious manual work not directly related to the main purpose of the web application.

The choice of a starting point involves the fundamental building blocks of a client-side web page: HTML, CSS, and JavaScript in the context of a web page running in a web browser. This is shown in Figure 5-1.

Figure 5-1. Client-side web page

The widest context to consider is the client itself. There are many possible web browsers. Each browser has many versions. Browsers are no longer specific to desktop applications, but run on mobile devices. Each browser instance runs on specific hardware that can have a wide range of capabilities. The hardware can vary in processor power, disk space, memory, screen size, and display characteristics. This is perhaps obvious, but often forgotten by a developer whose view is restricted to a few browsers running on a developement workstation.

Starter projects can be oriented toward specific content, style, and/or behavior. HTML defines the fundamental structure and content of the page. CSS defines style and design presentation. JavaScript provides behavioral capabilities. Those with design skills might opt for a starter project that is more minimal or provides more flexibility in CSS stylings, but might want a JavaScript infrastructure that supports a wide range of plug-ins and requires minimal programming. A developer might choose a project that provides a passible design out of the box, but be comfortable with a bleeding-edge JavaScript library that takes advantage of the latest browser capabilities.

The choice of a starter project is also based on your application requirements and your audience. The goal of compatibility over the largest selection of available browsers might suggest one starter project, while the goal a highly optimized application for specific mobile devices would suggest another. For example, frameworks like PhoneGap (*http://phonegap.com*) include starter projects that specifically target mobile devices. If your project is a game or other graphically intensive project such as a simulation, starter projects (*http://bit.ly/1dKHlf9*) that include JavaScript libraries with graphics and physics engine capabilities are relevant.

Specific requirements can suggest a starting point that is not immediately apparent or popular. It is easy to become enamoured with a particular framework or design trend, but a project's idiosyncracies might require a different approach. For instance, if you need to actively target a particular browser (due to in-house browser standards, target web demographic, and so on), you might orient development to its particular quirks and choose a starting project that accounts for these. In addition, HTML, CSS, and JavaScript can be used to develop a range of applications outside of a standard web page such as browser extensions and native applications. A general-purpose approach targeting a range of browsers and devices is often optimal, but it is certainly not the only valid one.

In general, most serious web development projects today are intended to be fully featured applications that work on variety of devices. Most are also created with an expectation that they will grow to be relatively large and sophisticated. This suggests the use of a client-side JavaScript framework related to standard software patterns and code organization. Differences in display, browser capabilities, and device functionality imply the use of well-thought-out design that adapts to a range of devices and degrades gracefully when features are not available. The range of target device features that are expected to be leveraged over the life of the application imply the use of additional libraries and frameworks. These did not need to be considered in traditional, limited desktop browser applications.

The High Cost (or Value) of Early Decisions

This section might seem to belabor the obvious. Pick a starter project and let's roll!

The issue at stake in making well-thought-out early choices has its roots in their huge impact down the road. The idea is expressed by economists and social scientists using the term *path dependence* (*http://bit.ly/MOg4SM*). The basic idea is that early decisions are a "disproportionate cause of later circumstances." Problems introduced early in a project might be impossible to reverse at a later point. For instance, a choice of an immature JavaScript library can lead to numerous fixes and hacks being added to address browser incompatibilities. Though not obvious during initial development (where developers have focused attention on modern browsers), later support can become burdensome, and the large amount of additional code can lead to a situation where there is no turning back. Conversely, a well-thought-out starter project can reduce the support burden significantly far into a project's implementation.

Starting Point One: Responsive Web Design

On May 25, 2010, Ethan Marcotte's article titled "Responsive Web Design" (*http://bit.ly/ rwdarticle*) appeared on *A List Apart* (*http://alistapart.com*). *Responsive Web Design* (or RWD) has now become a general term used as a shorthand to capture the ideas he expressed. Rather than designing specifically for each device display, this style of design strives to provide an optimal viewing experience across a wide range of devices. Like software design patterns (*http://oreil.ly/HF-Design-Patterns*) (which were inspired by Christopher Alexander's architectural patterns), the concept finds its origin in building architecture. Responsive architecture considers how physical spaces can adapt as people pass through them. Responsive Web Design seeks to adapt to user experiences on a variety of device displays with diverse methods of interaction based on device capabilities. Three components of RWD are:

Fluid grids (http://bit.ly/1guxBdt)
> Adapt the typographic grid for use on the Web. They take advantage of relative sizing available in CSS to provide display of a grid and its components in a manner properly proportioned to its context.

Flexible images (http://bit.ly/1aYRMAU)
> Include using the CSS `max-width` to cause images and other media to render within their containing element and related techniques to avoid fixed-point styling that does not adapt to all device displays.

CSS3 media queries
> Inspect the physical characteristics of the context where the page is rendered and respond with a specific display fixed-unit format.

The fluid layout and flexible images (which rely on relative sizing) combined with CSS3 media queries (allowing adaptive layout targeting fixed sizing) provide the basis of RWD. Fluid layout is proportionately scaled, and adaptive layout breaks at given points. This prevents the skewing that occurs with a fluid approach alone or the lack of adaptation to intermediate display possibilities from a purely adaptive design.

By using the three constructs of RWD, a single well-constructed set of web resources can produce pages that can be viewed and used effectively on a variety of devices. Marcotte later developed the ideas introduced in the article in a book (*http://bit.ly/ LXddpW*) on the subject. A number of projects have been developed based on these principles, among them HTML Boilerplate and Twitter Bootstrap.

HTML5 Boilerplate

HTML5 Boilerplate (*http://html5boilerplate.com*) provides a set of resources that satisfy the requirements of RWD. Its features include a standard directory structure and template files related to a website and web server configuration. It includes CSS that incorporates *normalize.css* (*http://bit.ly/normalcss*) (a stylesheet that provides consistent rendering in line with modern standards across browsers), some additional CSS defaults, common helpers, placeholder media queries, and print styles. The jQuery and Modernizr JavaScript libraries are provided as well.

Bootstrap

Twitter Bootstrap (*http://bit.ly/1fjDC9o*), was initially described by its creators (*http://bit.ly/1lJ5Uzq*) as "a front-end toolkit for rapidly developing web applications. It is a collection of CSS and HTML conventions. It uses some of the latest browser techniques to provide you with stylish typography, forms, buttons, tables, grids, navigation and everything else you need in a super tiny (only 6k with gzip) resource."

As such, it goes beyond the minimal resources provided in HTML5 Boilerplate. It was further enhanced in the second version (*http://bit.ly/1eWYtmn*) and continues to be refined (*http://blog.getbootstrap.com*) with input from the community that has grown around the project. Sites built with Bootstrap have been critiqued as being monotonous and predictable, essentially carbon copies of one another. Although similarity is to be expected due to the use of standard resources and styles, there is actually a great deal of flexibility available through manual customization or the use of themes. The framework has also become more "componentized" over time so that certain features can be included and excluded, and generators exist that can be used to create an out-of-the-box set of resources to differentiate it from the default.

There are many other similar projects. Zurb Foundation (*http://foundation.zurb.com*) has a smaller user base and claims a primary target of mobile devices. If you are interested in a more lightweight project that incorporates minimal responsive design and a basic grid system with some basic styling, Skeleton (*http://www.getskeleton.com*) might be worth checking out. But if you are working on a project that simply requires a responsive site with professional, balanced styling, Bootstrap (augmented with a theme and a few manual adjustments) is the best supported choice for the moment.

Starting Point Two: JavaScript Libraries and Frameworks

As a language matures, various standard libraries are added. In JavaScript, libraries don't require any special structure or packaging; they are simply other JavaScript files. Libraries have been created for almost every purpose you can imagine. But there are a few broad categories of general-purpose libraries that are applicable to client-server web applications.

Browser Compatibility

Although JavaScript is a de facto standard, the idosyncracies of certain browsers are the stuff of legend. The likelihood of browser vendors creating compatible implementation is small. There is too much effort dedicated to differentiating each browser and implementing functionality geared toward driving the standards process rather than adhering to estabilished standards or guidelines. Fortunately, a number of libraries in common use smooth over many of the rough edges and result in JavaScript code that provides consistent results (and less errors or disruptive results) regardless of the particular browser version. These libraries are shown in Table 5-1.

Table 5-1. Browser compatibility

Library	Purpose
jQuery (*http://jquery.com*)	DOM traversal and manipulation
Modernizr (*http://modernizr.com*)	Browser feature detection
Underscore (*http://underscorejs.org*)	Utility functions including object and array manipulation

jQuery and Modernizr are de facto standards in their particular realm. Underscore is a bit less established. There are a number of other libraries that provide similar functionality: consistent handling of objects and arrays in a concise, functional manner (Lo-Dash (*http://lodash.com*), for example, is intended to be an optimized replacement for underscore).

Frameworks

Direct DOM manipulation (á la jQuery) is a fine approach with small- to mid-sized JavaScript projects. With larger projects, it is much easier to manipulate JavaScript classes that incorporate interactive data and include additional functionality, such as data validation. These classes can then be populated and connected to the graphical elements in a page. This type of design has the beneficial effect of avoiding direct DOM manipulation. Instead, changes to the data are reflected on the page based on the state of the data in the containing objects. Interaction with the page (and data changes due to external events) result in changes to the state of the model that trickle down to all affected view components. The first MVC frameworks were created many years ago for this purpose, and the pattern has been adopted in modern JavaScript frameworks. There are several variations of MVC, which include *Model-View Presenter* (MVP) and *Model-View ViewModel* (MVVM) and so the term MV* is sometimes used as a general umbrella to identify these patterns as a group.

The choice of an initial framework can be rather daunting from the outside. If you do not have a particular bias, it can take a bit of effort to make a decision about which one to use. Some basic criteria beyond current in-house development skills are the functionality of a given framework and its popularity.

Functionality

The list of MV* frameworks is rather extensive and constantly changing. One site that provides immediate specific comparison of the functionality of popular frameworks is TODO MVC (*http://todomvc.com*). TODO MVC allows you to compare the implementation of a simple fully functional TODO list application in a variety of different MV* frameworks.

Popularity

Although the most popular selection might not be the best, it is a reasonable proxy for general support for a project and whether it has a viable ecosystem for education, enhancements, and bug fixes. Google Trends (*http://www.google.com/trends*) displays the number of searches being made for certain search terms, and the number of Stack-Overflow tags (*http://stackoverflow.com/tags*) can also give an idea of developer chatter on a subject. To get a better sense of what code is actually in use, view popular GitHub repos (*https://github.com/popular/starred*) (and statistics on new projects that have not yet catapulted to the top of the list) or get a sense of total deployment base using statistics from a site like BuiltWith (*http://builtwith.com*).

If you decide to work with one of the major JavaScript MV* frameworks, you will want to review and possibly start with whatever project the community has produced and actively supports. Table 5-2 lists starter projects for several popular frameworks.

Table 5-2. Starter projects for JavaScript MVC Frameworks

Framework	Starter project
Backbone (*http://backbonejs.org*)	Backbone Boilerplate (*https://github.com/backbone-boilerplate/backbone-boilerplate*)
Angular (*http://angularjs.org*)	Angular Seed (*https://github.com/angular/angular-seed*)
Ember (*http://emberjs.com*)	Ember Starter Kit (*https://github.com/emberjs/starter-kit*)

Each of these frameworks is rather extensive and an exhaustive overview is not possible here. O'Reilly's books on Angular (*http://oreil.ly/angularJS*) and Backbone (*http://oreil.ly/dev_backbone_js_apps*) go into much greater detail.

These are by no means the only options. JavaScript frameworks have dependencies and inspire libraries that extend their core functionality. jQuery is a prerequisite to many other projects, and `underscore.js` is a dependency for Backbone. Backbone developers tend to use `require.js` for script loading and code organization; it also inspired the alternative MV* framework Spine (*http://spinejs.com*). Angular-UI (*http://angular-ui.github.io*) provides user interface components. jQuery has inspired an entire ecosystem of related libraries, plug-ins, and extensions, among them large libraries such as jQuery UI (*http://jqueryui.com*) that provide widgets of all kinds and small specialized libraries like TouchPunch (*http://touchpunch.furf.com*) for touch screen event handling.

There are also starter projects, which combine a JavaScript library with another starter project oriented toward browser compatibility and responsive design. A project that combines Angular UI and Bootstrap (*http://bit.ly/MOgZCP*) is available and comparable to one created for jQuery UI and Bootstrap (*http://bit.ly/NFESxA*).

Beyond MVC frameworks, if you are creating a jQuery plug-in, the jQuery Boilerplate (*http://jqueryboilerplate.com*) can be used to set up a properly structured project for that purpose. The bottom line is that if you find yourself writing boilerplate code for a task that you are confident others have encountered, it behooves you to check around online to find out if starter projects exist.

Obtaining Starter Projects

There are a couple of different ways to obtain a starter project to jumpstart your development.

Download Directly from Repositories

Most of these projects are maintained online in public source code repositories (generally at GitHub (*https://github.com*)).

GitHub Repository Hall of Fame

For that matter, starter projects, resources that promote responsive web design, and JavaScript libraries are among the most popular repositories on GitHub (*https://github.com/popular/starred*).

- Responsive design resources
    - Modernizr (*https://github.com/Modernizr/Modernizr*)
    - Normalize CSS (*https://github.com/necolas/normalize.css*)
- Starter projects
    - Bootstrap (*https://github.com/twitter/bootstrap*)
    - HTML5 Boilerplate (*https://github.com/h5bp/html5-boilerplate*)
- JavaScript libraries
    - jQuery (*https://github.com/jquery/jquery*)
    - Backbone (*https://github.com/documentcloud/backbone*)
    - Foundation (*https://github.com/zurb/foundation*)
    - Angular (*https://github.com/angular/angular.js*)
    - Underscore (*https://github.com/documentcloud/underscore*)
    - Ember (*https://github.com/emberjs/ember.js*)

— jQuery UI (*https://github.com/jquery/jquery-ui*)

— Knockout (*https://github.com/knockout/knockout*)

Download from Starter Sites

Sites like Initializr (*http://www.initializr.com*) or HTML5 Reset (*http://html5reset.org*) ultimately rely on source code repositories, but include commentary, comparison, and documentation related to starting web projects and general development and design topics as well.

IDE-Generated Starter Projects

IDEs like WebStorm (a commercial project created by JetBrains) include options to create new projects from templates, as shown in Figure 5-2. WebStorm includes several of the starter projects discussed in this chapter as well as Node.js (Node.js boilerplate (*http://bit.ly/LXec9K*) and Node.js express (*http://expressjs.com*)) or Dart (*http://www.dartlang.org*) starter projects.

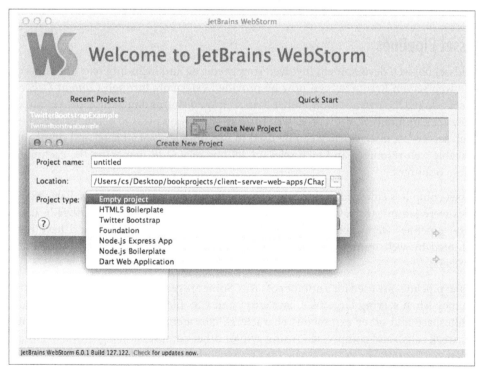

Figure 5-2. Client starter projects

The Rise of the Front-End Engineer

By now, it should be clear that the degree of sophistication involved with web development has expanded greatly from its humble beginnings. It is unlikely that a designer without significant developer skills and focus will be capable of keeping up with the latest advances. Likewise, it is unlikely that most server-side developers will have mature design abilities or an awareness of recent developments that are focused on the client side. This has given rise to a new occupation: the *front-end engineer*. If the topics introduced to this point don't convince you of the explosion of new information, consider these additional nuances related to client-side development and processes.

Client-Side Templating

Some of the JavaScript frameworks previously discussed bundle a JavaScript templating solution. A wide variety of others exist independently, many of which can be swapped in at your discretion with a variety of frameworks. LinkedIn engineering (*http://linkd.in/1dnFOzZ*) considered 26 client-side templating technologies before settling on dust.js (*http://bit.ly/1nvWrut*). There are some fascinating developments in this area, including the possibility of implementing client-side JavaScript templates that can failover to server-side rendering if needed.

Asset Pipelines

Old-school web development involved simply editing and including relevant assets on the web server. Resources can now be provided externally through *Content Delivery Networks* (CDNs). In addition, rather than simply editing and including the resources, they are commonly now preprocessed in a variety of ways prior to being served on the web server. An *asset pipeline* can be used to precompile, concatenate, and minify applicable web resources and take relevant actions related to managing the caching of these resources.

Asset compilers emerged in the Ruby community in the last several years. Early examples were Jammit (*http://bit.ly/1g1wEr1*) and Sprockets (*http://bit.ly/1lJ99H7*). Later, asset pipelines were incorporated into Rails (*http://bit.ly/1mcWjV8*) and have been adopted by web frameworks in other languages such as Java's Play2 (*http://bit.ly/1iScu5z*).

Asset pipelines are used for a number of tasks. Some are geared toward reducing network latency when serving large files. JavaScript and CSS files can be minified (removing whitespace and other extraneous characters), concatenated (resulting in fewer total network calls), and compressed (using gzip or other compression algorithms). Others relate to caching. For example, the Play framework uses ETag HTTP Headers (*http://bit.ly/MOi5OZ*) to append a value generated from the resource name and the file's last modification date and also provides the option of setting Cache-Control headers.

In addition, having a preprocessing step available opens up the possibility of compiling other languages to JavaScript (such as CoffeeScript (*http://coffeescript.org*) and Dart (*http://www.dartlang.org*)). This provides a range of possibilities for those who find the JavaScript language itself distasteful.

CSS can also be preprocessed, which reduces the amount of duplicated code. Less duplicated code makes the application styling more easily maintainable at the expense of adding an additional build step. A precompiler processes an initial file at some point prior to being referenced in an HTML page and resolves references in the code so that a standard stylesheet is rendered. Examples of the type of preprocessing available through a CSS compiler include:

- Definition of variables that replace values throughout a stylesheet (for example, a color used in various CSS classes)
- Creation of methods to assign a set of values to a class based on a variable passed as an argument
- Implementation of inheritence of CSS classes

CSS processors originated among Ruby developers but have been gaining acceptance in the Java community. For instance, a LESS CSS Maven plug-in (*http://bit.ly/1jaIEbW*) has been created.

The precompiling step involved in the implementation of an asset pipeline is somewhat controversial. Designers who have never only worked with hardcoded CSS files can find the programming possibilities introduced by a preprocessor daunting. And though developers are likely to be more accepting of the concept of a preprocessor (based on their usage in other programming contexts), changing anyone's workflow can be disconcerting. This is where a new role, that of a front-end engineer, serves a needed role in bridging the gap between developers and designers. This role includes a unique workflow and set of tools suited for the expansion of responsibility that has occurred on the client tier.

Development Workflow

A node-based package called Yeoman (*http://yeoman.io*) provides a development workflow utilizing three tools: yo (*https://github.com/yeoman/yo*) (for scaffolding), grunt (*http://gruntjs.com*) (for building), and bower (*http://bower.io*) (which provides package management). Other node-based packages such as karma (for running tests) and Docco (for documentation) also apply to development worflow and build processes.

Project

In the interest of seeing the value of the simplest possible example of a framework along with how it relates to fully featured starter projects, consider the following examples using Angular:

```html
<!doctype html>
<html ng-app>
  <head>
    <script src="http://code.angularjs.org/1.0.6/angular.min.js"></script>
  </head>
  <body>
        Angular Expression 1 + 2 evaluates to:  {{ 1 + 2 }}
  </body>
</html>
```

The use of the Angular framework is immediately apparent because there are a number of XML attributes (called directives) that are not part of standard HTML included in the document. In this example, ng-app (*http://bit.ly/1cz42D9*) (in the HTML tag) is required to auto-bootstrap an app. One attribute of this type can appear per HTML page. It designates the root of the application and (though it is empty in this case) can optionally include a module name. The script tag indicates that Angular is in use; other Angular scripts that provide additional functionality might also be included. Finally, the bit of visible Angular functionality that will be demonstrated is an expression (*http://bit.ly/1jBEwFh*). An Angular *expression* is JavaScript-like code snippets placed in bindings (double braces) that are evaluated to produce output.

This is a very minimalistic example that only evaluates an expression. It does not even demonstrate Angular as an MV* framework as it includes no controller or data binding. It simply serves to illustrate the absolute minimum features required to create an Angular application. The next example incorporates a model and controller:

```html
<!doctype html>
<html ng-app>
  <head>
<script src="http://ajax.googleapis.com/ajax/libs/angularjs/1.0.6/angular.min.js">
</script>
    <script>
        function HelloCntl($scope) {
                    $scope.name = 'World';
            }
    </script>
  </head>
  <body>
    <div ng-controller="HelloCntl">
      Your name: <input type="text" ng-model="name" />
      <hr/>
      Hello {{name}}!
    </div>
```

```
    </body>
</html>
```

A controller (*http://bit.ly/MfMkhY*) in Angular is simply a function used to implement behavior in a given scope. In this case, the controller is used to bind a model (*http://bit.ly/1fjFrTK*) (the name variable) that can be modified in a text field. Each time a keystroke is registered in the input text field that references the "name" model, the change is reflected in the expression referencing the model. A significant remaining bit of functionality is the framework's functionality related to Ajax calls to remote servers. The final example illustrates this:

```
<!doctype html>
<html ng-app="GoogleFinance">
  <head>
<script src="http://ajax.googleapis.com/ajax/libs/angularjs/1.0.6/angular.min.js">
</script>
    <script src="http://code.angularjs.org/1.0.6/angular-resource.js"></script>
    <script>
      angular.module('GoogleFinance', ['ngResource']);

      function AppCtrl($scope, $resource) {
        $scope.googleFinance = $resource('https://finance.google.com/finance/info',
              {client:'ig', q: 'AAPL', callback:'JSON_CALLBACK'},
              {get: {method:'JSONP', isArray: true}});

        $scope.indexResult = $scope.googleFinance.get();

        $scope.doSearch = function () {
          $scope.indexResult = $scope.googleFinance.get({q: $scope.searchTerm});
        };
      }
    </script>
  </head>
<body>
  <div ng-controller="AppCtrl">
    <form class="form-horizontal">
      <input type="text" ng-model="searchTerm">
      <button class="btn" ng-click="doSearch()">
      Search
      </button>
        </form>
      Current Price: {{indexResult[0].l_cur}}<br/>
      Change:        {{indexResult[0].c}}<br/>
  </div>
</body>
</html>
```

Angular resource (*http://bit.ly/1g1xmVg*) is used to make the backend calls. The script that defines it needs to be included, and it needs to be referenced as a parameter in the controller. Because we are making a call to a site under a different domain, JSONP is specified as a method. The model (searchTerm) is used to specify a stock symbol to search for using the Google Finance API. The results are returned as a JSON array, and the current price and change fields are displayed upon retrieval.

These three examples are helpful for educational and demonstration purposes. They are stripped-down versions that highlight exactly what features are required and how they relate.

With a small amount of effort, Bootstrap's stylesheet and some basic stylings can be added. Additional changes found in the code of this chapter add to the previous example by linking to the `bootstrap.css`, creating a container class and view rows, and adding a search icon and some other design adjustments. These all remain in a single self-contained file; a standard starter project breaks these resources up and organizes them in a standard directory structure.

These examples can be included in a starter project such as AngularJS seed or Bootstrap by adding relevant portions of the preceding code to the index page (or relevant included view). Ideally, inline JavaScript code presented in these examples is extracted into a separate file (to start: modules into `app.js` and controllers into `controllers.js`).

Conclusion

In any successful development team, each member has unique strengths that she brings to bear for the benefit of the project. The focus of one member allows others to pay closer attention in other areas, effectively limiting the problem scope under their attention. Starter projects and JavaScript frameworks insulate developers from details of BOM and DOM implementations, browser compatibility issues, initial concerns with code organization, and other challenges.

Hardware improvements and JavaScript performance optimization has made it possible to create large-scale JavaScript applications. Large-scale applications are much easier to manage when standard design is used, and project focus is enhanced by eliminating repetitive tasks required in every web development project. The frameworks introduced in this chapter are specific examples of projects that can jumpstart your next development effort and focus your team's attention immediately on the functional concerns of your project.

## CHAPTER 6

Java Web API Servers

A man wrapped up in himself makes a very small bundle.

—Benjamin Franklin

Packaging makes it possible to extend the capabilities of a language by including reusable components. The packaging available for a given language affects deployment options. Packaging schemes include consideration for standard naming conventions, metadata files, digital signatures, code obfuscation, arrangement of code, inclusion of related files/ resources, and compression mechanisms.

Packaging necessarily impacts deployment. The de facto deployment options available in a language tend to suggest the structure of a project and its development workflow. In Java, this is even more pronounced than other languages. Java source file names reflect the name of the public class they contain. Java packages follow the directory structure of the file system. Java utilizes several specific package types. General purpose source code is included in *Java Archives* (JARs), web applications are stored in *Web Application Archives* (WARs), and groups of related web applications can be packaged together in *Enterprise Application Archives* (EARs). WARs can be deployed to servlet containers, while EARs require full Java Enterprise Edition support, which is available in application servers like JBoss.

Java's packaging paradigm has many benefits but has resulted in a constrained view of deployment possibilities. Standard web application development practices in place since Java's initial development required independently installed and configured application servers. These are not, in fact, required to deploy Java web applications. Even if a web container is used, it is possible to avoid the overhead of installing and configuring it prior to beginning development.

Simpler Server-Side Solutions

The explosion of client-side technologies is overwhelming due to the inherent challenges of web browsers as a platform, the JavaScript language itself, and the JavaScript libraries created to help manage the complexity. An additional complexity is device-specific development, which can involve either mobile web applications or native applications that make HTTP web service calls. One pleasant surprise in the new client-server web paradigm is a corresponding simplification of a portion of server-side code.

A web application traditionally has been a relatively large construct that ran in an application server, web container, or web server. At the time of this writing, the venerable Apache web server (*http://www.ohloh.net/p/apache*) had over *two million lines of code* and required *hundreds of man-years of effort* to complete. J2EE development was notoriously complex (resulting in its being vastly simplified in more recent JEE versions). Server-side Model-View-Controller projects (Struts) and dependency injection frameworks (Spring) provided organization and eased the configuration burden, but highlighted the size and scale of a typical server-side implementation that appeared to be required to develop a Java-based web application.

Client-server web applications use servers that do not maintain session state and consist largely of simple APIs. Though such servers can certainly take advantage of middleware and supporting services, these are often not necessary. Due to direct and indirect influence from the scripting language world, it is now trivially easy to set up a minimal server to provide adequate functionality for front-end developers to work without a need for the full-scale server implementation. Java and JVM languages allow for many possibilities that allow a developer to include server functionality in a project without the need to install, configure, and maintain a full server implementation. This opens up possibilities for very different workflows than were previously possible. In addition to benefits during development, the practice of horizontal scaling in cloud-based production deployments is eased by having a lightweight server solution.

A "containerless" web application server can be constructed by simply using Java on the JVM or by taking advantage of libraries. Figure 6-1 illustrates the ones used in this chapter and their relationship to each other. Libraries located higher on the diagram have greater infrastructure, are more opinionated, and (in theory) are a more productive starting point for a framework suited to a domain. They are not exhaustive, but could be extended in various directions. For example, the various JVM languages have corresponding web frameworks (Sinatra or Rails for JRuby, and Django for Jython). Typeset (*http://typesafe.com*) is a Scala framework built on top of Play. vert.x (*http://vertx.io*) distinguishes itself as supporting several JVM languages.

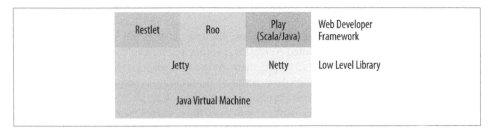

Figure 6-1. Server libraries

The examples in this chapter are confined to a Java-centric workflow and build process. JVM languages vary in their workflow practices depending on their origins. Groovy and Scala were created with their initial target being the JVM, whereas Ruby and Python were languages that were ported to the JVM. Techniques and practices in Groovy (and to a lesser extent Scala) tend to be traceable to problems or patterns familiar to Java developers. JRuby and Jython, having independent origins, tend to have original approaches that are less familar to Java developers (but are recognizable to those moving from other implementations to the JVM). These tend to require you to use the development installation procedures, toolchain, and commands specific to their community.

Java-Based Servers

Servers can be written in Java alone or can use one of several higher-level libraries. The same basic pattern is used in many cases: a server class delegates requests to a handler, which extends an abstract class or implements an interface, which defines a handle method. Figure 6-2 illustrates the basic relationship between the server class, which uses a handler class. The handle method is implemented by the concrete handler. In the examples that follow, the handler will return a JSON object.

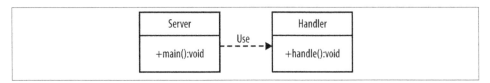

Figure 6-2. Server-handler class diagram

Note on Examples

Like other examples in this book, the examples in this chapter are intentionally simplified to isolate specifics relevent to the topic under discussion. For example, many of the following JSON responses are simply text strings. In practice, it is much more common to use Jackson or other such libraries when constructing a response. Most developers will work using a high-level, full-featured framework, but it is clearer to use strings to illustrate what is happening in code displayed in a book. The use of libraries along with annotations is very neat, efficient, and declarative in the context of a project, but hides so much functionality that sample code is unclear at best.

The point of these examples is to demonstrate that application servers are *not* always needed, and that writing functional, special-purpose servers is a relatively straightforward task. Many developers will choose to use higher-level frameworks, but having a knowledge of what is going on in lower-level libraries can assist when debugging or interpreting error stack traces and log messages.

Java HTTP Server

Java Standard Edition ships with an HTTP server API that allows the creation of simple, functional, embedded HTTP servers. The following program requires no external dependencies. It listens on port 8000 and responds to requests by returning an HTTP success response (200) with JSON content:

```
{"testResponse":"Hello World"}
```

A single Java source file consists of a class that defines a main method. Within the main method, a server instance is created that delegates to a static handler class (defined here as a static inner class) based upon the URL context:

```java
import java.io.*;
import com.sun.net.httpserver.*;
import java.net.InetSocketAddress;

public class HttpJsonServer {

    public static void main(String[] args) throws Exception {

        HttpServer server = HttpServer.create(
            new InetSocketAddress(8000), 0
        );
        server.createContext("/", new MyHandler());
        server.setExecutor(null);
                System.out.println("Starting server on port: 8000");
        server.start();
    }
```

```
static class MyHandler implements HttpHandler {

    public void handle(HttpExchange t) throws IOException {
        String response = "{\"testResponse\":\"Hello World\"}";
                    t.getResponseHeaders().set(
            "Content-Type",
            "application/json"
        );
        t.sendResponseHeaders(200, response.length());
        OutputStream os = t.getResponseBody();
        os.write(response.getBytes());
        os.close();
    }
  }
}
```

This example is so simple that there are no external dependencies and no build scripts. Just compile and run:

```
$ javac HttpJsonServer.java
$ java HttpJsonServer
Starting server on port: 8000
```

The server can be hit from a separate command-line session using Curl:

```
$ curl -i http://localhost:8000
HTTP/1.1 200 OK
Content-type: application/json
Content-length: 30
Date: Sun, 09 Jun 2013 01:15:15 GMT

{"testResponse":"Hello World"}
```

Obviously, this is not a particularly full-featured example. But it does suggest that the development of functional HTTP servers using Java is a relatively simple attainable goal.

Embedded Jetty Server

Jetty (*http://www.eclipse.org/jetty*) is a Java-based HTTP server and Java Servlet container maintained by the Eclipse Foundation. Besides being included as part of the Eclipse IDE, it is embedded in or used by a variety of other products such as ActiveMQ, Maven, Google App Engine, and Hadoop. It is more than merely an HTTP server because it also supports the Java Servlet API and the SPDY and WebSocket protocols. Because of its inclusion in so many projects, many developers are at least aware of its existence and functionality. Less are aware of how easily it can used as a component in a custom Java-based server.

Because a Jetty-based server needs to include external modules, a build script is in order. One challenge with describing Maven configurations in a book is that the *pom.xml* files tend to be relatively large and verbose. Gradle configuration is more terse and focused.

The following Gradle configuration includes Jetty and add a task that can be used to start the server:

```
apply plugin:'java'

repositories{mavenCentral()}
dependencies{compile 'org.eclipse.jetty:jetty-server:8.1.0.RC5'}

task(startServer, dependsOn: 'classes', type: JavaExec) {
    main = 'com.saternos.embedded.TestJettyHttpServer'
    classpath = sourceSets.main.runtimeClasspath
    args 8000
}
```

The pattern followed is similar to the simple Java-based example. A handler class is defined to return a JSON response:

```
package com.saternos.embedded;

import java.io.IOException;
import javax.servlet.ServletException;
import javax.servlet.http.HttpServletRequest;
import javax.servlet.http.HttpServletResponse;
import org.eclipse.jetty.server.Request;
import org.eclipse.jetty.server.handler.AbstractHandler;

public class JsonHandler extends AbstractHandler
{
    public void handle(
        String target,
        Request baseRequest,
        HttpServletRequest request,
        HttpServletResponse response
    )
        throws IOException, ServletException
    {
        response.setContentType("application/json;charset=utf-8");
        response.setStatus(HttpServletResponse.SC_OK);
        baseRequest.setHandled(true);
        response.getWriter().println(
            "{\"testResponse\":\"Hello World\"}"
        );
    }
}
```

A main method creates an instance of a server. The server object delegates requests received to the handler:

```
package com.saternos.embedded;

import org.eclipse.jetty.server.Server;

public class TestJettyHttpServer
```

```
{
    public static void main(String[] args) throws Exception
    {
        Server server = new Server(Integer.parseInt(args[0]));
        server.setHandler(new JsonHandler());
        System.out.println("Starting server on port: " + args[0]);
        server.start();
        server.join();
    }
}
```

Build and run the server using Gradle:

```
$ gradle build startServer
```

And the response via Curl is what you might expect, along with a reference to Jetty as the server in use:

```
$ curl -i http://localhost:8000
HTTP/1.1 200 OK
Content-Type: application/json;charset=utf-8
Content-Length: 31
Server: Jetty(8.1.0.RC5)

{"testResponse":"Hello World"}
```

If you are inclined to write a custom API server from the ground up, the basic building blocks are included in Java and expanded on in libraries like Jetty. Jetty is also used behind the scenes by other projects relevant to authoring web APIs such as Restlet.

Restlet

The Restlet API (*http://restlet.org*) is designed with direct references to REST concepts like resource, representation, connector, component, and media type. REST APIs can be implemented naturally in this framework. While not particularly RESTful, the following example demonstrates how little code is required to create a server that returns JSON. The class is a `ServerResource` that is attached to the root context and responds to HTTP GET requests by returning JSON:

```
package com.saternos.embedded;

import org.restlet.*;
import org.restlet.data.*;
import org.restlet.resource.*;
import org.restlet.ext.json.JsonConverter;

public class TestRestletHttpServer extends ServerResource {

    public static void main(String[] args) throws Exception {
        Component component = new Component();
            component.getServers().add(Protocol.HTTP, Integer.parseInt(args[0]));
            component.getDefaultHost().attach("/", TestRestletHttpServer.class);
```

```
        component.start();
    }

    @Get ("json")
    public String getGreeting() {
        return "{\"testResponse\":\"Hello World\"}";
    }

}
```

Roo

Roo (*http://bit.ly/MfMxBL*) allows you to create a project in a few minutes. The new project runs on an embedded Jetty (or Tomcat) server. An in-memory database is available (you can design your data models and they are automatically propagated to the selected database). So with zero time spent in server configuration, you can create a traditional web application that includes a web application server and database backend through interaction with a REPL.

Download the latest version of Roo (*http://bit.ly/1dKJ9EN*), extract it, and add the path to roo.sh (or roo.bat) to your path. Run roo.sh and you will be prompted to complete some initial setup (agree to terms of use). At this point, you can type help or hint at various points to be prompted with what options are available:

```
$ roo.sh


    ____  ____  ____
   / _ \/ _ \/ _ \
  / /_/ / / / / / / /
 / _, _/ /_/ / /_/ /
/_/ |_|\____/\____/    1.2.4.RELEASE [rev 75337cf]


Welcome to Spring Roo. For assistance press TAB or type "hint" then hit ENTER.
roo>
```

Roo's CLI responds like an expert system for creating Spring-based web applications. Type **hint** to find what options are available at a given point in development. You will be directed to set up a datastore, define entities and fields, and create a web application.

Note that there are times where you will need to work outside of the interactive prompt. For example, if you enter an entity or field incorrectly, these need to be deleted from the generated code.

The following set of commands run within the context of Roo will create a standard JEE web application that includes JSON services (output from each is not included):

```
project com.saternos.bookshop

jpa setup --provider HIBERNATE --database HYPERSONIC_IN_MEMORY
```

```
entity jpa --class ~.domain.Author --testAutomatically
field string --fieldName name --sizeMin 2 --notNull

entity jpa --class ~.domain.Book --testAutomatically
field string --fieldName name --notNull --sizeMin 2
field number --fieldName price --type java.math.BigDecimal
field set --fieldName authors --type ~.domain.Author

json all --deepSerialize
web mvc json setup
web mvc json all

web mvc setup
web mvc all --package ~.web
```

The application provides CRUD operations related to a list of books. After initial project creation, an in-memory datastore is configured. Two entities (and their corresponding fields) are then configured. The next set of three commands is required to expose the enties via a JSON web API. A JEE admin application based on the entities is generated by the final two commands.

The application can be built and run on Jetty:

```
mvn clean install jetty:run
```

Authors can be created through the JSON API using Curl. The first example shows how to create a single author; the second, a collection of them.

```
curl -i -X POST -H "Content-Type: application/json" \
-H "Accept: application/json" \
-d '{name: "Simon St. Laurent"}' \
http://localhost:8080/bookshop/authors


curl -i -X POST -H "Content-Type: application/json" \
-H "Accept: application/json" \
-d '[ {name: "Douglas Crockford"}, {name: "Michael Fogus"} ]' \
http://localhost:8080/bookshop/authors/jsonArray
```

The main page of the web application is available from *http://localhost:8080/book-shop/* and rendered with a professionally styled design by default, as shown in Figure 6-3.

The same URL can be used to remove a record using an HTTP delete:

```
curl -i -X DELETE -H "Accept: application/json" \
http://localhost:8080/bookshop/authors/1

curl -i -X DELETE -H "Accept: application/json" \
http://localhost:8080/bookshop/authors/2

curl -i -X DELETE -H "Accept: application/json" \
http://localhost:8080/bookshop/authors/3
```

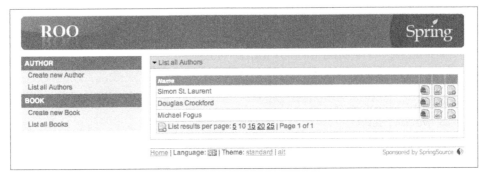

Figure 6-3. Roo web application author list

Books along with associated authors can be added by nesting the reference to the authors. Figure 6-4 shows the changes reflected in the "List all Books" page after the following curl calls are run:[1]

```
curl -i -X POST -H "Content-Type: application/json" \
-H "Accept: application/json" \
-d '{name:"JavaScript: The Good Parts",'`
    `'price:29.99,'`
    `'authors:[{name: "Douglas Crockford"}]}' \
http://localhost:8080/bookshop/books

curl -i -X POST -H "Content-Type: application/json" \
-H "Accept: application/json" \
-d '{name:"Functional JavaScript",'`
  `'price:29.99,'`
  `'authors:[{name: "Michael Fogus"}]}' \
http://localhost:8080/bookshop/books

curl -i -X POST -H "Content-Type: application/json" \
-H "Accept: application/json" \
-d '{name:"Introducing Elixir",'`
  `'price:19.99,'`
  `'authors:[{name: "Simon St. Laurent"}]}' \
http://localhost:8080/bookshop/books
```

1. Formatting code for human consumption is challenging. This is because computers and people interpret whitespace and linebreaks differently—and the fact that this book appears in both paper and digital formats. In practice, the preceding curl commands are best executed at the command line using no line breaks and minimal whitespace. Unfortunately, this results in either invalid word-wrapping or text flowing outside of the margins of the page. Within a bash session, long commands can be broken up over multiple lines using a backslash (\) at the end of each line. We follow that convention throughout this book, but it does not work in every case. The preceding examples break up a JSON string into separate lines, and include backticks (`) that cause the spaces and intervening newline to be ignored. We take advantage of this quirk of bash for the benefit of folks who are copying the commands from digital versions of this book.

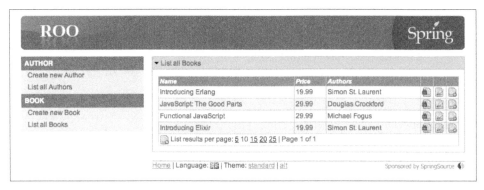

Figure 6-4. Roo web application book list

To retrieve the list of authors and books inserted:

```
curl http://localhost:8080/bookshop/authors
curl http://localhost:8080/bookshop/books
```

A single object in the array of results can be accessed by ID:

```
curl http://localhost:8080/bookshop/books/1
```

Format JSON at the Command Line

There are a number of ways to format JSON returned at the command line. You can redirect the output to a file and open it with an editor that supports JSON formatting. There are also special purpose utilites (like jq (*http://bit.ly/1kEGnti*)) that can format JSON data piped to it. If you have Python installed, formatting is as simple as:

```
curl http://localhost:8080/bookshop/books | python -mjson.tool
```

With the web API in place, standard HTML pages can be created and used in place of (or in addition to) the *jspx* page created through the Roo scaffolding command. Create a file named */src/main/webapp/test.html* and it will be available from *http://localhost:8080/bookshop/test.html*. The GET book listing calls can be accessed using jQuery using the getJSON method:

```
<html>
<head>
  <title>Book List</title>
<script src="http://ajax.googleapis.com/ajax/libs/jquery/1.10.1/jquery.min.js">
</script>
</head>
<body>

  <h3>Books</h3>
  <ul class='booklist'></ul>
```

```
<script>
  (function() {
    $.getJSON('/bookshop/books', function(books) {
      $.each(books, function(nil,book) {
        $('.booklist').append('<li>' + book['name'] + '</li>');
      });
    });
  })();
</script>
</body>
</html>
```

Roo is one of the most accessible tools available because of its interactive nature. If you want more extensive coverage on working with the framework, *Getting Started with Roo* (O'Reilly) is available as a free download (*http://bit.ly/LXfi5j*), and *Spring in Action* (Manning Publications) provides additional insight.

Embedded Netty Server

While Jetty has been associated with the Eclipse Foundation, a project with some overlapping use cases emerged from the JBoss community. Netty (*http://netty.io*) is used to create optimized network applications (protocol servers and clients). Optimized network applications scale better than general purpose alternatives. The fact that Twitter (*http://bit.ly/1gz2LPq*) leverages Netty to address performance concerns suggests something of its maturity and capacity for scaling.

A sample application using Netty is analagous to the one just demonstrated using Jetty in that it follows a similar basic pattern. Again, a class with a main method instantiates and starts the server and a handler class is defined to process incoming requests:

```
package com.saternos.embedded;

import io.netty.bootstrap.ServerBootstrap;
import io.netty.channel.socket.nio.*;

public class TestNettyHttpServer {

    public static void main(String[] args) throws Exception {

            ServerBootstrap bootstrap = new ServerBootstrap();

            bootstrap.group(new NioEventLoopGroup(), new NioEventLoopGroup())
                    .channel(NioServerSocketChannel.class)
                    .localAddress(Integer.parseInt(args[0]))
                    .childHandler(new JsonServerInitializer());

            System.out.println("Starting server on port: " + args[0]);
        bootstrap.bind().sync().channel().closeFuture().sync();
    }
}
```

The handler class extends ChannelInboundMessageHandlerAdapter, which allows the class to be included in the server's pipeline. The messageReceived method has access to the request and creates the response:

```java
package com.saternos.embedded;

import io.netty.buffer.Unpooled;
import io.netty.util.CharsetUtil;
import java.text.SimpleDateFormat;
import io.netty.channel.*;
import java.util.*;
import io.netty.handler.codec.http.*;

public class JsonHandler extends ChannelInboundMessageHandlerAdapter<HttpRequest> {

    public void messageReceived(ChannelHandlerContext channelHandlerContext,
                                HttpRequest httpRequest) throws Exception {
        StringBuffer buf = new StringBuffer();
        buf.append("{\"testResponse\":\"Hello World\"}");

        SimpleDateFormat dateFormatter = new SimpleDateFormat(
                                        "EEE, dd MMM yyyy HH:mm:ss zzz",
                                        Locale.US
                                        );

                dateFormatter.setTimeZone(TimeZone.getTimeZone("GMT"));
                Calendar time = new GregorianCalendar();

        HttpResponse response = new DefaultHttpResponse(HttpVersion.HTTP_1_1,
                                        HttpResponseStatus.OK);

response.setHeader(HttpHeaders.Names.CONTENT_TYPE,
                "application/json;charset=utf-8");
response.setHeader(HttpHeaders.Names.CONTENT_LENGTH, buf.length());
response.setHeader(HttpHeaders.Names.DATE,
                dateFormatter.format(time.getTime()));
response.setHeader(HttpHeaders.Names.SERVER,
                TestNettyHttpServer.class.getName() +
                ":io.netty:netty:4.0.0.Alpha8");
response.setContent(Unpooled.copiedBuffer(buf, CharsetUtil.UTF_8));
channelHandlerContext.write(response).addListener(
                ChannelFutureListener.CLOSE);
    }
}
```

A class that implements ChannelInitializer (*http://netty.io/4.0/api*) is also required to set up the pipeline.

The initializer's initChannel method has a reference to the Channel interface, which is used to create and access a pipeline for the /SocketChannel. Pipelines transform or manipulate the values passed to them. The HttpRequestDecoder (*http://bit.ly/*

1gz3znF) receives the raw bytes and uses them to construct HTTP-related objects, and the `HttpChunkAggregator` normalizes requests with a transfer encoding of *chunked*. The next two pipeline classes encode and chunk the response, which is then passed to the sample application's specific handler class (where headers and the actual response are created):

```java
package com.saternos.embedded;

import io.netty.channel.socket.SocketChannel;
import io.netty.handler.stream.ChunkedWriteHandler;
import io.netty.handler.codec.http.*;
import io.netty.channel.*;

public class JsonServerInitializer extends ChannelInitializer<SocketChannel> {

    public void initChannel(SocketChannel socketChannel) throws Exception {
        ChannelPipeline pipeline = socketChannel.pipeline();
        pipeline.addLast("decoder", new HttpRequestDecoder());
        pipeline.addLast("aggregator", new HttpChunkAggregator(65536));
        pipeline.addLast("encoder", new HttpResponseEncoder());
        pipeline.addLast("chunkedWriter", new ChunkedWriteHandler());
        pipeline.addLast("handler", new JsonHandler());
    }
}
```

Building and running the application results in a response similar to the preceding ones:

```
$ gradle build startServer
$ curl -i http://localhost:8000

HTTP/1.1 200 OK
Content-Type: application/json;charset=utf-8
Content-Length: 30
Date: Fri, 14 Jun 2013 14:02:57 GMT
Server: com.saternos.embedded.TestNettyHttpServer:io.netty:netty:4.0.0.Alpha8

{"testResponse":"Hello World"}
```

Netty is a relatively low-level, general-purpose network library. This provides a great deal of flexibility for creating optimized applications at the expense of the additional overhead of setting up applicable pipelines and handlers. The example is somewhat longer and more complex, but worth being aware of because Netty provides the foundation for several higher-level frameworks such as Play and Vert.x. Norman Maurer, a core developer of Netty, has written *Netty in Action* (Manning Publications), a book that goes into greater detail about the capabilities of this sophisticated framework.

Play Server

The Play Framework (*http://www.playframework.org*) is a lightweight, stateless framework well suited for creating API servers. A play application can be generated with a few simple commands, and a routes file can be configured to indicate HTTP methods and paths that reference controller methods. Code can be written in Java or Scala, and the influence of the Scala community is apparent in many places such as the use of SBT and Scala-based templates. Play project changes are reflected immediately in a browser; no separate build step is required.

With Play installed (*http://bit.ly/1jaLHkr*), create a new play application by running play new, naming the application, and choosing the Java template:

```
$ play new play-server

       _            _
 _ __ | | __ _ _  _| |
| '_ \| |/ _' | || |_|
|  __/|_|\____|\__ (_)
|_|            |__/

play! 2.1.1 (using Java 1.7.0_21 and Scala 2.10.0), http://www.playframework.org

The new application will be created in /Users/cs/Desktop/tmp/play-server

What is the application name? [play-server]
>

Which template do you want to use for this new application?

  1            - Create a simple Scala application
  2            - Create a simple Java application

> 2
OK, application play-server is created.

Have fun!
```

This command generated an application structure similar to that of a Ruby on Rails application. Subsequent command and file modifications are in the context of the newly created directory:

```
cd play-server
```

In this example, an application will return JSON from a URL (/json). To define this API call, modify conf/routes and add the following line:

```
GET     /json                   controllers.Application.json()
```

Finally, modify the Java controller code referenced in the routes file.

Note that this example departs from the previous practice of "Hello World" in a JSON string. Instead, an object is created and serialized as JSON in the response (using Jackson under the covers).

This process of creating an object and then serializing it to a target format in the server response is also used in JAX-RS (the JEE Java API for RESTful) web services:

```java
package controllers;

import play.*;
import play.mvc.*;

import views.html.*;

import org.codehaus.jackson.JsonNode;

import play.libs.Json;
import org.codehaus.jackson.node.ObjectNode;
import org.codehaus.jackson.node.ArrayNode;

// pretty print
import org.codehaus.jackson.map.ObjectMapper;

public class Application extends Controller {

    public static Result index() {
        return ok(index.render("Your new application is ready."));
    }

    public static Result json() {

            ObjectNode result = Json.newObject();

                // How to nest a JSON object
                ObjectNode child = Json.newObject();
                child.put("color", "blue");
                result.put("NestedObj",child);

                //  Adding Strings
                result.put("status", "OK");
                result.put("something", "else");

                // Add Integers
                result.put("int", 1);

                // Add a JSON array
            ArrayNode collection = result.putArray("coll");
                collection.add(1);
                collection.add(2);
                collection.add(3);
                collection.add(4);
```

```
//  comment out this line -VVV- and uncomment the /* */ below to format the JSON
                  return ok(result);
/*
// To return json pretty-printed, need to render it as a formatted
// string and then explicitly set the response
// http://www.playframework.com/documentation/2.1.0/JavaResponse
//
//
        ObjectMapper mapper = new ObjectMapper();
        String s="";
        try{
            s = mapper.defaultPrettyPrintingWriter().writeValueAsString(result);
        }catch(Exception e){}
return ok(s).as("application/json");
*/
    }

}
```

The application's internal server can be started from within the application directory:

```
$ play ~run
```

In the code listing above,

```
return ok(result);
```

can be removed and the lines that follow it can be uncommented. Refresh the browser to see the JSON change from unformatted to formatted output.

No Browser Refresh Required

With the use of a Chrome plug-in created by James Ward (*http://bit.ly/1nvXESt*), even the browser refresh can be avoided. Instead, the browser refreshes whenever a file is saved. To accomplish this, install the Play Chrome plug-in (*http://bit.ly/1cz54iB*) and modify *project/plugins.sbt* and add the following line:

```
addSbtPlugin("com.jamesward" %% "play-auto-refresh" % "0.0.3")
```

Other Lightweight Server Solutions

These are by no means the only options available for building APIs. Dropwizard (*http://dropwizard.codahale.com*) is a Java framework (similar in intention to Restlet) for developing HTTP/JSON web services. It is built on other "best of breed" technologies (Jetty for HTTP, Jackson for JSON, and Jersey for REST). Containerless and minimally embedded server solutions are somewhat novel to the Java community, but are taken for granted by programmers working with other languages.

JVM-Based Servers

Besides the options available for Java itself, the JVM can serve as a compilation target for languages other than Java itself. The support for additional languages on the JVM has grown with each release of Java. In fact, the play framework previously introduced supports Scala as its preferred language. If you are specifically interested in the expressive possibilities available through alternate JVM languages, Vert.x (*http://vertx.io*) is a web server that allows you to create applications using JavaScript, CoffeeScript, Ruby, Python, Groovy, or Java.

A JVM language can be invoked from within a Java application, or a project can be assembled that invokes the Java class specified as the interpreter for the language. The following code excerpts show basic examples of how to create simple servers that run on the JVM.

Jython

If you have Python installed, you can launch a web server to serve files from your current local directory by running the following command:

```
$ python -m SimpleHTTPServer 8000
```

Jython is a JVM implementation of Python that can perform a similar task with a bit more effort. Create a *build.gradle* file with a task to invoke Jython and call a small Python script that will invoke the HTTP server:

```
apply plugin:'java'

repositories{mavenCentral()}
dependencies{compile 'org.python:jython-standalone:2.5.3'}

// Example running a Jython Server
task(startServer, dependsOn: 'classes', type: JavaExec) {
    main = 'org.python.util.jython'
    classpath = sourceSets.main.runtimeClasspath
    args  "http_server.py"
}
```

The http_server.py consists of navigation to the directory where files will be served and a bit of code to create and start the server:

```
import SimpleHTTPServer
import SocketServer
import os

os.chdir('root')
print "serving at port 8000"
SocketServer.TCPServer(("", 8000),
SimpleHTTPServer.SimpleHTTPRequestHandler).serve_forever()
```

Create a directory named *root*. Whatever files are placed in the *root* directory will be served by the SimpleHTTPServer. Those files with a *.json* extension will have a content type of `application/json`.

Quickest Mock Server Ever
With this simple setup, client-side developers can begin work while working server-side code is not yet available. Mock JSON responses can be created in files within a directory structure that reflects the API paths. These JSON response files can also be used to essentially document the API and even serve as validation server-side unit tests.

Web Application Servers

There are of course full-scale web application server solutions for deploying production code developed in Java or in Python (using django-jython (*http://bit.ly/MOjBRl*), for example) or Ruby (using warbler (*https://github.com/jruby/warbler*)). Tomcat is a Servlet container and (available immediately in the Roo framework mentioned previously) and so can run any web application that can be deployed as a WAR. A project with a group of WARs that need to be packaged together in an EAR (or individual WARs that require certain JEE services) needs a full-fledged JEE application server like JBoss.

Development Usage

It is clear that the clear separation of client and server tiers provides various possibilities for client development using simple servers that are created quickly while server development progresses in parallel. At its most basic, an HTTP server could be created to return hardcoded JSON. With little more effort, the JSON could be stored on the file system in filenames that reflect the API URLs. If database access is required, Roo includes easy database integration using technologies that are also available in other Java-based projects. It is even possible to continually extend the server to include disparate datasources, application caching, and other such features that will allow it to serve as the basis of the production server. This type of development is not possible when developing monolithic applications that do not provide a clear partitioning of client and server applications.

Conclusion

The examples in this chapter highlight the progressive simplification of server-side development, which contrasts with the growing complexity of client-side code. Java developers entrenched in a view based on traditional Java packaging methodologies and application server deployment should be aware of the alternatives that better fit a client-server paradigm.

Creating a lightweight, specialized API or HTTP server is possible without a deep knowledge of network minutiae and low-level languages. Simple, lightweight server-side code and simplified deployment options emerged out of a necessity to create highly scalable solutions that are practical for large-scale deployments. The shift also has a profound effect on the day-to-day workflow for programmers. These effects, which are positive for the most part, are the subject of the next chapter.

## CHAPTER 7

Rapid Development Practices

To find my home in one sentence, concise, as if hammered in metal. Not to enchant anybody. Not to earn a lasting name in posterity. An unnamed need for order, for rhythm, for form, which three words are opposed to chaos and nothingness.

—Czeslaw Milosz

Developer Productivity

Conciseness, efficiency, and simplicity are highly valued in modern culture. Perhaps this is because of the relative abundance and complexity that distinguishes our time from previous generations. A web application built using simple, concise code and efficient and streamlined practices will result in a final product that is easier to maintain, easier to adapt, and will ultimately be more profitable. Likewise, a programmer's workflow and tools should be efficient and avoid unnecessary complexity. Because there are so many options available, it is particularly important for a developer to step back from coding and consider if the workflow in use is truly optimal and productive.

Along with a fundamental shift to a client-server web paradigm, there has been incremental changes and improvements to development workflows. These improvements eliminate extraneous, unnecessary work by using reasonable defaults and removing rarely used configuration options. Simplification of workflows results in smaller, tighter feedback loops. Frequent feedback promotes quicker recognition and elimination of problems. The early identification and remediation of bugs results in increased productivity—and happier programmers. Furthermore, it introduces the possibility of creating complex, high-quality software that ironically requires less time and resources to construct and maintain.

Copious Hand-Waving…

Measuring programmer productivity is notoriously difficult. Measures such as hours worked, lines of code per day, or defects resolved are objectively measurable, but not terribly meaningful. The unique purpose, time frame, and intended longevity of a project make it difficult to compare to others. A truly formal and objective measurement that fairly and accurately reflects productivity across all projects simply does not exist. In practice, most software development managers engage in a bit of artful spreadsheet manipulation and develop a knack for accurately assessing the degree of correlation between the estimates given by their developers and actual outcomes. With that understood, a general assumption that improvements to processes can be made to the benefit of individual and group performance will be accepted.

Agile methodology was initially presented as a correction to waterfall methods, which tend to be encumbered early on with a large amount of effort and activity that actually prevent meaningful progress. Limiting this tendency toward "analysis-paralysis" and recognizing the need to immediately begin creating a workable product was refreshing when introduced. Unfortunately, the term has become diluted over time and now can often simply suggest a "ready-fire-aim" approach where there is a great deal of activity early on with no well-defined goal. In this context, though it might seem counterintuitive, being truly productive requires one initially to *cease working*. Obviously, this is meant as an absolute cessation of activity. It is the ability to sacrifice immediately measurable and visible progress for long-term project quality and productivity.

This is a significant challenge. Management wants to see progress on the project at hand. Developers like coding. Users want evidence that work has commenced. But starting prematurely can result in the wrong (or at least less than ideal) tool or approach to be adopted. An inapplicable convention or tradition introduced to a project can be very damaging. An early deviation can set a project on a bad trajectory and lead to problems that compound as the project progresses. It takes a bit of vision to realize that *ceasing work* to do some up-front analysis can result in far more productive work and higher-quality results.

Up-front analysis has suffered quite a bit with the adoption of *pseudo-agile* methodologies ("pseudo" is intended to indicate that what is suggested here is not opposed to an agile approach). It is far more beneficial to measure twice and cut once. This applies on many levels. Development team leads need to make decisions relevant to their projects. Individual developers need to remain aware of the best practices and emerging techniques that might be applicable to the problem at hand. Having the right tool or approach for a given job can reduce the time and effort required to complete the initial work, and done correctly, can result in a system that is simpler and easier to maintain in the long run. The pressure to focus all energy and attention on whatever task is deemed most urgent must be resisted to make the fundamental adjustments required to work productively. An agile approach that welcomes changing business requirements throughout the project can be used, but foundational technical decisions and related developer workflow should generally not be significantly affected.

Productivity in Isolation

It should be apparent that a focus on productivity alone is inadequate. If productivity were to be considered in absolute isolation, then doing nothing might be considered the best option! Software quality, reliability, clear communication, correctness of functionality, and adherence to processes and conventions are important values as well. All other things being equal, it is better to complete a required task through fewer actions using less resources. So changes to processes in the name of productivity still need to be considered in light of this wider range of concerns. Besides, a truly productive process will tend to promote quality, reliability, and other important values as well.

It is somewhat disappointing that there is no simple plan or theory that will result in productivity gains. True software productivity improvements are discovered and enacted in practice during specific projects in an ad hoc manner. Work is done, and over time, improvements to the process are identified and implemented, and the cycle repeats. The knowledge gleaned is a source of reflection on areas that can be improved, optimized, or even eliminated on other projects.

In the abstract, a software project requires that one or more tasks be completed, ideally in the most effective and productive manner possible. Productivity is often most easily comprehended and measured when isolated to a defined task. Every software development task involves one or more people and one or more computers. Each person and computer can interact with other people and computers over the course of a project. All of these are likely to be geographically dispersed. This is shown in Figure 7-1.

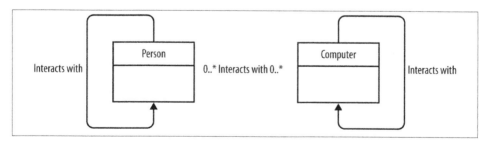

Figure 7-1. Interactions between people and computers

With this in mind, productivity improvements can be made to interactions between:

- People (with each other)
- Computers
- People *and* computers

People and computers are the resources that perform the work required to complete a task, as shown in Table 7-1. To increase productivity:

- Redefine the task.
- Increase efficiency (of a given resource or in interactions between resources).
- Increase resources.
- Increase effort (get more out of each resource through additional work).

Table 7-1. Areas for productivity improvement

Action	Humans	Computers
Redefine the task	Identify requirements, plan, architect, manage	Languages, software, programming paradigms
Increase efficiency	Develop skills, minimize distractions	Automate, preprocess, compress, optimize, tune
Increase resources	Developers, consultants	Scale, add hardware/processing power
Increase effort	Time management, workload	Parallelize

These areas are important to recognize on a couple of counts. A failure to take advantage of productivity improvements in one area (such as recent technical innovations classified under the Computers column) result in an increase in factors affecting productivity in the Humans column (additional hours or personnel). A bit of reflection about these areas as they relate to a project can help to suggest actions that might require relatively minor effort and result in significantly better results.

Acknowledgement of this more holistic view can help avoid overemphasis on a single category for solving all problems. A well-known example is the irrational hope that increasing workload and adding developers late in a project will result in meeting an overly ambitious deadline. Another is the sophomoric developer trap of believing that everything can be automated through additional homegrown software development regardless of the nature of the task. The particular emphasis of this book is in the Computers column.

Optimizing Developer and Team Workflow

Iteration involves repeating a process with the aim of approaching (and eventually completing) an intended result. Each part of a project includes tasks that are iterated times, as shown in Figure 7-2. This basic observation can be applied to many different aspects of software development, including requirement-gathering, design, development, testing, and deployment.

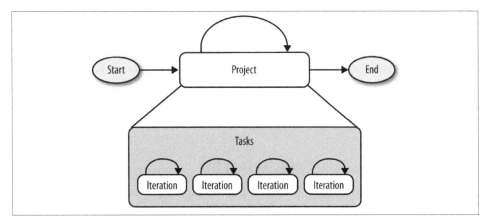

Figure 7-2. Project iterations

There are a couple of key insights to keep in mind:

- An iteration should conclude with an observable result. This result can be compared with the state prior to completing the iteration as well as with the intended result. If the result is not observable, there is a problem. What is observable can be measured and improved. What is not visible cannot be evaluated, fixed, or enhanced. An iteration can also be thought of as a feedback loop, beginning with an action and resulting in a response that must be evaluated.

- An iteration (or feedback loop) can be small or wide. A single code change made by a developer is a small iteration, while the final delivery of an entire large-scale system is relatively large. Feedback from a deployment can be automated or manual. Automated feedback can provide a general indication that a deployed system is functioning as expected but cannot replace an actual end-user response to a release.

- Shorter iterations allow for increased feedback. Increased feedback is essentially increased visibility. Increased feedback is desirable for many reasons. It results in a quicker identification of problems (and even opportunities), and it is easier to make corrections to the project trajectory early in the process. The smaller the loop and more immediate the feedback, the better.

- By its very nature, any gain to a given iteration will result in a much more significant gain to the overall project due to the fact that it is repeated. The challenge is to recognize that a task is being repeated and to make improvements to tasks that will have the greatest overall impact to the entire project.

- Any optimization to a task in the project is worthwhile. An optimization to a task that is repeated many times is generally even more beneficial. It is better to automate a task altogether if possible. What is somewhat counterintuitive to those geared toward "doing work" is that the best option, if available, is to eliminate unneeded tasks altogether.

These observations are rather obvious and boil down to simple common sense. But as those who have spent any time in the software development world can attest, developers are creatures of habit. Many get comfortable with a certain sequence in a workflow or a given set of tools. This can result in a large amount of unnecessary work that complicates projects and produces suboptimal results, to say the least.

Faster Is Better

Boyd decided that the primary determinant to winning dogfights was not observing, orienting, planning, or acting better. The primary determinant to winning dogfights was observing, orienting, planning, and acting faster. In other words, how quickly one could iterate. Speed of iteration, Boyd suggested, beats quality of iteration...

I'll state Boyd's discovery as Boyd's Law of Iteration: In analyzing complexity, fast iteration almost always produces better results than in-depth analysis.

— Roger Sessions, "A Better Path to Enterprise Architectures"

Most of us are not going to create the next big thing that is going to revolutionize software development processes. But simply stepping outside of one's own programming culture can be an eye-opening experience. There are plenty of improvements available that can be leveraged, and delving a bit deeper into well-established technologies can provide significant results for individual developers let alone wider project considerations. A few examples might help illustrate this.

Example: Web Application Fix

A change needs to be made to a Java JEE web application (an EAR comprised of several WARs) built using Maven and deployed to a JBoss web application server. The developer who needs to make the change will need to make several code changes (likely making a mistake or two in the process). One way to approach the problem involves a few different steps. First, make code changes. Next, type out commands to do a standard full build, followed by a deployment of the application. This second step might take several minutes to complete depending on the size of the application, the number of unit tests being run, the build, and other factors. What improvements to the process might be made?

- To start, there are numerous shell command options that might be of use. Command history (and searching) immediately come to mind.

- Does every step in the build process need to be performed? For example, in Maven, the `-DskipTests` parameter might shorten the build time significantly.

- Is a full deployment even required? It might be possible to hot deploy code depending in a manner that no build is required to test a change.

- Does the change require an initial deployment at all? Initial test might be done by testing within the browser (if they relate primarily to HTML, CSS, or JavaScript). For server-side code, attaching the remote debugger and observing relevant objects and variables in their immediate, populated context might allow enough discovery to prevent a few unnecessary iterations. The Java code might be able to be evaluated in a unit test outside of the full deployment as well (which suggests a productivity benefit of Test-Driven Development).

Example: Testing Integration

This example is regarding the same web application project, now well underway. There is a general recognition of the need to include testing as part of the SDLC. This can occur at many stages and at many levels:

- A QA resource or developer peer testing might do a good job validating initial requirements and code match-up, but people do not tend to be consistent or exhaustive.

- Unit tests (using JUnit) are created. They provide more extensive testing but are of little use if not run consistently.

- Unit tests are quickly integrated into the Maven build. The build is done on a continuous integration server so developers are quickly alerted of a change that breaks the build. Yet it is difficult to tell how extensive or valuable the tests are.

- A coverage report can be generated to provide some indication of code coverage. One area noted is that testing is specifically server-side. This is an issue because the browser-side code in the project is significant.

- Fortunately, our crafty front-end engineers have already begun doing unit testing using Jasmine. These can be integrated into the Maven build using a plug-in. In addition, JavaScript developers run unit tests on their client-side code using Karma installed on their individual workstations.

- As the project proceeds, the project flow solidifies, and broader functional tests that reflect user experiences can be written. These functional tests can then be run on various browsers using Selenium.

The focus with this testing scenario has been on increasing feedback regarding project status rather than quality itself. The value in optimization is evident, as bugs are quickly identified and fixed. In addition, incongruities between requirements and implementation are easily identified. New developers can be added to such a project because they can learn about code in relative isolation by observing and running tests. A project with significant test coverage can survive sweeping refactoring changes. The confidence to undertake such refactoring is a result of having suites of automated tests that verify a significant subset of existing functionality.

Example: Greenfield Development

As a software architect on a new project, you need to choose the best set of tools and set up an initial application structure. As a cloud-deployed, highly scalable web application, a client-server architecture described in this book is selected. It is accepted that the team will adopt some new tools and processes, but Java is mandated as the programming language due to organizational practices and in-house abilities (which eliminate possibilities like Rails and Grails that rely on other JVM languages):

- Maven/JEE is initially considered. Although JAX-RS is suitable for server-side development, JSF development does not fit due to a tendency for developers to use sessions.

- After a bit of investigation, it turns out that the entire build/deployment to an application server can be mitigated by using a server-side framework like Spring Roo or the Play framework. Play is selected, and a server-side web API is generated that serves some sample JSON files from the filesystem. These mock services will later be replaced with integration from a variety of other backend services.

- Yeoman can be used to generate a front-end project that uses the JavaScript framework and relevant HTML5 starter project. A quick npm search yeoman-generator yields a few likely candidates that are used to generate not just one but several client-side projects—each in its own directory. A few hours of evaluation (hooking up the frontends to the existing services) provides a sense of the value each generated project brings, and one is selected.

- Some cleanup is done, including providing example server-side and client-side tests that run automatically when a file is saved. Automated documentation utilities are set up for Java and JavaScript. Code is checked into SVN, and the project is registered and configured on the continuous integration server. The server also generates documentation when code is built and publishes it to a known central documentation server. An IDE template is set up that includes acceptable defaults for code formatting.

With this initial work in place, many of the most significant and important decisions have been made prior to individual developers implementing more specific business requirements. These decisions have led to a process that allows for relatively isolated (parallel) client and server development. It also includes immediate feedback using unit tests and specific examples for developers to copy as they add tests for new functionality. Published auto-generated documentation and an IDE template encourage relatively homogeneous coding and commenting practices.

These examples are subjective and will undoubtedly be changed and improved as new technologies emerge. The point is to provide an example of the analysis that can be done to make incremental improvements to processes rather than blindly following previous practices and conventions. The section that follows is intended to help you brainstorm and identify areas of your projects that are applicable targets for improvement.

Productivity and the Software Development Life Cycle

Productivity needs to be considered at each point in the software development life cycle. This is because a glaring inefficiency in a fundamental step in the process cannot necessarily be overcome by productivity gains in another. In general, tasks related to productivity can be prioritized in order of diminishing returns. Although each project and team is unique, some general statements can be made concerning which areas will tend to have the greatest overall effect. Generally, management and cultural decisions are foundational, followed by overall technical architecture, specific application design, and lower-level programming and platform concerns. Given an accurate analysis and prioritization of tasks, optimal results can be obtained by addressing productivity issues in order.

Management and Culture

In general, the largest gains can be had when considering the overall scope of a project involving many individuals working on a team. Although not the focus here, management actions, team dynamics, and work culture have a profound impact on the work that will be accomplished. These broad environmental considerations set the stage for the work to be done and the value proposition for the overall organization as well as each individual. They are significant and often the primary areas that should be addressed. One challenge that can be significant—especially in larger organizations—is to align goals. Charlie Munger (*http://ycombinator.com/munger.html*), the businessman and investor best known for his association with Warren Buffett, described the challenge that Federal Express once faced to align the goals of workers with the organizational mandate to eliminate delays. The solution to the problem involved making sure all parties involved had the proper incentives:

> From all business, my favorite case on incentives is Federal Express. The heart and soul of their system—which creates the integrity of the product—is having all their airplanes come to one place in the middle of the night and shift all the packages from plane to plane. If there are delays, the whole operation can't deliver a product full of integrity to Federal Express customers.

> And it was always screwed up. They could never get it done on time. They tried everything—moral persuasion, threats, you name it. And nothing worked.

> Finally, somebody got the idea to pay all these people not so much an hour, but so much a shift—and when it's all done, they can all go home. Well, their problems cleared up overnight.

So getting the incentives right is a very, very important lesson. It was not obvious to Federal Express what the solution was. But maybe now, it will hereafter more often be obvious to you.

—Charlie Munger (*http://ycombinator.com/munger.html*)

Other "big-picture" considerations: basic well-known organizational and management principles hold true. Assign responsibility, centralize documentation, and use version control. These concerns are obvious yet frequently ignored.

Technical Architecture

The overall architecture of a system dictates many facets of subsequent technology selection and implementation. A highly scalable, cloud-based application targeted for a widespread public deployment involves a more sophisticated setup than an application that is going to be used internally by an organization. There is far more margin for error in the latter case. The overall productivity of a team will be severely hindered if members are required to either code with consideration for scenarios that will never occur or make changes late in the project to address unexpected architectural requirements. A clear sense of project scope should be reflected in architectural choices.

A similar concern is the choice of data storage medium. Traditional relational databases are a relatively well-understood resource that provide services like referential and transactional integrity that developers tend to take for granted. New NoSQL solutions offer the ability to optimize write operations and store data in a manner that is far less constrained. Each has its benefits, but there is no single silver bullet that will address all concerns. A NoSQL solution might be selected because of initial scalability concerns related to incoming data. But if reporting capabilities are not also considered up front, data might not be stored in a way that will allow for efficient reporting. Individual developers might be remarkably capable and productive, but will not be able to overcome a fundamentally incorrect data storage decision through isolated effort on a specific reporting task.

Each programming language has dogmatic adherents who enter into epic debates on the relative virtues of their language. What is certain is that there are characteristics of a language that make it simpler to complete a given programming task in less time. For instance, if a compilation step can be eliminated (through the use of automated compiling in an IDE or the use of a scripting language), a task will require less time. Languages like Java have a huge number of available supporting libraries, while some newer languages like Scala and Groovy boast fundamental language differences that reduce the amount of code that needs to be written to perform an equivalent task. Scripting languages like Ruby and Python have their own unique workflows that have been effective on their own and influenced the development of tools and processes elsewhere.

Software Tools

Selection of programming languages, development tools, and frameworks is a major area where an architect steers project direction. The power and constraints available to individual programmers throughout development of a project are influenced heavily by these decisions. Technologies and their associated workflows were created with a variety of values in mind. Productivity will inevitably be impacted this selection.

In *Software Tools* (Addison-Wesley Professional, 1976), Brian Kernighan famously said, "Controlling complexity is the essence of computer programming." The range of software tools that have assisted in the attempt to tame complexity touch on every part of the software development life cycle: version control systems, automated documentation, coverage and quality reports, testing tools, issue management systems, and continuous integration servers, to name a few. Besides these, the simple everyday tools a developer has mastered can be the difference that makes a developer an order of magnitude more effective than his peers.

Each language has associated build tools. Although you can mix and match languages and build tools, there is a close associate between Maven for Java, Gradle for Groovy, SBT for Scala, and Rake for Ruby. Each language has associated frameworks for developing client-server web applications. Java is known for JEE and Spring (which is also available through a highly automated utility called Roo) as well as for newer frameworks like Play (which also supports Scala). The same could be said for Ruby and Rails, Groovy and Grails, and Python and Django. Most of these frameworks include embedded servers that tend to promote developer workflow. They also tend to be coupled with starter projects that can eliminate a significant amount of time-consuming, boilerplate coding. The selection of a relevant framework can result in reduced build time, the elimination of a build altogether, the benefits of preprocessing of an asset pipeline, and easy incorporation of integrated test suites.

IDEs include features such as code completion, intelligent searching and code navigation, refactoring functionality (encapsulating code in a new method, and renaming a variable across files of different types), unit test integration, and background compilation. They are a mainstay in the Java community. They provide tremendous value when working in a language like Java, so much so that some developers find it hard to believe that every programmer does not use one for every task.

Developers using scripting languages (particularly those that were not initially created for the JVM) tend to use lighter-weight *code editors*. If working at the command line in an *nix type environment,[1] vi (or vim) and Emacs along with a few of the built-in utilities can provide analogous (or even superior) mechanisms for a variety of software devel-

---

1. For the uninitiated, an asterisk is a wildcard in programmer-speak. *nix is shorthand for "Unix or Unix-like systems such as Linux." The term *nix also includes Apple's OS X but excludes Windows. Windows can run an emulation environment like Cygwin to make it look like a Unix system.

opment tasks. Even if you're not working all the time at the command line, it is worth-while to be conversant at this level because so many support tasks (deployment to a server, viewing logs, and checking server performance) take place in an environment where only the command line is available.

Performance

Applications that perform well can be debugged more quickly. Minimizing the time required for an iteration (the size of the feedback loop) makes for a larger number of possible changes and validation. The optimization of a poorly performing section of code can provide time for developers to work on other issues that would otherwise be spent waiting for a system to respond. The initial selection of APIs, algorithms, data storage mechanisms, and related processing has a tremendous downstream effect in this regard. Even the choice of programming language paradigms has an effect; for example, functional programming (which is widely publicized for its virtues of limiting side effects), commonly utilizes highly efficient caching mechanisms. It can also be used to efficiently traverse structures with an extremely terse, easily understood code representation. It simplifies processing and requires fewer lines of code that need to be sifted through when refactoring. Both actual application performance as well as human readability can benefit with the use of the right technology (with the right team). Even in a mature project, there are often areas that are candidates for optimization. For instance, network performance in many web applications can benefit from simple compression or reduction of calls. These details can be overlooked early in a project but can often be implemented later in a nondisruptive manner. And the gains for improving performance always extend the specific area addressed as time is freed up for developers to actively program and test rather than wait for the system to respond.

By way of more general application design, the benefits of RESTful application constraints promote productivity. A client-server paradigm allows for parallel development, easier debugging and maintenance, and simplification of otherwise complex tasks. These benefits also apply to the practice of creating discrete modules elsewhere in a system. Proper modularization of a project can allow an initial creation of a project using a highly productive but less scalable solution that can later be rewritten. Good design tends to promote later productivity.

Testing

Once done in a largely haphazard and ad hoc manner, testing has become a much more formalized discipline. Automation of testing (along with integrating tests into builds) is required to ensure confidence in large-scale refactoring and is foundational to practices like automated deployment. Automated tests were initially run intermittently and infrequently. With available processing power, it is now feasible to run build suites every time a project is built (or even every time a file is saved). The extent of testing might vary a bit as a project matures but is a necessity in some form in most nontrivial modern web development. Testing has become firmly established in the JavaScript community, allowing for the development of larger projects that perform reliably across browsers and devices. New forms of testing are being developed to address cloud-based deployments such as Netflix's Chaos Monkey (*http://nflx.it/1dkWwjE*), which assists the development of resilient services by actively causing failures.

Testing, when properly instituted, can fulfill a unique roll in facilitating communication between programmers and computers as well as programs and other members of their team. This might not be obvious at first; after all, the purpose of testing is generally understood to validate the reliability or functionality of software. Certain types of testing can also contribute significantly to the overall productivity of a large-scale project. This is immediately evident when tests reduce the pain of integration and result in quality improvements that require fewer fixes. In a somewhat more subtle manner, tests that follow the Behavior-Driven Development paradigm can improve productivity by creating a means of consistent communication between project team members representing different areas. As stated in *The Cucumber Book: Behaviour-Driven Development for Testers and Developers* (*http://bit.ly/prag-cucumber*):

> Software teams work best when the developers and business stakeholders are communicating clearly with one another. A great way to do that is to collaboratively specify the work that's about to be done using automated acceptance tests…When the team writes their acceptance tests collaboratively, they can develop their own ubiquitous language for talking about their problem domain. This helps them avoid misunderstandings.

Better communication results in less time wasted due to misunderstandings. Better understanding results in greater productivity.

When Testing Opposes Productivity

There are times when running tests can become burdensome and inhibit productivity. Constructing and maintaining tests takes time. Running extensive test suites requires time and resources. Like any other development task, effort and time are required for testing that could be spent elsewhere. This has led to many developers and other parties dismissing testing efforts in large part.

It has become relatively easy to integrate testing into web applications at many levels. Many starter projects include testing configured out of the box. To get the maximum value from testing, a culture is required that values the benefits of tests and considers their maintenance to be real work and worth the effort. It is hard to sell testing in terms as directly benefitting productivity. For most projects that have any significant lifespan, its value cannot be understated.

Underlying Platform(s)

The operating system along with installed infrastructure software comprises the underlying local deployment platform. A reasonably powerful workstation or two (along with an extra monitor for added screen real estate) is the equivalent of a supercomputer from a few years ago. Initial setup to allocate sufficient JVM memory or to shut off unneeded programs from consuming resources might be of some value, but often, fundamental aspects of application design play a larger factor. In some cases, having a faster file system will make a noticeable impact on build time.

The use of centralized databases versus developer-maintained copies can be an important decision. In a developer-maintained scenario, migration frameworks like Fly-WayDB (*http://flywaydb.org*) can be of assistance. If working with remote resources, networking can become a significant concern, particularly when working with distributed teams.

Conclusion

By design, there is no sample project with this chapter. Productivity, or simply efficiency during the development process, requires a step back to consider available options and how they fit with the project at hand. Each stage of a project includes macro- and micro-level tasks that might be simplified, automated, or performed more efficiently. There is no substitute for "coming up for air" and giving the appearance of leisure that allows sufficient reflection on the best options available.

## CHAPTER 8

API Design

In theory, there is no difference between theory and
practice. But, in practice, there is.

—Author Unknown

There are two basic ways to solve problems: start with a comprehensive theory and work out the details, or start with particular facts and develop a theory that ties them together. "Detail people" derive solutions by studying the minutiae of a particular problem. "Big-picture people" fit problems into categories that relate to their overarching theories. Each approach has value, and much problem-solving involves adeptly switching between them.

Waxing Philosophical

In philosophy, Plato describes "universals" as abstracted to the highest and most fundamental "realm of ideas." His student Aristotle instead finds them in specific, particular, real-world things. These starting points are more than an intellectual curiosity. In design analysis, starting points affect the ultimate outcome of the process. The best solutions are often the result of both approaches being applied in a complementary manner. These ancient starting points are related to modern data science techniques by the authors of *The Handbook of Statistical Analysis and Data Mining Applications* (Elsevier):

> Traditional statistical analysis follows the *deductive method* in the search for relationships in data sets. Artificial intelligence (e.g., expert systems) and machine learning techniques (e.g., neural nets and decision trees) follow the *inductive method* to find faint patterns of relationship in data sets. Deduction (or deductive reasoning) is the Aristotelian process of analyzing detailed data, calculating a number of metrics, and forming some conclusions based (or deduced) solely on the mathematics of those metrics. Induction is the more Platonic process of using information in a data set as a "spring board" to make general conclusions, which are not wholly contained directly in the input data.

REST and practical web API design are representative of these starting points as well. REST was articulated by Roy Fielding in purely abstract terms. RESTful web APIs, while inspired by the ideals of REST, are created to solve specific problems and accept implementation details that don't fit the theory in its purest form. Much of the disagreement that occurs in discussions concerning REST can be traced to the starting points chosen consciously or unconsciously by each party.

Obviously, REST does specify constraints that provide immediate practical value for web API authors. The discrete division between client and server tiers, the use of HTTP verbs, and identification of web resources have been clearly demonstrated to be useful in the creation of a variety of real-world web APIs. The fact remains that HATEOAS, while theoretically compelling, has proved difficult to implement consistently. It is especially challenging to reconcile due to the widespread adoption of JSON as the de facto data transport format for web APIs.

A Decision to Design

Although web services have existed in one form or another for years, the shift to using them as a foundational design element did not occur immediately. The gradual adoption of Ajax and the creation of JSON and related lightweight web APIs initially impacted existing systems built on server-side MVC. As developers pushed the limits of these technologies to create sophisticated single-page applications, it became clear that an server-driven MVC approach did not adapt well to pervasive use of the new technologies. This lead to a fundamental change to the design of web applications that broke continuity with previous practices. See Figure 8-1 for a timeline illustrating the technological progress that led to client-server-style web applications.

A Shift to a Client-Server Approach

The technologies used in a client-server approach to web development are not new. The programming languages used have matured but are not fundamentally different, and servers, browsers, and the HTTP protocol have been around since the Web was created. However, the design methodology applied in a consistent manner is a more recent development and is largely a result of various technologies being developed.

The first web pages were simple, static content served by web servers and rendered in browsers. Dynamic content was introduced in the mid-1990s as CGI programs on the server and JavaScript in the browser. JavaScript was relatively slow, and client computers were not powerful, so the focus was on utilizing server-side processing to create dynamic content. The complexities involved resulted in the introduction of patterns such as Model-View-Controller (MVC) to the server side.

The MVC pattern remains a staple of server-side Java development and appears in major standards like JEE and frameworks like Spring. Further JavaScript innovations like Ajax and JSON immediately influenced server-side MVC developers, who used these technologies in an ad hoc, piecemeal manner. Frameworks have not disappeared, but their design and use has been significantly affected. In terms of design, MVC frameworks like Spring have adopted "pretty URLs" that reflect resources being acted on. In terms of use, APIs can of course be used in conjunction with traditional MVC. Regardless of the framework in use, many applications today are based on web APIs without MVC, which is effectively a client-server approach.

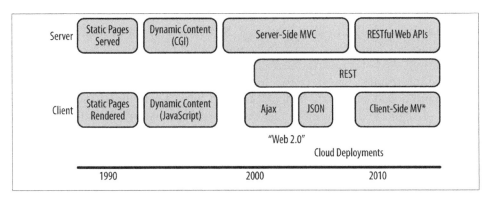

Figure 8-1. History of technologies related to client-server web development

A client-server approach involves a specific design decision to develop RESTful web APIs to deliver data to client-side views and to avoid generating views server-side. This begs the question of how to best design web APIs in a consistent, supportable manner. Design decisions of this type always elicit a range of opinions, but there is a fairly established consensus. The general agreement is that web APIs should be significantly influenced by REST without being rigidly restricted by controversial or impractical constraints.

Practical Web APIs Versus RESTful APIs

While what is practical might be subject to interpretation, there is widespread agreement that web APIs should be easy to use. They should be easily understood by an outside developer, consistent, predictable, and conform to many parts of REST. Implementation of certain aspects of REST provides this kind of ease-of-use by design. This is despite the fact that REST was not originally specified with any particular intention about short-term productivity or developer ease-of-use as it is sometimes understood.

Roy Says...

REST is software design on the scale of decades: every detail is intended to promote software longevity and independent evolution. Many of the constraints are directly opposed to short-term efficiency.

—Roy Fielding (*http://bit.ly/roy-gbiv-restAPIs*)

So which parts of REST are most easily applied in a practical manner? The consistent identification of resources as nouns that are acted upon by HTTP verbs is fundamental to REST, and especially clear in applications that rely on CRUD operations. "Pretty URLs" are one result of such identification. REST makes no specific demands involving performance but does reference cachable resources that promote systems that perform and scale well. And of course, the clear client-server distinction is of immense value as described in previous chapters. REST has been so influential because its very design tends to promote development of applications in concert with the design of the Web itself. Well-engineered applications that can be easily understood and extended result when these parts of REST are in use.

There are qualities of practical web API design that do conflict with REST. Most notably, the use of JSON leads to a lack of linkability defined in the media type itself. The use of a media type that is not linkable immediately results in an API that is not self-describing, and therefore requires documentation. What is perhaps even more challenging is determining a course of action when considering areas not directly touched upon in REST. Securing and supporting changes to APIs are relevant topics outside of the scope of REST.

Even though Fielding does not address all issues related to web API design, he does make many observations that are applicable in other areas. For example, though ease-of-reading for an API response is not a particular concern of REST itself, Fielding highlights the lack of visibility incurred when using solutions like Java applets. This concern could imply that in many situations, formatted JSON would be beneficial. The clarity provided to a client-side developer often outweighs the few spaces saved in a compacted message (not to mention that server compression is more effective for improving transport size and performance).

REST was conceived of as an abstract model. Abstract models stand outside of space and time. As such, it does not directly take into account the fact that systems change over time. The ease-of-use value suggests that changes should be made in a manner that is backward compatible if possible. Versioning of APIs provides a great deal of flexibility in this area.

Recall that one of the constraints of REST is a uniform interface. A uniform interface is almost completely self-describing. Ideally, a system with such an interface needs no documentation beyond a system entry point. This is a stark contrast to protocols like SOAP, which often include a *Web Services Description Language* (WSDL) to describe a web service's functionality. A RESTful system would provide links to all resources and not require any additional description. In practice, web APIs are far more usable if they are well documented.

Guidelines

Unlike technologies whose specifications are dictated by standards committees, web APIs can be constructed at the whim of a developer. In practice, it makes sense to create APIs that conform to the expectations of the broader development community. The following sections reflect the significant influence of REST on development of light-weight web services. They are suggested guidelines for designing easily understandable and usable web APIs.

Nouns as Resources; Verbs as HTTP Actions

As dictated by REST, *resources* are *nouns*. Nouns in a RESTful system are represented in the URL path and are used to manipulate the resource referenced. *Actions* are *verbs* that correspond with functions and are used to manipulate the resources. Verbs in a RESTful system are specifically related to HTTP operations.

Resources correspond with objects, entities, or tables in other design approaches. Nouns are modeled as *classes* in UML class diagrams. They are modeled as *entities*, which are often later implemented as *tables* in relational databases in *Entity Relationship Diagrams* (ERDs).

 UML class diagrams and ERDs are related in that they are notations based on mathematical graphs, but include additional semantics to indicate what nodes and edges represent.

UML and ERDs are not unique in giving special attention to nouns. REST gives them a place of prominence as well. Table 8-1 shows the correspondence between these systems. In REST, nouns are represented as resources; in UML class diagrams, they are classes; and in ERDs, they are entities that are implemented as database tables. Methods used to decompose domains for presentation on class or ERD diagrams can be used when analyzing and modeling a system for a REST API. This is especially true in systems that map well to CRUD operations.

Table 8-1. Noun representation in modeling system

Architecture	Entity that a noun represents
Object-oriented class hierarchy	Class
Relational database	Table
REST API	Resource

When designing a system that includes CRUD operations, consider the applicability of every action on every resource. This can prevent the need to later change a system to include required functionality that was simply overlooked. For example, a blog engine might be modeled to include users, blog posts, and comments as resources. Most blog systems need to be able to create, read, and delete these resources. The ability to update a user or change a comment might not be necessary. Such a system is shown in Table 8-2, where the first column identifies the resources (nouns) and each row identifies the actions (verbs).

Table 8-2. Sample API design grid for a blog

	Create	Read	Update	Delete
User	X	X		X
Post	X	X	X	X
Comment	X	X		X

But I Have No Nouns...

REST model resources are a fundamental unit of the architecture. Analysis of REST resources using techniques similar to those used in UML class diagrams and ERDs map well to CRUD-type applications. An application that is not resource based might be thought of as a group of verbs. Such an application might be better represented as a series of remote procedure calls. This type of system cannot easily be represented in RESTful terms.

In many cases, such a system can be redesigned to be resource based, but this is not always possible. Abstractions might be good enough to model certain systems but insufficient for others.

Query Parameters as Modifiers

While nouns are significant parts of the URL, and verbs relate to HTTP actions, they do not tell the whole story. Other parts of a URL can include additional information. As is the case in the grammar of spoken languages, additional parts of speech are used to qualify or clarify the intent of nouns and verbs.

Query parameters can be useful when referencing a collection of resources. Parameters can be used to filter a collection to only return a subset of the set. They might return a selected number of resources, such as only the first 10. They can also be used to sort the results.

Pagination is a special case of filtering. Parameters can be used to explicitly reference a subset of returned results. Query parameters are better suited for limiting the set of data included in a collection request (serving as adjectives or adverbs, if you will). Pagination has implications beyond the use of query parameters, most notably, linking.

GitHub's API provides a good, well-documented example (*http://bit.ly/1guCZgz*) of pagination parameters. The `page` parameter indicates which page of those available is returned, and the `per_page` parameter limits the results returned to 100:

```
curl https://api.github.com/user/repos?page=2&per_page=100
```

HTTP GETs with Request Bodies

Request parameters tend to "uglify" URLs that were otherwise pretty. In some circumstances, it might be necessary to take an action that seems to map to an HTTP GET and yet involve a request object that is more easily defined as a hierarchical data structure. One example is the retrieval of a number of items that each require several fields for lookup. Roy Fielding and the HTTP spec (*http://yhoo.it/1hfR4SD*) seem to allow for it, though lack of any formal requirement for the server to parse the body suggests that while it works in many instances, this should not be used in a system as a long-term solution.

Web API Versions

REST does not demand that a web API be designed for updates and modifications, but its constraints tend to promote a system that is more easily changed. Versioning APIs is an important consideration not touched upon in Fielding's thesis. Including a portion of a URL with a version number prevents changes to an API from disrupting client activities. Without versioning, it is necessary to coordinate a parallel upgrade to client-side code to account for server-side modifications (which in many cases is not even possible, let alone practical). Though a version identifier lacks theoretical simplicity and elegance, using one can greatly improve a system. Because there is a range of opinion on their usage and they are not self-describing, version segments in web API URLs need to be clearly called out and documented to be effective.

There is a range of opinion on where a version might be included. Some suggest that the version be included in the URL path. Others suggest that it be specified as a query parameter. Still others prefer that a version not clutter the URLs and suggest that it be communicated as an HTTP header.

HTTP Headers

A version identifier is only one of many uses (*http://bit.ly/1bs2O21*) for request and response headers. Other "out of band" information can be stored here as well. Twitter reports rate limit data (*http://bit.ly/1a1l2ly*) in headers to alert a developer when her application is approaching a limit. ETags (*http://bit.ly/1cz6auK*) can be used to control caching, and other headers apply to security authentication and authorization. Headers are often used to communicate secondary but essential information. They don't neatly fit into an abstract model, but they have many practical uses that need to be considered.

Accept and content type headers can be used to impact how the server responds to a request and what sort of response it provides. Besides the obvious differentiation between XML and JSON content, these are used to return padded JSON (JSONP) rather than straight JSON. This is part of the magic that allows JSON content to be sent to a remote server without violating cross-domain restrictions. In essence, it allows access to a JSON API by wrapping a JSON payload in a function call. An example of this is provided in the project later in this chapter.

Linking

Pagination presumes the ability to link to the previous and next resources relative to the subset being displayed. Some API designers recommend including the entire link for the next and previous page in the results of your API, while others recommend only the inclusion of IDs to save space and eliminate repeated text. While providing links is often a good decision and limits the need for additional documentation, strict HATEOAS is not practical or possible for every situation at this point.

Responses

Having an API that is self-describing is an excellent ideal. If resources are specified and reflected in the URLs and HTTP verbs are leveraged, this can be accomplished to a significant degree. Following convention in the use of HTTP response codes (for example, 400 reflects client concerns while 500 indicates server issues) will contribute to this as well. Ideally, your system's error messages will provide immediate, actionable descriptions to address their triggers. But in most systems, some documentation will be needed at least in a few basic areas. Error codes and messages are often a bit terse. They should therefore be keyed to documentation. Ideally, errors will be described in documentation at a level that is impractical in a system error message (for instance, identifying each field in a PUT/POST/PATCH and the errors it can cause).

Documentation

Documentation should be easy to locate, search, and understand. One convention adopted by some web API developers is to use a *Web Application Description Lan-*

guage (WADL), which is a machine-readable description of a web application, generally in XML format. These are often easy to locate, but will not be sufficient if simply generated by a utility. Providing examples that can be replicated by a developer using Curl at the command line can go a long way toward clarifying the intent of your API. If an API is directed toward third-party developers, even more attention will be required.

Documentation on RESTful web APIs will involve manual effort, but there are tools that can ease this burden by automatically generating documentation. Some servers create a WADL as a resource available from the web API server. For example, Jersey generates a basic WADL at runtime that you can request using a GET to */application.wadl*. Additional information can be included in the WADL by specifying selected directives. If you are using a server that does not generate a WADL out of the box, a package like Enunciate (*http://enunciate.codehaus.org*) can be added and configured for your project to generate one. There are also websites like *http://apiary.io* where you can design and document your API outside of the context of any specific project.

Formatting Conventions

Finally, following simple format conventions can make an API much more approachable. Developers need to actually view and read documents during initial development as well as ongoing support. Because JSON is JavaScript, it makes sense to follow idiomatic JavaScript practices like using camel case for naming fields.

Another simple practice is to pretty-print JSON responses to make it easier for people to read. The usual argument against this is that pretty-printing JSON increases the response side and hurts performance, but greater performance gains are possible by configuring JSON responses to be GZipped. The few spaces added in a formatted response can be worth the performance hit because developers can view returned responses without first formatting it in an IDE or using a command-line utility like jq (*http://bit.ly/1kEGnti*).

Security

REST does not provide specific guidelines related to security. This is because it was designed with the assumption that APIs would be publicly available on the Internet. It is often also a good idea to serve APIs over HTTPS rather than HTTP. For APIs that are not intended to be restricted to a server, a JSON API can be made public via JSONP or CORS.

Project

The following project demonstrates how Jersey can be used to return JSON, XML, or JSONP content. A single resource (greeting) is used in this Hello World-style application. The project is available on GitHub (*http://bit.ly/LXhEB8*).

Running the Project

The project is configured to run a Java class from Maven. The class contains a main method that starts a local HTTP Server on port 8080. A single command can be used to build and run the application:

```
mvn clean install exec:java
```

Server Code

The server code consists of three Java classes. App.java contains a main method that runs the server. It creates an instance of a Grizzly (*https://grizzly.java.net*) HTTP server and defines /api as the context root for the web API. It then adds a static HTTP handler to serve the HTML and JavaScript code:

```
package com.saternos.jsonp;

import org.glassfish.jersey.grizzly2.httpserver.GrizzlyHttpServerFactory;
import org.glassfish.jersey.server.ResourceConfig;
import org.glassfish.grizzly.http.server.*;

public class App {

  public static void main(String[] args) throws java.io.IOException{

    HttpServer server = GrizzlyHttpServerFactory.createHttpServer(
      java.net.URI.create("http://localhost:8080/api"),
      new ResourceConfig(GreetingResource.class)
    );

    StaticHttpHandler staticHttpHandler =
    new StaticHttpHandler("src/main/webapp");
    server.getServerConfiguration().addHttpHandler(staticHttpHandler, "/");

    System.in.read();
    server.stop();
  }

}
```

GreetingBean is a POJO with an annotation related to rendering XML responses:

```
package com.saternos.jsonp;
import javax.xml.bind.annotation.*;

@XmlRootElement(name = "greeting")
public class GreetingBean {

  @XmlAttribute
  public String text;

  public GreetingBean() {}
```

```
    public GreetingBean(String text) {
      this.text = text;
    }
}
```

GreetingResource provides the ability to return the data contained in a Greeting
Bean through the server. Jersey (*https://jersey.java.net*) is the JAX-RS reference implementation that maps web requests to Java methods. JAX-RS applies *annotations* to Java
objects. Annotations became available in Java in version 1.5. They are used by frameworks to apply behaviors to classes and methods and effectively reduce the amount of
code needed to complete common tasks. These annotations effectively provide a DSL
that maps pretty clearly to underlying HTTP functionality.

The @GET annotation indicates the HTTP request verb in view. The @Path annotation
describes the URL path in context, and the @Produces annotation describes what content
type will be produced by Jersey when returning the bean from the method. The @Quer
yParam is used to assign the query parameter as a method argument to getGreeting.
Table 8-3 presents representative annotations.

Table 8-3. Selected JAX-RS annotations

Annotation	Description
@GET	Requests a representation of a resource
@POST	Creates a resource at the URI specified
@PUT	Creates or updates a resource at the URI specified
@DELETE	Removes a resource
@HEAD	Provides an identical response to GET, without the content body
@Path	The relative path for a resource
@Produces	Indicates the media types a service can return
@Consumes	Indicates the media types a service can accept in a request
@PathParam	Binds a method parameter to a segment of the URI path
@QueryParam	Binds a method parameter to a query parameter
@FormParam	Binds a method parameter to a form parameter

There are a number of other annotations available in JAX-RS. See *RESTful Java with
JAX-RS* (O'Reilly) for more information:

```
package com.saternos.jsonp;

import org.glassfish.jersey.server.JSONP;
import javax.ws.rs.*;

@Path("greeting")

public class GreetingResource {
```

```
@GET
@Produces({"application/xml", "application/json"})
public GreetingBean getGreeting() {
  return new GreetingBean("Hello World Local");
}

@Path("remote")
@GET
@Produces({"application/x-javascript"})
@JSONP(queryParam = JSONP.DEFAULT_QUERY)
public GreetingBean getGreeting(
        @QueryParam(JSONP.DEFAULT_QUERY) String callback
        ) {
  return new GreetingBean("Hello World Remote");
}
}
```

Curl and jQuery

The client-side code included with the project uses jQuery (*http://jquery.com*) to call API URLs. The jQuery library has a wide range of Ajax capabilities and hides some of the complexities and cross-browser challenges related to the core JavaScript XMLHTTPRequest object. The calls used in the application can also be replicated using Curl, as illustrated below. Table 8-4 shows web API URLs used in this example.

Table 8-4. Application URLs

URL	Description
/	HTML and JavaScript in the web app directory
/api/greeting	JSON or XML from getGreeting()
/api/greeting/remote	JSONP from getGreeting (string callback)

Curl can be used to return a web page in HTML:

```
curl http://localhost:8080
```

When using Curl, the -i argument can be specified to include header information. The HTTP response code and content type are of particular interest. For instance, if you specify a URL path that is not recognized by the server, it will return a "Not Found" response:

```
curl http://localhost:8080/api -i
```

The application returns XML in the response by default:

```
curl http://localhost:8080/api/greeting
```

By modifying the HTTP Accept request header, a JSON response can be returned instead:

```
curl http://localhost:8080/api/greeting -H 'Accept: application/json'
```

Finally, a call to return JSONP will often include the specification of a JavaScript function name as a query parameter. The same response returned in the JSON call results, padded by a JavaScript function. Because JavaScript files can be downloaded from different domains, the content is returned. They would otherwise be forbidden by the JavaScript same-origin policy:

```
curl http://localhost:8080/api/greeting/remote?__callback=myCall
curl http://127.0.0.1:8080/api/greeting/remote?__callback=myCall
```

Theory in Practice

REST in its pure theoretical form remains an ideal standard. It serves as a measure of projects implemented with it in view. It ought to be studied and understood. But the value of other technologies, namely JSON, has been proven as well. JavaScript-based clients easily consume JSON. The lack of a universally accepted mechanism for linking in JSON has not deterred developers from adopting it as the data transport of choice. Supplementing such APIs with documentation and other practical considerations has made the difference between theoretically perfect systems that are never delivered and practical solutions that meet immediate needs.

The applicability of RESTful web APIs to the practical problems faced by developers has grown over time and resulted in the change in architectural approaches. Such APIs can be consumed by devices with a wide array of capabilities, including those created by third-party developers. They are lighter weight than SOAP and other web service implementations that include complex envelopes and exchange patterns. They can be used to create applications without problems related to stale data on the client. They effectively distribute processing to clients that have significant computing power. They are horizontally scalable by simply adding additional server applications when deployed in a cloud-based platform like Amazon Web Services. These and other characteristics have resulted in developers switching from occasionally implementing or consuming a service to developing entire applications with a consistent approach leveraging RESTful web APIs.

jQuery and Jython

*Language is no longer regarded as peripheral to our grasp of the world
we live in, but as central to it. Words are not mere vocal labels or
communicational adjuncts superimposed upon an already given
order of things. They are collective products of social interaction,
essential instruments through which human beings constitute
and articulate their world. This typically twentieth-century view
of language has profoundly influenced developments
throughout the whole range of human sciences.*

—Roy Harris

Programming languages have an immediate and tangible impact on the lives of those
who use them and on those who are not even aware of their existence. Amusingly
enough, programmers often spend precious little time working with the fundamental
features of a language. After gaining an understanding of these, they immediately look
for ways to avoid reinventing the wheel. An *abstraction level* or generalization can become so popular that it becomes practically conflated with the original language.

The jQuery library is such a technology related to JavaScript. It has been widely adopted,
and most JavaScript developers have used it extensively. Some consider it not just a
library, but more of a *internal Domain Specific Language* (DSL). Thought of this way,
jQuery is a small language with a focus on DOM manipulation, Ajax processing, and
other common JavaScript tasks. In any case, jQuery use is so prevalent that you will find
questions online of the form, "How to do X in JavaScript?" that are answered using
jQuery idioms.

The abstraction layer that has made Java so successful is at a lower level than the language
itself; it is the Java Virtual Machine (JVM) which processes the bytecode generated by
the Java compiler. Java was intentionally designed from the onset with the JVM as an
abstraction layer. Its independent existence has made it possible to create compilers for
non-Java programming language implementations that target the JVM. The JVM is a

well-engineered, highly optimized program and is the result of years of research and development. Developers who have no particular interest in the Java language can still benefit from this underlying technology.

The project created in this chapter will use jQuery and Jython (a JVM-based Python implementation) to demonstrate how simply a client-server web application can be prototyped.

Server Side: Jython

The Python (*http://www.python.org*) programming language was initially released in the mid-1990's by Guido van Rossum (its principal author and "Benevolent Dictator For Life"). Python is known for its clear, readable, and regular syntax. It departs from many of the idioms of C-based languages (like curly brackets). Because of its consistency and clarity, it has been adopted in many educational settings as the language taught in introductory programming classes. Python generally requires fewer lines of code than Java to perform a given task.

Jython (*http://www.jython.org*) is an implementation of Python that runs on the JVM. This allows for the creation of clear, concise Python programs that are run wherever Java is installed. Jython programs also can interact with Java objects, which introduces a range of possibilities for embedding Jython or using it in conjunction with native Java libraries.

Python Web Server

As a scripting language, Python also can be used in ways unfamiliar to Java developers. For instance, to run a static web server that serves files from an arbitrary directory without writing an original line of code, you can simply navigate to the directory in question and invoke the following:

```
python -m SimpleHTTPServer
```

Jython Web Server

Creating a Python-based web server using the SimpleHTTPServer referenced above requires only a few lines of code:

```
import SimpleHTTPServer
import SocketServer
import os

os.chdir('src/main/resources')
httpd = SocketServer.TCPServer(("", 8000),
SimpleHTTPServer.SimpleHTTPRequestHandler)
print "serving at port 8000"
httpd.serve_forever()
```

Jython can be invoked from the command line or embedded inside of a Java application. For example, this script can be called from inside of a Java class:

```java
package com.oreilly.jython;

import java.io.File;
import java.io.IOException;
import org.python.util.PythonInterpreter;
import org.apache.commons.io.FileUtils;

public class Server
{
    public static void main( String[] args ) throws IOException
    {
        new PythonInterpreter().exec(
                    FileUtils.readFileToString(
              new File("python/http_server.py")
            )
                );
    }
}
```

The project, including its dependencies, is available on GitHub (*http://bit.ly/ 1bPlMKG*). It can be built using mvn clean install and run by calling mvn exec:java.

Mock APIs

A static web server has significant limitations. Most notably for a web app developer, it cannot produce dynamic content. However, it is possible to mock out APIs by simply creating files that contain representative data. For example, a directory named *api* with a file called *groups.json* can be created and would be available from the *http://localhost: 8000/api/groups.json* URL. The content of this JSON file is an array of groups, each of which is an object that has a name, description, and URL:

```json
[
    {
        "name":"duckduckgo",
            "description":"Internet search engine founded by Gabriel Weinberg",
            "url":"http://duckduckgo.com/"
    },
    {
        "name":"angular",
            "description":"Open source JavaScript framework initially created" +
                " by Adam Abrons and Miško Hevery",
            "url":"http://angularjs.org/"
    },
    {
        "name":"twitter",
            "description":"Online social networking service and microblogging" +
                " service created by Jack Dorsey",
            "url":"http://twitter.com/"
```

```
            },
            {
                    "name":"netflix",
                    "description":"American provider of on-demand Internet streaming "+
                            "media Marc Randolph and Reed Hastings",
                    "url":"http://netflix.com/"
            }
    ]
```

Directories relative to the root directory are reflected in the URL path, and many web servers will respond with the desired content type if a corresponding extension is specified. Client-side developers can work in parallel using a mock API like this while server-side configuration and development proceeds.

Client Side: jQuery

Since its release in 2006, jQuery has simplified cross-browser development in several different ways. It was created by John Resig with the intention of changing the way that developers write JavaScript. Specifically, it sought to remove common repetitive tasks and replace obscure, verbose JavaScript with a clear, succinct syntax.

When encountering jQuery for the first time, the number of dollar signs that appear in code can be surprising. This is because $ represents the jQuery object in the namespace for the library. So the following are equivalent:

```
jQuery('a')
$('a')
```

Running JavaScript after a page loads is accomplished in standard JavaScript using the body onload event. The load event occurs after a page is fully rendered (including all assets such as images). jQuery provides an event that runs slightly earlier, after the DOM is ready. There are several different syntaxes to specify this handler. The recommended one is the verbose version:

```
$(document).ready(function() {
// Handler for .ready() called.
});
```

which is equivalent to:

```
$(function() {
// Handler for .ready() called.
});
```

In general, the pattern of jQuery usage involves finding DOM elements and then doing something with them. Finding DOM elements is accomplished using a string pattern of some sort (CSS Selectors or XPath). Doing something might be as straightforward as reading the contents of the element, or could involve its contents or style or associating a behavior with it through an event handler. jQuery also provides a consistent interface for Ajax processing. It is also designed to be extended using plug-ins.

DOM Traversal and Manipulation

Much of the criticism leveled at JavaScript is due to difficulties in interacting with the browser DOM. jQuery eases interaction between HTML and JavaScript by providing an elegant interface for DOM selection, traversal, and manipulation. This is most frequently accomplished using CSS selectors from CSS 1-3, as well as some specific to jQuery. *CSS selectors* are strings containing patterns that can simply refer to an element by name or specify a complex series of matching conditions. If all conditions specified by a pattern are true for a given element, the selector matches it. Table 9-1 gives some jQuery examples.

Table 9-1. jQuery examples

Selector	Description
`$('$div')`	All divs
`$('#myElement')`	Elements with an ID of `myElement`
`$('.myClass')`	All elements with a class of `myClass`
`$('div#myDiv')`	All divs with an ID of `myDiv`
`$('ul.myListClass li')`	All list items inside of a ul with an class of `myListClass`
`$('ul.projects li:first')`	The first list item in uls with a class of projects

As shown in Table 9-2, other attributes can also be accessed, even if only part of the value searched for is known.

Table 9-2. jQuery partial values

Selector	Description
`$('input[name*="formInput"]')`	Input elements with a name with a substring of `formInput`
`$('input[name^="formInput"]')`	Input elements with a name that starts with `formInput`

Characters with special meanings must be escaped using two backslashes. For example, if you had an input text field with an ID of `myForm:username`, the following selector could be used to identify the element:

```
$('input#myForm\\:username')
```

CSS selectors are very expressive, but at times result in an array of objects that need to be further processed. Many jQuery methods return a jQuery object that you can then use to call another method. So for instance, a subtree of the DOM can be searched to find a specific element:

```
$('div.projects').find('.project1')
```

Utility Functions

jQuery also provides a number of utility functions (*http://bit.ly/1g1BkgF*) that can handle similar tasks on collections of elements, as shown in Table 9-3. Libraries like under score.js overlap somewhat with jQuery but provide even more capabilities for manipulating lists and objects. The JavaScript language has been augmented over time to include similar methods. jQuery's methods will likely continue to be used for the near future due to the benefit of compatibility with legacy browsers.

Table 9-3. Utility functions

	jQuery	Underscore	JavaScript 1.6
iteration	each	each	forEach
transform	map	map	map
filtering	grep	filter, where	
find index	inArray	indexOf, lastIndexOf	

After an object has been located, it is trivial to do something with it. Function chaining makes manipulating elements especially convenient:

```
$('div.items').find('.item1').text('Hi World').css('background-color', 'blue')
```

The modification of specific elements in the DOM leads into the development of dynamic interactive user interfaces that respond to a user's actions.

The pattern of "find an element" and "do something with it" is simple, powerful, and immediate. To appreciate this, simply pop open a browser web console on a page that includes jQuery and begin writing some selectors that return objects. When you have located some, try changing their text or styling. If you want to try this pattern on a page that does not include jQuery, you can load it by running a few simple commands in advance:

```
var script= document.createElement('script');
script.type= 'text/javascript';
script.src= 'http://ajax.googleapis.com/ajax/libs/jquery/1.9.1/jquery.min.js';
document.head.appendChild(script);
```

Effects

jQuery includes convenient methods for modifying CSS to show or hide elements. It also includes methods related to animation, including fading and sliding effects:

```
$('form#myForm').hide()
$('form#myForm').show()
$('form#myForm').slideUp('slow')
$('form#myForm').slideDown('slow')
$('form#myForm').fadeIn('slow')
$('form#myForm').fadeOut('slow')
```

Event Handling

jQuery selectors can be used to attach event handlers to specific elements. The actual syntax used to this end has varied a bit over time. Methods such as `bind`, `live`, and `delegate` have been superseded by `on` and `off`. One challenge introduced with increasingly dynamic interfaces is that you might want to define an event handler for an element that could come into existence at some later point depending on user interaction. The solution to this challenge using jQuery is to bind the event at a higher level of the DOM. When the event is fired, even though the event is not directly associated with the element, it will be propagated up and handled when the selector is matched:

```
$(document).on('click','.myClass', function(){
        console.log('Hey you clicked me.');
});
```

Ajax

jQuery wraps the `XMLHttpRequest` browser object into a more usable, simple form that behaves in a consistent manner across browsers. `jQuery.ajax` is a general Ajax requester, and more specific functions provide a shorthand for commonly used HTTP GET or POST commands. Because of the popularity of JSON communication in Ajax applications, it includes a `getJSON` method as well and also provides the ability to make calls using JSONP.

jQuery is an amazing but relatively simple library. The concepts introduced in this chapter cover the bulk of what it is designed for at a high level. Books like Cody Lindley's *jQuery Cookbook* (O'Reilly) are very helpful in showing how the library can be used for specific tasks.

jQuery and Higher-Level Abstractions

jQuery greatly simplified cross-browser development and made it possible to develop a class of web applications with significant Ajax interactions, event handling, and DOM manipulation much more easily. Its popularity (*http://bit.ly/1eSnqkn*) suggests that it will continue to be influential and popular for many years. But as web apps have grown in size, new approaches have emerged to tame the complexity. Larger-scale design patterns (MVC) and programming paradigms (functional programming) provide alternatives and compliments to the functionality available in jQuery.

Consider, for example, the simple practice of assigning variables. This basic task becomes burdensome as the number of variables in a program (with dependencies on one another) begins to grow. Object-oriented programming was popularized with the notion that an object could encapsulate a group of variables that represent the state of an object. The object would be given defined methods to allow access to and manipulation of an object's state.

Object orientation (in the classical sense) is not particularly influential in the JavaScript community, but other solutions address the challenge of keeping variables in sync. These include two-way data binding between model and view components (AngularJS) and Functional Reactive Programming, which defines data types that represent a value over time (rather than being concerned only about a variable's value at a particular instant).

Functional Reactive Programming

Functional Reactive Programming (FRP) is a declarative approach to GUI design that has been garnering recent attention. Its selling point is that many of the constructs addressed directly by jQuery (event handlers, callbacks, and DOM manipulations) are not done directly.

---

jQuery has its limitations, and separate projects have sprung up to provide niceties like client-side templates, modularization of code, and management of callbacks. Others seek to simplify the complexities of direct DOM manipulation. Many of these can be used in conjunction with jQuery, and jQuery's success in taming browser incompatibilities and providing a consistent interface for DOM manipulation have made it an established presence in JavaScript development.

Project

The Jython-based HTTP server introduced earlier in this chapter simply responds to requests for files in the specified directory. This is sufficient to serve up HTML and JavaScript files. Although the server itself provides little functionality, there are ways to effectively expand the server tier by making external calls to third-party APIs. One API that is publicly available and requires no special setup or API keys is the GitHub API. The application described will do anything from lookups on GitHub data to listing members of select GitHub Groups (as shown in Figure 9-1).

Figure 9-1. GitHub Groups

Basic HTML

The application can be "built out" from scratch starting with a simple HTML file with a bit of embedded CSS. Although stylesheets are better externalized for production projects (consistent with the previous discussion related to Unobtrusive JavaScript (*http://bit.ly/1guPBTM*)), it is simpler to keep all the code in view when developing in this manner:

```
<html>
<head>
        <title>index</title>
        <style type="text/css" media="screen">
                img {width: 50; height: 50;}
                span {padding: 7px;}
        </style>
</head>
<body>
        <select id="selected_group">
          <option>Select Group</option>
        </select>
        <div id="images"></div>
</body>
</html>
```

JavaScript and jQuery

Underneath the closing style element, add a reference to jQuery, which is available from Google:

```
<script src="//ajax.googleapis.com/ajax/libs/jquery/1.8.3/jquery.min.js">
</script>
```

The options that will appear in the dropdown will be loaded in a JSON file listed earlier.

The jQuery code to load this JSON file calls $.getJSON and iterates through each record returned and appends the option to the select element. When an option is actually selected, a function called getGroup is called:

```
<script>

$.getJSON("/api/groups.json",
        function(data) {
                        $.each(data, function(i,item){
                                        $("<option>"+item.name+"</option>").
                appendTo("#selected_group");
                        });
                }).error(function(){ console.log("error");});

$(document).ready(function() {
        $('#selected_group').bind('change',
        function (){
            getGroup();
        });
});
});
</script>
```

The getGroup() function clears any previous display, then makes a call to GitHub to retrieve the data for the selected group. The names and avatars for each group member are then displayed:

```
function getGroup(){
        $("#images").empty();
                $.getJSON("https://api.github.com/orgs/"+
            $('#selected_group').val()+"/members",
                        function(data) {
                                $.each(data,
                function(i,item){
                                                $("<span>" +
                        item.login +
                    "</span><img/>").
                        attr("src", item.avatar_url).
                        appendTo("#images");
                                });
                }).error(function(){ console.log("error"); });
        }
```

This example shows how straightforward it is to use jQuery to make local or remote web API calls and display the results. The entire client side consists of fewer than 40 lines of HTML, CSS, and JavaScript. Add to this cross-browser support afforded by jQuery and it is apparent why it was so quickly and widely adopted.

That said, the project does leave something to be desired. It's not exactly pretty or terribly responsive to different devices. The strings containing snippets containing HTML might also make you cringe and wish for a templating solution of some sort. You might also feel that the nested function calls are a bit foreign and that there might be a way of providing a more natural functional syntax to the calls. You are not alone in having this reaction. The JavaScript world has developed projects and libraries that will be discussed in later chapters.

Conclusion

A client-server approach to web development requires only a few minutes of initial setup. The server project contained in this chapter simply serves static assets. Static HTML files and mocked-out API calls stored in JSON files can be created on the file system and require no build to update. Once in place, jQuery can be used to make local or remote API calls and display the resulting data. A project of this nature does not require a deep dive into Java or Python, and even simplifies the amount of JavaScript that must be mastered. The result is a simple dynamic web application that can be viewed in a variety of browsers.

## CHAPTER 10

JRuby and Angular

We live in a beautiful and orderly world,
not in a chaos without norms, even
though that is how it sometimes appears.

—M. C. Escher

Sorting and filtering are activities that have been used since ancient times to organize the world. Ancient acrostics used each letter in an alphabet to start a line of a poem. This involves both filtering (selection of first letter) and sorting (alphabetical). The Sieve of Eratosthenes (*http://bit.ly/1fjJi38*), shown in Figure 10-1, can be visualized (*http://bit.ly/1g1BULt*) by writing out, in order, the integers from two to the upper bound in question, and then filtering out composites (nonprime numbers) as the multiples of primes.

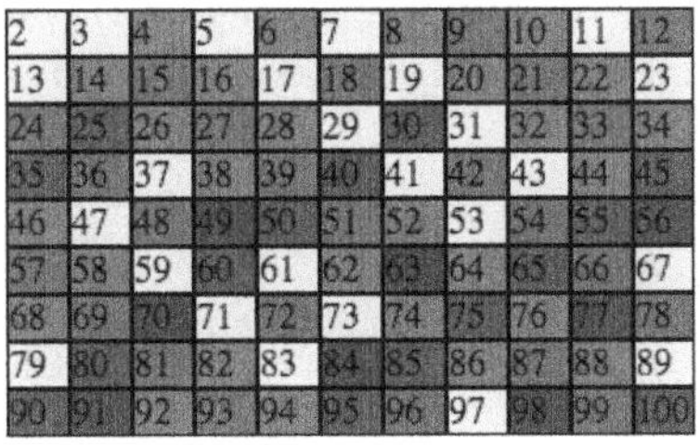

Figure 10-1. Sieve of Eratosthenes

A quick search on filtering and sorting returns many results geared toward the manipulation of data in spreadsheet programs. The project in this chapter will show how, with a relatively small amount of code, JRuby and Angular can be used to filter and sort an HTML table containing data from Google Finance stock market data.

Server Side: JRuby and Sinatra

Simple, dynamic web APIs can be created using Ruby and a microframework called Sinatra. Sinatra is essentially a Ruby-based wrapper of HTTP.

Ruby was developed by Yukihiro "Matz" Matsumoto, who incorporated parts of his favorite languages (Perl, Smalltalk, Eiffel, Ada, and Lisp) to create a new language that balanced functional and imperative approaches. Although it was released in 1995, and he wrote a book called *Ruby in a Nutshell* about it in 2001, it saw a significant spike in popularity when Ruby on Rails (or simply Rails) became popular several years later. The language is, in the words of its author "simple in appearance, but is very complex inside, just like our human body." Matz coauthored a more recent book (*http://oreil.ly/ruby-prog-lang*) on Ruby that goes into the details of this fascinating language.

Rails (*http://rubyonrails.org*) is the Ruby MVC web framework that first brought Ruby to the attention of many developers. David Heinemeier Hansson extracted the framework from Basecamp (*https://basecamp.com*) (a project management tool he worked on at 37signals (*http://37signals.com*)) and released it in 2004. In many languages and frameworks, writing no code results in no behavior. In Ruby (as well as Rails and other Ruby projects), default behavior is included when no code is written. The Rails philosophy expresses this under the principle of *convention over configuration*. This greatly limits the amount of setup required to get a project up and running. This principle is evident in other web frameworks written in Ruby, most notably Sinatra (*http://www.sinatrarb.com*), which is much smaller than Rails and ideal for creating streamlined applications that don't require all of the bells and whistles of a larger framework.

Workflow

One approach to using JRuby (or other JVM language) is incorporating them from a Java perspective. The module containing the language implementation can be included in a project as a dependency:

```
<dependency>
    <groupId>org.jruby</groupId>
        <artifactId>jruby-complete</artifactId>
        <version>1.6.3</version>
        <type>jar</type>
        <scope>compile</scope>
</dependency>
```

In the case of web applications, this makes sense if you have Java application servers already installed. Warbler (*http://bit.ly/1aYZAm6*) can be used to bundle Rack applications into WAR files, and there are some interesting experiments like the Rack Servlet from Square Engineering (*http://bit.ly/MfPQsr*) to embed a Ruby-powered servlet into an existing WAR.

A Java developer who approaches Ruby in this manner will have the benefit of focusing on differences in syntax, but will miss the tools and workflow that have helped make the language so successful. These differences begin with the very tools used to initially set up the language and associated packages.

Interactive Ruby Shell

The *Interactive Ruby Shell* (IRB) is a shell for executing Ruby commands. It is comparable to an OS shell in that it provides an immediate result for any expression it evaluates. This sort of exploratory programming using a read–eval–print loop (REPL) is available in a number of other languages. When experimenting, learning a new bit of syntax, or when it is not clear what algorithms or data structures might be used, the usual cycle of edit/compile/run/debug can be burdensome. Java does not have any directly comparable tool. Executing a bit of code while paused in a debugger is similar, and the Eclipse IDE has a feature called a Scrapbook Page, which is similar. IRB is worth exploring when learning Ruby, and when using JRuby, it can also be used to access Java classes.

For an example of how IRB can be used to explore Java JARs, see Appendix A.

Ruby Version Manager (RVM)

Rather than accessing JRuby as a dependency of a Java project, a JRuby environment can be set up using the *Ruby Version Manager* (*https://rvm.io*) (RVM). RVM is not limited to JRuby, but can be used with many other Ruby implementations. RVM supports deployments of multiple Ruby environments. Each one is self-contained and includes a specific version of Ruby, and associated set of required gems. RVM makes it easy to set up projects with a specific set of gems dependent on a particular Ruby version and keep these projects independent of ones using other versions of Ruby. It is interactive and gives intelligent advice during installations regarding additional configuration or troubleshooting. If you are working on multiple Ruby projects, it lets you develop in a given environment and switch to another environment with a single command.

Ruby/JRuby/RVM/Dependency Management

JRuby can be used in several different ways, which can be the source of some confusion.

Ruby is a programming language in its own right. *JRuby* is a version of the Ruby programming language that runs on the Java Virtual Machine. *RVM* provides a mechanism for managing several different versions of Ruby, *including JRuby distributions*. The RVM environment includes language installs and associated Ruby packages and is maintained locally on a machine outside of a project. RVM provides a way of working with Ruby implementations, including JRuby, from a Ruby perspective.

JRuby can also be included as a standard module dependency in Maven or other build tool. RVM is not used in this case, and JRuby is treated from a Java perspective.

To identify which version of Ruby RVM is using:

```
$ which rvm-auto-ruby
/Users/cas/.rvm/bin/rvm-auto-ruby

# Generally, you don't call this directly...
$rvm-auto-ruby --version

# The version in Ruby in use will match the one in the previous command
$ruby --version
```

To list installed Ruby interpreters and the version currently in use:

```
rvm ls
```

To switch to an environment, call the rvm use command along with a portion of the Ruby interpreter name:

```
rvm use 2.0.0
```

Other RVM Functions

RVM does a great deal more than simply let you interactively maintain Ruby versions. With it, you can set up project-specific Ruby environments called gemsets (*https:// rvm.io/gemsets/basics*) that are independent of other Ruby projects. It can be called at the command line to execute scripts that use a specific Ruby version and gemset. It can even go beyond simple diagnostic advice; for instance, SSL certificate issues can sometimes be resolved by simply running the following RVM command:

```
rvm osx-ssl-certs update all
```

Packages

Ruby packages are called gems and are maintained using the gem utility. Gems can be released with various versions, and a project can be developed that uses a rather specific set of dependencies. A set of gems can be associated with a single RVM environment, which allows for simultaneous development of several different Ruby projects that use different versions of Ruby and different sets of gems. In order to deploy a given project to other machines, the specific set of dependencies can be maintained declaratively using the bundler gem (*http://bundler.io*). Bundler dependencies are listed in a Gemfile.

Using RVM, you can set up a new Ruby environment. You can then install a bunch of gems individually and tweak the environment until all of the correct dependencies and versions are available. When these are available, populate a bundler Gemfile with all of the versions in use in your current environment. The following sequence of bash commands can be used to create a new Gemfile, add a comment referencing the Ruby version in use, and include a list of gem dependencies that matches the current environment. The bulk of the work is done in the last command, which lists the gems available in the current environment, formats the list, removes references to `rvm` and `bundle`, and uses the list to create the corresponding gem entries in the Gemfile:

```bash
#!/bin/bash
bundle init

echo "# Ruby Version: `ruby --version`">>Gemfile

gem list --local |
grep -v '\*\*'|
sed 's/[)(,]//g' |
egrep -v 'rvm|bundle'|
awk '{print "gem \""$1"\",\""$2"\""}' >>Gemfile
```

The generated Gemfile can be distributed to other machines that need the same environment (such as other development machines or separate deployment environments). These otherwise would have to be set up using a Ruby installation or RVM, and a tedious manual gem installation.

Sinatra

Sinatra (*http://www.sinatrarb.com*), as described on its website, is a DSL for "quickly creating web applications in Ruby with minimal effort." It essentially wraps HTTP in a Ruby-accessible interface that runs on Rack (a common interface for Ruby web servers and web frameworks). A Sinatra application is made up of *routes* (each one an HTTP method paired with a URL-matching pattern). A route is associated with a block, which can be used to fulfill the request (by executing Ruby code, rendering a template, and so on).

Sinatra can also serve static files from a directory named *public* by default (see Figure 10-2). This makes it ideal for creating a set of web APIs in Ruby that back HTML/ CSS/JavaScript applications. It is by no means limited to this approach. A standard server-side MVC approach involves Ruby-based templates (ERB) in the *views* directory (by default).

Sinatra is minimal and thus sometimes referred to as a microframework. Like the best of other Ruby libraries, it stays out of your way and exposes a clear interface that can be referenced as you see fit.

Or perhaps more accurately stated, as a Domain Specific Language (*http://bit.ly/ 1md4cKg*), it improves programmer productivity and communication due to its close alignment with the domain it represents: HTTP for web applications.

Sinatra lends itself to being expanded from trivial apps (designed in *classic* style) to a form considered more suitable for production deployments (written *modular* style). So it is feasible to begin work on a tiny Sinatra app that is gradually built out into a final application. Because of its simple and transparent nature, it can also be used for prototyping, which results in an application that is essentially formal documentation that can be used to implement a separate system.

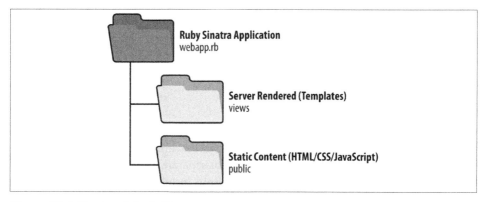

Figure 10-2. Sinatra default directory structure

Sinatra is a relatively simple framework with great (*http://bit.ly/1md4fG1*) documentation (*http://bit.ly/1g1CpoH*) online and has garnered enough attention to have a book (*http://oreil.ly/Sinatra-UR*) written on it as well. It is worth learning for its own sake, and has inspired a variety of similar frameworks in other languages.

JSON Processing

The JSON gem is rather straightforward; it converts Ruby objects to and from JSON strings. With a straightforward mapping between JSON types and Ruby types, it makes working with JSON data a breeze. Consider the following IRB session:

```
>require 'json'
 => true

> o = {:A=>[1,2,3], :B=>{:C=>:D}}
 => {:A=>[1, 2, 3], :B=>{:C=>:D}}

> o.class
 => Hash

> s=JSON.pretty_generate(o)
 => ...

> puts s
{
```

```
  "A": [
    1,
    2,
    3
  ],
  "B": {
    "C": "D"
  }
}

s.class
 => String

o2=JSON.parse(s)
 => {"A"=>[1, 2, 3], "B"=>{"C"=>"D"}}

o2.class
 => Hash
```

There are some subtleties that Ruby aficionados will notice (Ruby symbols and strings are both converted to JSON strings, for example). But in general, the example shows that it is very simple and straightforward to parse and generate JSON using this package.

Client Side: AngularJS

AngularJS (*http://angularjs.org*) (often referred to simply as *Angular*) is an MV* Java-Script framework developed in 2009 by Miško Hevery and Adam Abrons. As of 2014, a team at Google that includes Igor Minár and Vojta Jína maintain the project. Angular reads the DOM of its associated HTML document, processes custom elements and attributes (directives), and binds data in an associated model to the page.

Angular seeks to provide a comprehensive approach to the development of web applications. It recognizes the declarative nature of HTML and enhances its behaviors. It is a very sophisticated framework that has entire books (*http://bit.ly/angularJS*) dedicated to in-depth coverage. The purpose here is not to exhaustively describe the project, but to demonstrate how to quickly get up and running with it. There are a number of concepts related to Angular that need to be understood in order to use it effectively.

Model

If you have done server-side MVC development, you probably think of a model as a class that contains attributes and is associated with a relational database. Hibernate and iBatis are used by Java developers, and ActiveRecord is included in Rails to serve in this capacity. There are also JavaScript frameworks like Backbone that include a specific model object that is recognized by the framework.

Angular is quite different in this regard. Unlike some other JavaScript frameworks that have a specific model object, an Angular model is a plain JavaScript object. The *model* in Angular is simply the data. Because of how little attention is given to the model in Angular, some have seen it as more of a templating solution, as cited in the Angular FAQs (*http://bit.ly/NFMEYm*). However, the rest of the features of the framework, including bidirectional data binding, make Angular more than simply a templating system.

Views

The *view* is a representation of the model through an HTML template. Whenever the model changes, Angular's two-way data binding is activated so that updates to the view are rendered as needed. *Expressions* are JavaScript-like snippets of code enclosed in bindings, such as *{{ _expression_ }}*.

Directives can be included to effectively extend the capabilities of HTML. During DOM compilation, directives are executed to perform a wide range of tasks, including DOM manipulation (showing or hiding elements, looping and creating new elements, and so on) or a variety of other tasks. Angular comes with a set of directives, and programmers can add additional ones that effectively serve as independent web components.

One of the most pervasive problems with JavaScript is issues related to the use of globals. Angular mitigates this to prevent pollution of the global namespace. *Scopes* allows the template, model, and controller to work together. They are nested in a hierarchical structure corresponding to the structure of the DOM. Scopes detect model changes and provide the execution context for expressions.

Controllers

A controller constructs the model and publishes it to the view. A JavaScript function contains the code associated with the controller, and the `ngController` directive attaches a controller function to the view.

The Angular Seed (*http://bit.ly/1md6hpB*) project provides an example of how requests can be routed to various controllers. The `$routeProvider` service is associated with a function that matches the portion of the URL after the hash with a corresponding template and controller.

Services

A variety of services are built into Angular. The `$parse` service processes expressions. A single *injector* per Angular application is used to locate services. As is the case with directives, programmers can encapsulate their own logic in custom services as needed.

Comparing jQuery and Angular

It is natural to compare jQuery and Angular. Both are popular, influential libraries. jQuery is a clearly established leader, and Angular promises to address a slew of issues encountered when using jQuery alone. A cursory look at the Angular documentation reveals that Angular is compatible with jQuery, and viewing a few sites will establish many examples of jQuery and Angular being used in the same page. Though both are effective tools in developing large-scale web applications, there are some areas of consideration that influence successful design and development.

DOM Versus Model Manipulation

Angular does work with jQuery if it is present. If it is not present, Angular uses a built-in subset of jQuery. In this sense, the libraries are compatible, and both manipulate the DOM.

However, it is safer to consider Angular as primary when both libraries are present. This is because there is a fundamental difference in how each library maintains application state. A jQuery application directly manipulates the DOM and views it as containing the application state. An Angular application treats the *model* rather than the DOM as the "source of truth." The model, *not* the DOM, is directly manipulated. Changes to the model result in the DOM being updated. Relying on jQuery DOM manipulation in an Angular application leads to subtle problems that are hard to address because the Angular model gets out of sync and doesn't know about changes made by jQuery.

Due to this fundamental difference in approach, it is difficult to integrate Angular into an existing jQuery-based application. Angular DOM manipulation should be done using Angular *directives*. Packaging up jQuery functionality into directives from an existing application can be challenging. It is far easier to write an application from the ground up using Angular.

Unobtrusiveness of Angular

There are some differences of opinion on whether Angular is in line with the principles of unobtrusive JavaScript, but connecting presentation and behavior needs to occur at some point in an MV* framework. The problem can be seen in the following examples.

Placing JavaScript in HTML has widely been regarded as a bad thing:

```
<button onclick='someFunction()'>Click Me</button>
```

In jQuery, an HTML element is identified using a CSS selector. A common way of selecting an element is based on its ID:

```
<button id='myButton'>Click Me</button>
```

A connection between HTML and JavaScript can be made by binding the element using a jQuery selector event handler:

```
$("#myButton").on('click', function(){someFunction();});
```

Angular makes the point of connection within the HTML page using directives (customized attributes):

```
<button ng-click="someFunction()">Click Me</button>
```

This does not really violate the goals of unobtrusive JavaScript. Angular attributes have the distinct advantage of having a single, well-understood meaning. jQuery selectors require the use of arbitrary HTML attributes (ID and class). Use of these standard attributes introduces ambiguity. It is not evident whether the value affects presentation, behavior, or both. HTML5 introduced data attributes that help mitigate this problem a bit.

HTML5 Data Attributes

A *data attribute* is an attribute that starts with "data-" and does not affect layout or presentation. Such attributes are specifically used to store data instead. Multiple attributes are differentiated by the string that follows "data" in the attribute name.

```
<li class="pet" data-name="Katniss" data-type="Civet" >
Hi Kat
</li>
```

Project

There are two basic approaches to working with any JavaScript framework. You can start with the smallest possible project and expand it, or you can start with a fully featured starter project and fill in pieces in the set of largely empty files that comprise the project. Both approaches are valid and suited for particular circumstances.

The smallest possible examples are excellent for troubleshooting and communication (especially when demonstrating working examples at sites like JSFiddle (*http://jsfiddle.net*)). The starter projects provide stable foundations for subsequent development of full-scale projects. The following example starts with the smallest possible example and gradually adds functionality.

The application can be run using JRuby 1.7.4 and the Sinatra and JSON gems. Each page iteratively adds additional functionality.

To run the application, download the code (*http://bit.ly/1aZ1jI1*), install RVM and a version of JRuby, install the dependent gems, and kick off the server:

```
$ rvm list

rvm rubies

   jruby-1.7.4 [ x86_64 ]
=* ruby-1.9.3-p194 [ x86_64 ]
   ruby-2.0.0-p247 [ x86_64 ]

# => - current
# =* - current && default
#  * - default

$ ls
README.md    public    webapp.rb

$ ruby webapp.rb
[2013-08-13 21:20:01] INFO  WEBrick 1.3.1
[2013-08-13 21:20:01] INFO  ruby 1.9.3 (2013-05-16) [java]
== Sinatra/1.4.3 has taken the stage on 4567 for development...
[2013-08-13 21:20:01] INFO  WEBrick::HTTPServer#start: pid=71632 port=4567
```

The root of the web app displays a list of links based on HTML files residing in the public directory. Although a bit of a gimmick, this requirement is a fun example of how concise and expressive Ruby can be. The API call defined in `webapp.rb` in the following code is about as long as the English description of what it does:

```
get '/' do
  Dir.entries('public').entries.map{|f|
    "<a href='#{f}'>#{f}</a><br/>" if f=~/.*\.html/
  }.join
end
```

Normally, HTML is generated server side and rendered in separate templates; or JSON, XML, or another data type is returned. Sinatra, being essentially an HTTP DSL, does not place many restrictions on what is returned. Figure 10-3 shows the index page for the web application, which lists links to several AngularJS examples.

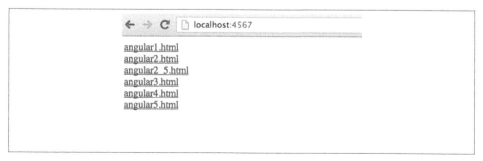

Figure 10-3. Web app links

The first example, shown in Figure 10-4, will simply display two text boxes. When the text is changed in one text box, the corresponding text will be displayed in the other as well.

Figure 10-4. Web app text boxes

A minimized version of the Angular JavaScript file (referenced in the following `script` tag) is available from the Google Hosted Library (*http://bit.ly/NFMLTw*). After this JavaScript file is loaded, the DOM is traversed to find Angular directives (which are represented as HTML element attributes). The `ng-app` directive identifies the tag it occupies as the outer boundary for an Angular application. The `ng-model` directive is used to identify a model, which can be modified in either of two text boxes and is updated in the other due to built-in, two-way data binding:

```
<!DOCTYPE html>
<html ng-app>
<head>
  <meta http-equiv="Content-type" content="text/html; charset=utf-8">
  <title>angular1</title>
<script src="http://ajax.googleapis.com/ajax/libs/angularjs/1.0.3/angular.min.js">
</script>
</head>
<body>
  <input type="text" ng-model="myModel" value="{{myModel}}" />
  <br />
  <input type="text" ng-model="myModel" value="{{myModel}}" />
</body>
</html>
```

The next example will show how an external service (in this case, Google Finance) can be called and the JSON object returned displayed, as shown in Figure 10-5. The Google Finance API has been deprecated (*http://bit.ly/1evKNdF*) but no shutdown date is currently scheduled. The initial example will not be terribly pretty or fully functional, but only a small amount of Angular functionality is required to perform all of this work.

Figure 10-5. Google Finance data for Apple

Obtrusive JavaScript for Consolidated Examples

In these examples, JavaScript is included inline to see all of the moving parts in one place. An unobtrusive approach dictates that such code should be externalized. In addition, Angular controllers ideally should be small, and complex code should be extracted into Angular services. These examples displayed in the context of a book are kept to a single file for ease of explanation. They are intentionally obtrusive for purposes of explanation and illustration. An unobtrusive approach is to be preferred for actual projects.

In the previous example, the ng-app directive stood alone. In this case, the angular module is specifically named *app* (the value assigned to the ng-app attribute in the HTML element). Angular is broken up into several different JavaScript files that can be included as needed. The Angular JavaScript library *resource* is included immediately after the base library and contains the code for the ngResource module. This module allows for RESTful interactions rather than using calls to the lower level $http service. The *app* module we defined is dependent on the ngResource module.

In this and our previous example, an ng-model mapped to a JavaScript variable. The ng-controller directive here references a JavaScript function called AppCtrl. Though all Angular controllers are JavaScript functions, the converse is not true. The look up() function is contained within the execution context (or $scope) of the control ler function. The function is called whenever the button is clicked as specified by the ng-click directive. The lookup function calls the $resource service, which is defined in the ngResource module. The parameters passed to the service reference the Google Finance API. An HTTP GET uses JSONP (required because the call requests data from a server in a different domain) and an array is expected to be returned. The array returned is assigned to $scope.result, the first record of which is displayed in its raw form within the pre element. The double brackets are bindings that contain Angular expressions that are processed by the $parse service:

```
<!DOCTYPE html>

<html ng-app="app">
<head>
  <meta http-equiv="Content-type" content="text/html; charset=utf-8">
  <title>angular2</title>
<script src=
"http://ajax.googleapis.com/ajax/libs/angularjs/1.0.3/angular.min.js">
</script>
<script src=
"http://ajax.googleapis.com/ajax/libs/angularjs/1.0.3/angular-resource.min.js">
</script>
<script>
angular.module('app', ['ngResource']);

function AppCtrl($scope, $resource) {

    $scope.lookup = function(){

      $scope.result  = $resource(
        'https://finance.google.com/finance/info',
        {
                    client:'ig',
                    callback:'JSON_CALLBACK'
        },
          {
                    get: {
                                method:'JSONP',
                                params:{q: $scope.stockSymbol},
                    isArray: true
            }
        }
                          ).get();
          }
    }
</script>
</head>
<body>
        <div ng-controller="AppCtrl">
                <input type="text" ng-model="stockSymbol" />
                <pre>{{result[0]}}</pre>
                <button ng-click='lookup()'>Lookup</button>
        </div>
</body>
</html>
```

The display of raw JSON can be replaced with a formatted display of the data it contains. For instance, to display the current price, use this:

```
{{result[0].l_cur}}
```

It is a bit unwieldy to show all of the code examples inline; the full code is available at GitHub (*http://bit.ly/1aZ1jI1*).

The *angular3.html* example, shown in Figure 10-6, adds the ability to add a stock to a "portfolio" displayed in a tabular form. An input text field can be used to filter data, and columns can be sorted by clicking on the headers. Records can also be deleted from the table. Unfortunately, there is no persistence in place, so refreshing the browser results in all records that have been added to the portfolio being forgotten.

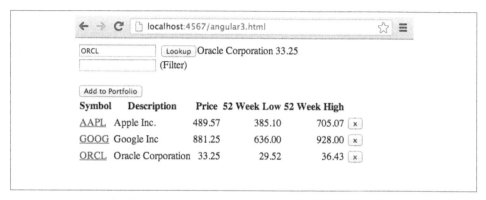

Figure 10-6. Portfolio listing

The *angular4.html* example remedies this situation by including server-side integration. Data is simply stored in server memory that persists until the server restarts. The we bapp.rb is a Ruby application built using the Sinatra microframework. The first two lines import the relevant Ruby and Java resources. Strictly speaking, Java could be omitted altogether and this would run in C-based Ruby implementations. It is included to illustrate how Java can be included, with a call to System.currentTimeMillis() included in a call to GET of */version*, as shown in Figure 10-7.

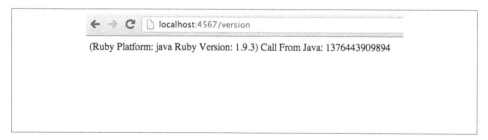

Figure 10-7. Page showing that both Java and Ruby are available and functioning

A class variable ($stocks) is defined as an array that holds the portfolio of stock records. HTTP PUT, DELETE, and GET can be used to perform CRUD operations on individual stock records, and the list of all stocks can be returned through the *stocks* GET URL:

```
%w{rubygems sinatra java json}.each{|r|require r}
java_import 'java.lang.System'

$stocks = []

get '/' do
  Dir.entries('public').entries.map{|f|
    "<a href='#{f}'>#{f}</a><br/>" if f=~/.*\.html/
  }.join
end

get '/version' do
  "(Ruby Platform: #{RUBY_PLATFORM} "+
  "Ruby Version: #{RUBY_VERSION}) "  +
  "Call From Java: #{System.currentTimeMillis()}"
end

get '/stocks' do
  $stocks.to_json
end

get '/stock/:t' do
  stock = $stocks.find{|e|e['t']==params['t']}
  if stock.nil?
    status 404
  else
    status 200
    body(stock.to_json)
  end
end

delete '/stock/:t' do

  stock = $stocks.find{|e|e['t']==params['t']}
  if stock.nil?
    status 404
  else
    $stocks.delete(stock)
    status 202
    body(stock.to_json)
  end
end

put  '/stock/:t' do
  o = JSON.parse(request.body.read)['data']
  puts "---\n  #{o['name']} \n---\n"
  $stocks << o
```

```
      status 200
   end
```

The *angular5.html* example is our first nod toward styling. Twitter Bootstrap CSS is included, a few styles are defined, and HTML elements that follow Bootstrap conventions are added, as shown in Figure 10-8.

Figure 10-8. Styled portfolio

At this point, it would make sense to refactor the project to extract CSS and JavaScript in HTML into external files. The entire project might be retrofitted into a starter project geared toward the intended audience and development tools.

Conclusion

Angular and Sinatra can be used to produce highly dynamic applications with far less code than is possible using other popular libraries. They are worth reviewing not only for their own value, but because of the continuing influence they are exerting on other technologies. Sinatra has inspired a number of other HTTP DSLs. Angular anticipates technologies like HTML5 *web components* with similarities such as declarative templates and data binding. They are mature technologies that are usable on current projects and also suggest the trajectory of future web development efforts.

## CHAPTER 11

Packaging and Deployment

> *The thought occurred to me, as I waited around that day,*
> *that it would be easier to lift my trailer up and, without*
> *any of its contents being touched, put it on the ship.*
>
> —Malcom McLean

Malcom McLean had an idea in 1937 that would lead to his legacy as the "the father of containerization." It came to him while waiting in Hoboken for cotton bales he had delivered to be loaded for transport overseas. It wasn't until 1956 that McLean developed the metal shipping container, which greatly simplified cargo handling and revolutionized the shipping industry. Innovations in packaging lead to efficiencies in shipping. In technology, deployment and distribution of applications is analogous to shipping. Java provides standardized packaging, which is foundational to the distribution of code and deployment of applications.

Java and JEE Packaging

Java packaging formats are fundamental building blocks in JEE applications. They are also used in more recent deployment processes that do not adhere strictly to the JEE specification.

Java developers initially develop code outside of deployment packages. A Java class corresponds with a file on the operating system. Confusingly enough, a Java package is not really related to packaging but instead is a namespace that reflects the path from an application root to a directory where a class resides. It is rare to encounter classes and packages on their own outside of a programmer's development environment. An application or module is compressed and packaged as a unit before it is deployed to a production environment or end user.

The *Java Archive* (JAR) file is used to bundle Java class files and related resources into a single archive. JAR files are compressed using a ZIP file format and include a manifest file with path name of *META-INF/MANIFEST.MF*. They can be created using the *jar* utility (*http://bit.ly/1eX8yjj*) included in the JDK. At its simplest, a JAR is a *.zip* file with a few additional characteristics defined in its *META-INF* directory.

JARs are not JEE-specific. They are part of standard JDKs and their specification (*http://bit.ly/1czakCX*) is included in the JDK documentation. JEE does describe several special usages of JAR files. *Application client modules* and *EJB modules* are packaged as JARs. All other JEE packaging formats are based on the JAR format as well. In fact, the remaining JEE-specific file formats *are* JAR files with a file extension specific to their function and contents. JEE archives can be constructed manually but are more often assembled using build tools like Ant, Maven, or Gradle.

A *web module* is the smallest deployable unit in the JEE world. Such a module contains web components and web resources, primarily static content. A web module can be packaged into a *web archive* or WAR. A WAR includes a */WEB-INF* directory that contains a file named *web.xml* that defines the structure of the web application and references other assets included in the archive. WARs are very flexible and can be deployed to a *web container* which supports a relatively small subset of the JEE specification.

Popular web containers include Tomcat (*http://tomcat.apache.org*) and Jetty (*http://www.eclipse.org/jetty*). Web container development tends to precede definition of technologies in the JEE specification, and significantly different sets of features are available in each one.

An *enterprise archive*, or EAR file, contains WAR files, JAR files, and an *application.xml* that references the included modules and defined security roles. As suggested by the name, EARs are intended for enterprise applications. EARs must be deployed to an *application server*, which supports a much greater portion of the JEE specification than a web container. They cannot be run on a web container because they require EJB support and other services. Application servers include JBoss (*http://bit.ly/1evPmEw*), IBM's WebSphere (*http://bit.ly/ibm-websphere*), and Oracle's WebLogic Server (*http://bit.ly/1oq3cRA*).

A less familiar JEE archive mentioned for the sake of completeness is the *resource adapter module* (RAR). This type of archive is used to allow connectivity to an *Enterprise Information System* (EIS). An EIS is typically a legacy system such as an ERP, Main-Frame, Queue, or other such service. A RAR's purpose is similar to that of a JDBC driver. It provides a consistent interface to a backend system but is not limited like JDBC to accessing relational databases. See Table 11-1 for a list with related file extensions.

Table 11-1. Java packaging formats

Extension	Name	Description
.jar	Java archive	Standard Java package format
.war	Web archive	Maps to a single web context root
.ear	Enterprise application archive	Contains multiple WARs and JARs
.rar	Resource adapter module	Communication with an EIS

WARs are of particular interest to web application developers, and their popularity is reflected in their adoption by modern frameworks based on other languages. The Play framework can create a WAR containing Scala resources, and a Ruby gem called Warbler (*http://bit.ly/1c216lP*) can be used to make a Java JAR or WAR file out of a Ruby application.

Existing Java and JEE packaging works well for client-server web development. The main consideration is maintaining independent server and client code in separate archives for projects that are of any significant size. An application can be deployed as an EAR that references a server WAR containing API code and a separate client WAR containing HTML, CSS, and JavaScript. The same two WARs could be deployed outside of the EAR to separate web containers. Unlike other areas that have been covered, there are no major innovations related to packaging itself.

Sample WAR

A single WAR used in illustrations later can be built from the code associated with this chapter (*http://bit.ly/1aZ5ELm*) using Maven. It includes both client and server code in a single WAR to provide minimal usage examples.

An archive considered as an independent package of related Java resources does not do much good in isolation. The archive has to be executed (if written as a self-contained executable) or deployed to a runtime environment. While packaging practices have remained constant, choices related to deployment *have* changed quite a bit.

JEE Deployment

At one time, options for deployment were severely limited. Decisions revolved primarily around the degree of automation to use. At the time of application deployment, it was assumed that the application server would have been previously installed and configured by a developer or systems administrator. To this day, the JEE specification itself remains oriented toward this expectation, particularly in the description of the actors involved in the deployment of an application. A JEE web app deployment setup is shown in Figure 11-1.

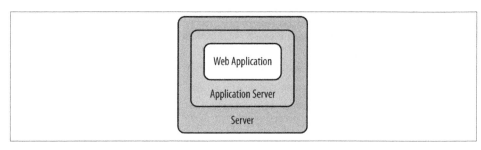

Figure 11-1. JEE web app deployment

JEE *roles* indicate functions that people fill during the development process, including a *deployer* and *system administrator*. The person or people acting as deployers are responsible for configuring the application for the operational environment, verifying that modules conform to the JEE specification, and installing the application modules on the server or servers. It is evident from this description that the target environment for a JEE application is expected to be an already-installed application server under the active management of the person or group. (It also suggests manual intervention at the time of deployment as opposed to the continuous delivery (*http://bit.ly/MfVk6A*) common in large-scale deployments.) As was already suggested, this is not the only possible way to deploy a Java web application, but it does appear to be the only one that conforms with the specification.

JEE and Cloud Deployments

JEE, like other somewhat monolithic efforts, seeks to maintain continuity with previous releases. It is also intended to relflect a wide range of deployment environments. This wide applicability is its strength in some cases and its weakness in others. It has been updated in more recent versions to reflect cloud deployments, but these seem to suggest minimal responsibilities for a deployer that are often absorbed in practice by the same person acting as systems administrator:

> For example, in the case of cloud deployments, the Deployer would be responsible for configuring the application to run in the cloud environment. The Deployer would install the application into the cloud environment, configure its external dependencies, and might handle aspects of provisioning its required resources...

> ...in a cloud scenario, the System Administrator would be responsible for installing, configuring, managing, and maintaining the cloud environment, including the resources that are made available to applications running in the environment.

> —JEE7 (*http://bit.ly/1g0H4KP*)

Having an already-installed application server following the JEE specification limits processes but does not dictate all deployment practices. It is possible to build a project on the server where the deployment will reside. This requires that build tools be available on all relevant servers and can result in performance degradation or disruption of service to the server. There is also the possibility of security vulnerabilities due to the installation of additional software or the deployment of untested code to a production server. These challenges suggest that it is better to build outside of the production server and transfer the packaged application to the machine for deployment.

With the advent of modern deployment involving large numbers of servers, it is even less common to build on a server that is a deployment target. In rare situations it might make sense; but in general, it is better to build archives on a nonproduction machine and transfer them to the target servers for installation. Even if not required in the early stages of a project, this provides greater flexibility should application usage grow over time and it becomes necessary to add additional servers. A variety of projects have been developed in recent years specifically geared to distributed remote execution of shell commands, which makes this sort of deployment much more manageable.

GUI Administration

Active application server administration involves user interaction through a graphical user interface. This is not always the case with web containers. In the distant past, some interfaces were old-school, native-client applications that made remote network connections to the application server. Today the GUIs are web applications in their own right. Those available after installation require additional configuration. Steps need to be taken to prevent the admin portal from being publicly available, which would present a security vulnerability. Adjustments need to be made to avoid an admin server's context root from conflicting with other deployed web applications. These configuration concerns lead many administrators to simply disable the administrative web application during initial installation.

One example of an application server with a web-based graphical administrative site is Red Hat JBoss Enterprise Application Platform 6 (JBoss EAP 6), as shown in Figure 11-2. After downloading it (*http://bit.ly/1mdc3rg*) and adding an administrative user, the standalone server can be started where the administrative console is available by default. By clicking a few buttons, an administrator can deploy and enable a WAR. This deploys the web application and makes it available from the indicated context root.

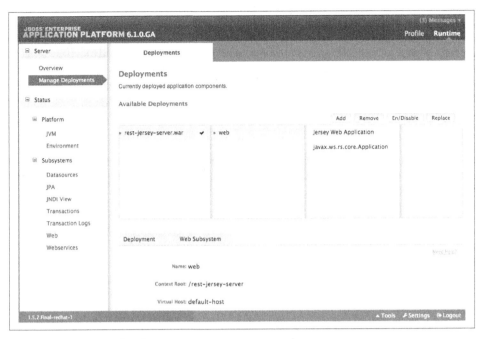

Figure 11-2. JBoss web admin

JBoss, being a full-featured application server, bundles many useful modules, which can minimize the amount of code you need to include with a WAR. It can also result in some obscure errors if similar modules exist both within JBoss and within your application. The WAR associated with this chapter includes Jersey among its dependencies. Including Jersey could result in an error during deployment. The error is reported by RestEasy (included with JBoss), which scans by default and identifies Jersey as a conflicting JAX-RS implementation. The solution is to add context parameters to the *web.xml* to disable this scan:

```
<context-param>
    <param-name>resteasy.scan</param-name>
    <param-value>false</param-value>
</context-param>
<context-param>
    <param-name>resteasy.scan.providers</param-name>
    <param-value>false</param-value>
</context-param>
<context-param>
    <param-name>resteasy.scan.resources</param-name>
    <param-value>false</param-value>
</context-param>
```

The solution is simple enough but highlights the point that although JEE specifies clearly defined packing mechanisms, it is ambiguous about which services will be included in a given deployment environment. These types of idiosyncracies are a major reason why mantras like, "Write once, deploy anywhere" can only be true with significant qualifications when applied to JEE deployment.

Command-Line Administration

Administrative GUIs are convenient for initial setup of an application. They present available administrative options in an easy-to-understand user interface. This clarity makes them ideal for learning an application server and reviewing available functionality. Like all GUIs, they do not lend themselves to scripting and subsequent automation as command-line alternatives. Though a mere convenience for small-scale deployment scenarios, they are essential to complex deployment scenarios (or even simple ones with a large number of servers).

JBoss includes a command-line interface that allows adminstrative actions to be taken from a prompt or script. Almost any action available in a GUI is available through a command-line equivalent. A command-line session is initiated by accessing the command-line interface and connect to a running application server. To do so, call the cli with the -c option (which immediately establishes a connection to the application server):

```
$bash bin/jboss-cli.sh -c
```

Once logged in, you can type **help** to get a list of available commands:

```
[standalone@localhost:9999 /] help
```

Knowledge of few basic ones is enough to perform most common actions. To view a list of contents available at the particular node path, use the ls command:

```
[standalone@localhost:9999 /] ls
```

The JBoss environment can then be navigated like an operating system file system using cd to change directory and ls to list the content at a given node path. To view the WAR that was deployed earlier:

```
[standalone@localhost:9999 /] ls deployment
rest-jersey-server.war
```

The syntax is not completely consistent with the corresponding operating system commands. For instance, additional information about the WAR in the deployment directory can be obtained by using the ls command and identifying the deployment using an equals sign:

```
[standalone@localhost:9999 /] ls /deployment=rest-jersey-server.war
```

This design does lend itself to executing JBoss CLI commands from an external script. The following command prints out the current list of deployments straight from an OS command prompt:

```
$bash bin/jboss-cli.sh -c --commands='ls deployment'
```

The availability of a CLI opens up the possibility of creating sophisticated scripts to interact with the application server as well as the operating system and other applications. The examples to this point have been limited to query operations, but the CLI is not limited to these. It can also take actions which modify the state of the application server, such as deploying or undeploying a WAR:

```
[standalone@localhost:9999 /] undeploy rest-jersey-server.war
[standalone@localhost:9999 /] deploy /tmp/rest-jersey-server.war
```

Administrators can replace manual GUI interaction with CLI scripting for a wide range of adminstrative tasks, but the CLI does have its own syntax and organization that takes some time to understand and use effectively. If the only administrative concern is to deploy the application, both the GUI and the CLI can be avoided by copying files to a designated deployment directory. Applications copied to this directory are detected by the JBoss *deployment scanner* and automatically deployed. Copying can be done interactively or via a script, so automated deployment is possible without learning the CLI at all. Developers requiring frequent deployment can copy applications and rely on the deployment scanner or rely on hooks integrated into their standard toolchain. Plugins (*http://bit.ly/1lJsurD*) have been written for Maven and other build tools and IDEs that couple the deployment of the application with the build process itself.

Non-JEE Deployment

For many years, Java web development was synonymous with Java Enterprise Edition. It can be jarring (pun intended) for Java developers to realize that the JEE model for web application deployment is not the only one available, and in fact, might not be the best one for a given system. Java technology encompasses far more than web application development, and JEE is but one approach to web application development possible on the Java platform. Figure 11-3 shows the Java web application development model.

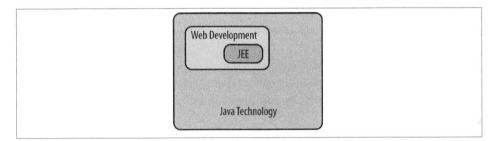

Figure 11-3. Web development in Java

A non-JEE web application deployment does *not* require the existence of a previously installed application server. From the perspective of a Java web application, the application server providing its context might be *outside*, *inside*, or *alongside* it. These options are not unique to application servers but also might apply to other software that provides an independent service (such as a database).

Server Outside

Application servers are complex, mature pieces of software that have been around for years. At one time, due to space and processing limitations as well as configuration complexities, the only real option was to expend a fair amount of time and effort up front installing them. Once installed, a web application could be installed and configured to connect to these existing services. The web app ran "on" a server, as shown in Figure 11-4. The app server functioned as the deployment target for the web application, *outside* of the web app itself.

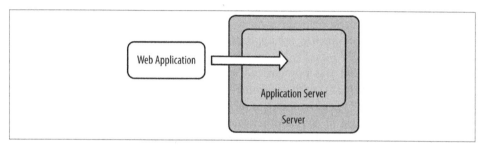

Figure 11-4. Server outside the web application

This approach is the de facto JEE method for deployment described earlier in the chapter. It works well when your application needs to be deployed to an internal system that is already running an application server, or when you want to host multiple web applications and JEE packages on a single web application. In many cases, there is precious little administration required for an application. An application server or servlet container might be required to run it, but no administration is expected. This led developers to defer deployment of the application server until the web application itself was deployed.

The Trend Toward Lightweight Containers

The trend away from large, monolithic, manually configured installations of application servers is part of a larger trend toward virtualization and lightweight deployment of applications. The advent of cloud-based deployments has led to a much more transient view of servers and their contents. This view mandates an approach to deployments to make them fast, as simple as possible, and highly automated.

Server Alongside

There are a few different ways to deploy a web application without first installing an application server. One is to bundle the web application with the application server. The application server, though separate and distinct, is installed *alongside* the application at the time of deployment, as shown in Figure 11-5.

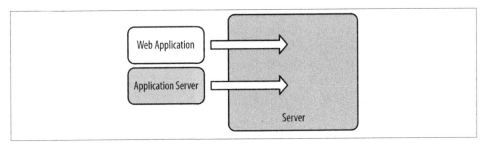

Figure 11-5. Server alongside the web application

This type of deployment was popularized with Rails, which includes a server (WE-Brick (*http://bit.ly/1guJCiT*)) with the framework itself. Play and Roo took a cue from Rails and use this type of deployment, but rely on Java web containers. The Maven Jetty plug-in (shown in Figure 11-6) is another example that allows an web application to be deployed and run immediately in a servlet container that requires no external maintenance or administration. Using the project provided in this chapter, you can build the web module and run the resulting WAR on Jetty with the following command:

```
mvn clean install jetty:run
```

Figure 11-6. Web app running in Maven Jetty plug-in

The application is then available on port 9090.

Maven is not needed to run a web application using Jetty. Jetty can also be included as a JAR at the command line using Jetty Runner (*http://bit.ly/1eSr5ig*). From the build directory, the Jetty runner can be called passing the path and WAR as arguments:

```
curl -O http://repo2.maven.org/maven2/org/mortbay/jetty/jetty-runn
er/8.1.9.v20130131/jetty-runner-8.1.9.v20130131.jar

java -jar jetty-runner-8.1.9.v20130131.jar \
--path /jersey-server \
target/rest-jersey-server.war
```

Tomcat Runner (*http://bit.ly/1iSnlMM*) is a similar project (*http://bit.ly/1eSr9i0*) that uses Tomcat. It takes the same arguments as the Jetty Runner:

```
java -jar webapp-runner-7.0.40.0.jar \
--path /jersey-server \
target/rest-jersey-server.war
```

Server Inside

Rather than using an external server, a Java server library can be included *inside* an application's code base, as illustrated in Figure 11-7. The server is run from *inside* the web application itself. Chapter 6 included several examples of libraries and frameworks that can be used to this end.

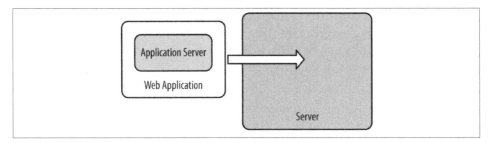

Figure 11-7. Server inside the web application

With a server available inside of an application, distribution can be reduced to creating and deploying a single executable JAR and executing it on a server. The JEE standard does not consider JARs or application servers in this way, but as described earlier, presumes that applications will be deployed to environments that provide services like HTTP processing, database connections, and related configuration.

Consolidated Executable JARs

Although it is common for Java projects to reference multiple JARs, a project can be packaged and deployed as a single executable unit. Utilities to package JARs inside of JARs include one-jar (*http://one-jar.sourceforge.net*) and build tool plug-ins like the Maven Shade plug-in (*http://bit.ly/1bsaamg*).

Implications of Deployment Choice

The method of deployment chosen has significant implications for security, scalability, and overall support of an application. Deployment methods vary in their flexibility for quick changes.

It is possible in simple deployments with a single server and an exploded EAR or WAR to *hot-patch* a system. A change to code or a configuration file can update the application without the overhead of doing a full deploy. This practice itself raises a host of process and security concerns, but is highlighted since it is not even possible to do this type of change in more complex deployment scenarios.

Credentials and connection strings are easy to modify in an externally administered application server. This is not the case in systems where the application server is deployed alongside or built into an application's packaging.

Deployments that do not rely on externally administered application servers provide tremendous flexibility in regards to horizontal scaling. By building intelligence into load balancers, it is possible to make quick changes with little downtime by creating new server instances with the desired configuration data rather than changing existing servers.

The nature of the deployment can impact the development process and the choice of modules that comprise the foundation of an application. The deployment target is best identified early in the development process to ensure that the required resources are available and the relevant processes enacted.

Load Balancing

Load balancing is closely related to deployment in that its implementation determines the network and server topology required to run an application. The goal of load balancing is to distribute incoming requests as efficiently as possible with available processing power. In the case of a web application, incoming HTTP requests are redirected from a designated load-balancing server (or cluster of servers) onto multiple web servers.

The decision of how to distribute the load varies based upon the amount of work involved to process each request, the power of the servers, and the choice of hardware and/or software that will perform load balancing operations. Tasks can be distributed evenly between the servers in a round-robin fashion, or weighted to distribute more work to servers with greater processing power. There are more sophisticated schemes that track the requests being processed by each server or allow each server to essentially pull tasks when they are available, which makes better use of available processing power. Some load balancers are able to detect node failures and will not route requests to dead nodes. Load balancing is illustrated in Figure 11-8.

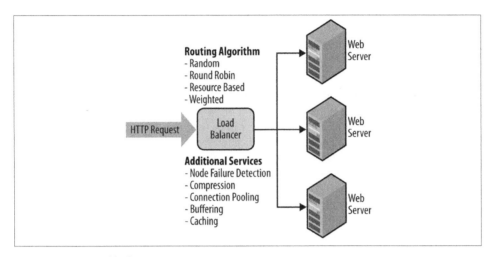

Figure 11-8. Load balancing

Not all of the functionality available in physical load balancers is replicated in software load balancers. This includes security concerns like distributed denial of service protection and SSL termination, as well as performance-enhancing features like compression, connection pooling, buffering, and caching. Such features are not necessarily inherent to load balancing, but in some cases are essential to use it effectively.

Loads More on Load Balancing

There are many facets to load balancing that are not really relevant in the context of client-server web development. JBoss includes internal load balancing (*http://bit.ly/ 1c22FjH*) for JNDI, RMI, and EJBs within a cluster. It and other Java web containers include a clustering feature to make sessions available to multiple application servers. Load balancing schemes vary in regard to whether multiple requests from the same client will be directed to the same server. *DNS-based load balancing* provides a similar functionality to round-robin processing, but clients that cache the IP will return to the same server after the initial lookup. Sticky sessions can be used to HTTP requests associated with the same session to be sent to the same server. The range of possibilities is very large and can range from internal management of load balancers for independent operations to cloud deployments like AWS Elastic Load Balancing (*http://amzn.to/1bsahhC*). Documentation (*http://amzn.to/1dKQPH3*) from these as well as older discussions of the basic techniques (*http://oreil.ly/server-load-balancing*) can provide information in greater depth.

Even if a developer is not involved directly with load balancing, it is important for him to understand enough to make relevant design and deployment decisions. Stateless processing where sessions are not used requires major adjustments. Security configuration can be affected. Ongoing support requires the interpretation of application of logs. Without knowing something about how networking is set up, the requests and responses recorded in the logs cannot be used effectively for troubleshooting.

Application Server Clustering

Clustering of application servers or web containers can be a viable alternative to load balancing. It can be used to achieve the same goal of distributing server-side application load. The implementation details are not standard and not available for all servers. Clustering is particularly common in commercial projects, but like other enterprise solutions, it can be expensive. Load balancing *might* involve expensive hardware and software but does not necessarily require it. In its basic form, load balancing is well understood and can be implemented with common, vendor-neutral networking configuration that does not jeopardize portability across different application servers.

Automating Application Deployment

A number of tools have been developed in an effort to tame the complexity of possible deployment scenarios. Ad hoc scripts gave way to *cfengine* as a way to automate the management of workstations in the 1990s. It is extremely lightweight and remains actively maintained. It supports a wide range of OS platforms (including Windows, Mac OS X, and others), which sets it apart from more specialized tools designed for the particular idiosyncrasies of web applications.

Capistrano is a utility for executing SSH commands in parallel on multiple remote machines. It is Ruby-based and geared toward web application deployment due to its origins in the Ruby on Rails ecosystem. A typical usage of Capistrano is to check out a web application from SCM and deploy it to multiple remote servers. *Fabric* is a Python-based Capistrano alternative. Because of the relatively transient server life span in cloud-based deployments, these utilities are often considered alongside configuration management tools like Puppet, Chef, Ansible, and Salt.

Project

Deployment of this chapter's project was illustrated earlier. The project itself is a simple client-server web application that provides CRUD operations to add, update, and delete books. This example has no backend data store. An array holds books that are added, so the data is lost when the server is restarted.

The structure of the application is reflected in the *pom.xml* and *web.xml*. The *pom.xml* includes Jersey-related modules as the dependencies that are used in the implementation of a JAX-RS-style API that produces JSON. The *web.xml* distinguishes the client and server portions of the API and lists the *index.html* welcome page as the client entry point to the application.

Client

The *index.html* contains the HTML, CSS, and JavaScript related to the application. jQuery is served by a CDN. The JavaScript for the application is included inline between script tags. The jQuery `getJSON` and `ajax` methods are used to make API calls. The jQuery `$( document ).ready()` function calls the `list` function, which retrieves a list of books in JSON format and iterates through the results, displaying each in a div (containing an anchor with the `delete` class) that is appended to the paragraph identified the `listing` CSS class. The DELETE call is bound to the document (rather than to each div) to ensure that all hrefs with the `delete` class respond to the event (if it were instead bound directly to the `delete` class, it would only be bound to elements that existed at the time the page was initially loaded). Bootstrap is also served by a separate CDN. It is not used much in the application to keep it minimal, but is included as a starting point for more detailed styling.

Again, this is minimal implementation, but writing an application to this point helps to highlight the limitations of this starting point, based on DOM manipulation and no MV* or significant use of a CSS framework.

For one thing, an inline style is included to center the page, which is a terribly un-Bootstrappy thing to do. Instead, Bootstrap and other responsive frameworks rely on grid-based layouts. Modifying the HTML to use a grid would make it better suited to viewing on different device displays.

In addition, DOM manipulation can be difficult to visualize. The state of the initial HTML does not closely resemble the state of the DOM after a few records have been loaded, suggesting that a view-templating system might be useful. Besides the JavaScript being a bit unwieldy inline, it is not split into distinct units that reflect the functionality of each chunk of code. An MV* framework provides an initial structure for an application that suggests better arrangement of JavaScript code.

Server

The web API is contained in a single `BookService` class that is mapped in the *web.xml* to the */api* URL path. The `@Path` annotation at the top of the class indicates that the class is referenced under */books*. The GET, PUT, and DELETE methods are included to retrieve, create, and destroy book resources. The `@produces` annotation indicates `application/json` as the expected format returned in each JSON call. The {book} referenced in several `@Path` annotations at the method level maps to the `@PathParam` passed as an argument in the corresponding methods.

Normally, a library is used to create JSON. In this case, Mention Apache IO Utils is used in the context of string concatenation to create JSON. The API calls can be validated and tested in the browser, or by using a tool like Curl. With the context path that is used by the Maven plug-in, a record can be added using:

```
curl -X PUT http://127.0.0.1:9090/api/books/4?title=Client+Server+Web+Apps
```

Conclusion

In years past, deployment of Java applications followed JEE processes that were rather well defined. While JEE style deployments remain applicable in many situations, the Java community has also adopted new approaches to deployment that are of particular interest to designers of client-server-style web applications. The next chapter will describe the rise of virtualization techniques used in cloud-based environments that contribute to the argument that, in many cases, it is better to deploy an application server inside or alongside an application rather than outside it, as has been done traditionally.

## CHAPTER 12

Virtualization

People don't appreciate the substance of things.
Objects in space. People miss out on what's solid.

— Jubal Early (*Firefly*, Objects in Space)

The word "computer" immediately brings to mind some image of machinery, perhaps a monitor and keyboard, a laptop, or a stack of servers. In each case, the image is a tangible, solid, material object. This common impression is not particularly useful in software development when the physical details of hardware are masked by additional abstraction layers. *Virtualization* is a term used to describe a technology that hides details and specific implementation characteristics. It applies to a range of technologies related to hardware platforms, operating systems, storage devices, and network resources. While it is not directly tied to client-server web development or any other paradigm, it is interesting because many such applications are intended for large-scale deployments built on virtualization solutions. Virtualization is a powerful concept that impacts practices related to active development, deployment, scaling, and disaster recovery.

Full Virtualization

Without virtualization, a server is defined by and limited to physical constraints. Server administrators build and configure servers with a specific set of options suited to their particular hardware and purpose. Individuals on a development team each install software and configure their machine to conform to the target server. Hardware limitations, performance bottlenecks, and capacity issues are often overcome by adding additional hardware to a given machine. Automation might be used to some degree, but in many cases, manual processes are the order of the day due to the unique details of a particular machine's hardware. In situations where there are a number of different servers to maintain, complex backup and recovery practices become imperative to system availability and reliability.

The type of virtualization that alleviates these challenges involves virtual machines that take the place of physical servers. *Full virtualization* seeks to provide a complete simulation of underlying hardware to the extent that a distinct unmodified operating system can run within a virtual machine. Figure 12-1 shows the continuum of virtualization, ranging from traditional, persistent, manually configured physical hardware to highly transient virtual machine instances that are automatically created and might only exist for a few seconds in a cloud.

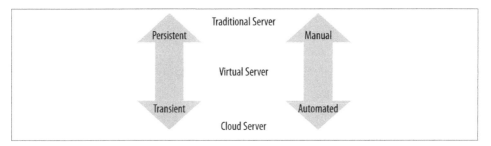

Figure 12-1. Server types

Challenges to maintaining physical servers are often alleviated using virtual machines. Since full virtualization involves a full simulation of physical hardware, individual developers can be given isolated environments for testing new software without the expense of purchasing and maintaining additional machines. Virtual machines can be created to test software on multiple operating systems on a single physical server. Entire software installations can be shipped in preconfigured virtual machines. The ability to create a snapshot that captures the state of a machine at a point in time opens up many possibilities related to managing disaster recovery. Rather than managing many physical machines with specific hardware concerns, servers can be replaced with virtual machines to reduce energy consumption and hardware costs.

One downside to virtual machines is that additional processing comes at a cost. Virtualization software must be purchased in some cases, and running them incurs additional processing power. Projects that require low-level hardware access are not good candidates for virtualization, but most web applications are. The problem with virtualization versus physical hardware is similar to the use of a high-level programming language versus a lower-level language like C or assembly. Tasks that require high performance can only be implemented "close to the metal" using specific, highly tailored solutions. A myriad of other tasks do not have such stringent requirements.

One other cost to consider is additional complexity. Rather than paying attention to one physical server, a virtual machine's behavior must be understood not in isolation, but also in relation to its host machine. A performance problem could be due to an issue on the VM itself or on the host machine. Virtualization layers can be nested several layers deep, adding additional complexity. Virtualization removes entire classes of problems, but does require specific technical awareness and know-how to use effectively.

The popularity of VMs in place of physical servers has resulted in a significant shift in server management and scaling practices. So-called cloud providers host virtualized computer resources in one form or another. In some cases, the virtualization provided is in the form of specific machines. In this case, the need to actively manage physical servers is eliminated altogether.

What About the "V" in JVM?

The Java Virtual Machine provides partial virtualization, allowing class files containing bytecode to be interpreted and executed on any hardware where a virtual machine can be run. It does not provide any sort of distinct container for isolating code and does not result in the creation of a distinct machine that can be managed as an independent server on a network. Any type of virtualization can be extremely effective in masking underlying implementation details, but different levels are applicable to specific problems.

Virtual Machine Implementations

Virtualization dates back to an IBM research system created in the 1960s called the CP-40. It was followed in 1967 by the CP 67, which was a virtual-machine operating system developed for the IBM System/360-67. Other virtualization solutions were introduced in the years that followed, most specific to particular operating systems. The applicability and popularity of virtualization grew as powerful hardware became available at lower costs to a larger number of developers.

Among the myriad virtual machine implementations available today, VMWare, VirtualBox, and Amazon EC2 are among the most popular. They are also specific targets of provisioned servers created with tools such as Vagrant (*http://bit.ly/1g1Knyi*) and Packer (*http://www.packer.io*).

VMWare

The first encounter many web developers had with virtual machines was VMWare (*https://www.vmware.com*) workstation released in 1999. VMWare now offers a range of related virtualization, cloud management, backup, and desktop products. Open source (*http://bit.ly/LXq3EN*) versions of VMWare software are available today as well.

VirtualBox

In January 2007, an open source version of VirtualBox (*https://www.virtualbox.org*) was released as a full virtualization solution that runs on Windows, Linux, and OS X. It was acquired by Sun and later by Oracle where it was rebranded as Oracle VM VirtualBox. It is comparable to VMWare's offerings in general functionality, but differs most substantially in non-technical fine points like licensing terms, paid features, ease of use, and availability of documentation.

Amazon EC2

An *Amazon Machine Image* (AMI) is a template that defines the server configuration that can be run on *Amazon Elastic Compute Cloud* (Amazon EC2). An AMI is selected when an instance is launched and afterward is available as a virtual server in the cloud. As such, AMIs are only relevant for deployments targeted for Amazon Web Services.

Management of Virtual Machines

Management of VMs becomes a significant undertaking as their number and complexity increases. Each implementation has proprietary mechanisms for defining and maintaining virtual machines. *Open Virtualization Format* (OVF) is an open standard for packaging and distributing VMs, and there are a number of noteworthy projects designed to assist in creating and maintaining them.

Vagrant

One challenge is that each virtualization technology has unique processes, scripts, and utilities for creating and maintaining an environment. Vagrant (*http://www.vagrant up.com*) provides mechanisms to configure reproducible and portable VMs provisioned on top of VirtualBox, VMware, AWS, or any other provider. The `vagrant` command is used to complete all related operations.

A `Vagrantfile` contains configuration for a given machine. Once this file is configured, a *box* (base image used to create VMs) must be available or added. It is an initial image that is cloned but never actually modified. With a box added, a machine can be started by running `vagrant up`, and the new machine can be accessed via `ssh` using `vagrant ssh`. Additional commands can be used to provision a machine as well as to stop and clean up old machines and boxes. Mitchell Hashimoto (*http://mitchellh.com*), the creator of Vagrant, has a book on Vagrant (*http://oreil.ly/vagrant-UR*) that covers it in depth. He has also more recently authored another project that further promotes simplified *cross-VM implementation* configuration called Packer.

Packer

As useful as Vagrant is, the creation and management of images remains a tedious, difficult, and largely manual process. Packer (*http://www.packer.io*) uses a template written in a single portable input format to generate images for multiple platforms in parallel. Packer is used to automate the creation of base boxes for various VM providers.

Components of Packer called *builders* create machine images for a given platform in a form known as artifacts. For example, Packer's VirtualBox builder can create VirtualBox VMs and export them in OVF format. *Artifacts* are comprised of IDs or files that represent a virtual-machine image. Packer also compliments Vagrant's functionaity, as it can take the artifact and turn it into a Vagrant box using *post-processors*.

A consistant syntax and workflow for configuring VMs for different providers does not address provisioning and maintenance concerns. Additional automation can initially be provided through a few shell scripts. Terminal enhancements like csshX (*https://code.google.com/p/csshx*) for OS X to run ssh commands on multiple machines or a tool like Capistrano (*http://www.capistranorb.com*) might suffice to manage multiple servers in a small-scale environment. These solutions are not sufficient for general-purpose systems administration when the number of servers grows beyond a small number.

DevOps Configuration Management

Simple Vagrant machines can be set up with individual commands or shell scripts referenced in a file named *Vagrantfile*. More complex configurations can use Chef (*http://www.opscode.com/chef*) or Puppet (*http://docs.puppetlabs.com*) to automatically install and configure VMs. Both Puppet and Chef are written in Ruby, but Puppet uses a JSON-based language to determine what to install based on dependencies defined, while Chef requires an install script written in Ruby itself. More recently, Ansible (*http://bit.ly/1bsclWT*) and Salt (*http://www.saltstack.com*) have emerged as alternatives (or in some cases compliments) to these. There is a tremendous amount of overlap between what can be accomplished with these tools, but each is particularly suited for certain projects and administrators.

Table 12-1 lists DevOps configuration management tools.

Table 12-1. DevOps configuration management tools

Tool	Initial release	Notes
CFEngine (*http://cfengine.com/downloads*)	1993	C-based, fast, lightweight, steep learning curve
Capistrano (*http://www.capistranorb.com*)	2005	Focus on Rails app deployment
Puppet (*http://docs.puppetlabs.com*)	2005	Inspired by CFEngine
Chef (*http://www.opscode.com/chef*)	2009	Ruby for configuration
Salt (*http://www.saltstack.com*)	2011	Fast, large-scale orchestration and admin
Ansible (*https://github.com/ansible/ansible*)	2012	Simple, agentless administration

The year of initial release is helpful for understanding the role of each tool and its relation to the existing ones. Puppet is inspired by CFEngine (*http://bit.ly/1bsd4Yd*). The authors of Chef used and learned from Puppet (*http://bit.ly/1mdgJ0n*) but took a somewhat different approach based on their admin experiences. More recently, Ansible (*http://bit.ly/1bsclWT*) and Salt (*http://bit.ly/MfYtmX*) have been gaining traction as simplified, streamlined tools akin to Chef or Puppet. They perform both initial configuration and provisioning of a server as well as execution of commands to retrieve results from arbitrary nodes.

DevOps

It often seems like as soon as the number of tools, techniques, and acronyms in a technical area gains a certain critical mass, a new job title appears. *DevOps* is the one that was introduced in 2009 to represent the role filled by professionals whose responsibility spans traditional development and operations tasks. While individual developers might not use the tools listed in this section in depth, it is beneficial to understand it and be able to interact intelligently with the DevOps professionals who do.

Containers

While full virtualization was an early goal with many useful applications, more limited forms have also had a great impact. *Partial virtualization* only attempts to emulate a portion of an entire operating system and does not provide a full-blown virtual machine. Instead, operating-system-specific *container technology* allows a limited form of virtualization.

Development of container technology was driven by the problem of obtaining process isolation and security beyond what is possible through other operating-system mechanisms. Traditional user and group management is cumbersome and incomplete for many situations. A limited isolation available since the late 1970s is the chroot utility. Though useful in some circumstances, it stops short of providing the capability of running a fully functioning independent container. Containers can be considered from a high level as partial VMs or from a low level as enhanced chroots.

Containers might be described as *operating-system-level virtualization* or with other vendor-specific terms. They provide user-space instances that allocate private resources within a container but execute commands against the host's kernel. Rather than emulating an entire *machine*, container technologies are focused on virtualizing an individual *operating-system process* such that it runs in an isolated, secure environment independent of the rest of the server.

LXC

LinuX Container (*http://linuxcontainers.org*) (LXC) virtualization is available on Linux. It allows one or more isolated containers to run on a single server. This provides a better balance between resource usage and security than is possible in a single monolithic system running standard OS-level processes. Containers run instructions native to the core CPU without intermediate steps required by standard virtualization techniques, and so are better performing. Since they do not have all of the overhead included in a full operating system, they are lighter weight and take up fewer resources than would be required in a full-blown VM. Linux containers will run regardless of the host system's kernel version or distribution.

Docker

Docker (*http://www.docker.io*) extends LXC with a high-level API. Like other container technologies, Docker is intended to simplify application packaging and deployment and the creation of individual private environments for end users. In large part, Docker makes the functionality available through LXC much easier to use. In this respect, Docker is to LXC as Vagrant is to the underlying virtual machine implementations it supports, as shown in Figure 12-2.

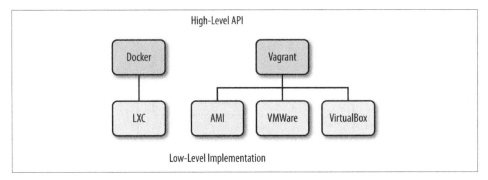

Figure 12-2. Docker and Vagrant high-level APIs

In Docker parlance, you run *containers* that are based on *images*. When exiting a container, its filesystem state and exit value are preserved but its memory state is not. Containers can be started, stopped, or restarted. A container can also be promoted to an image using the Docker commit command. The image can then be used as a parent for new containers.

Docker images can have parent images. Base images have no parent. A collection of images used to create containers are stored in a Docker *repository*. Repositories can be referenced in a *registry*. The implicit top-level registry is index.docker.io, so Docker also includes mechanisms to publish and share images.

Although it is a very new project, Docker has tremendous potential with its promise of standard containers to distribute environments. Used properly, the time spent by individual developers and administrators setting up machines could be eliminated. The popularity of Linux on a wide range of hardware suggests new possibilities for distribution of applications to anything from a fellow developer's machine, to a cloud service, to an embedded device.

Project

The project uses several of the virtualization technologies mentioned previously. The project requires Git, VirtualBox (*http://bit.ly/1mdhXZm*), and Vagrant (*http:// www.vagrantup.com*) as prerequisites. In just a few steps, Docker will be set up (in a Vagrant-managed VirtualBox). Figure 12-3 shows the Vagrant file that resides on an OS X host system and defines the configuration of a VirtualBox instance where Docker instances run. A Java SDK will be installed in a Docker container. The container will then be used to compile and run a Java program. This simple example includes all the steps required in larger, more extensive installations to Docker.

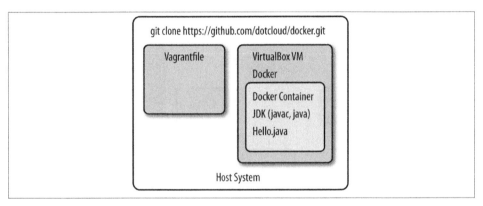

Figure 12-3. Java running on Docker for OS X

The directions for setting up Docker using Vagrant (*http://bit.ly/1gCvJMn*) varies slightly by operating system. In general:

1. Docker sources including the Vagrantfile for machine setup are fetched using Git.

2. The VM is started using Vagrant.

3. The user logs into the new VM using `ssh` and switches to the Docker user.

4. Docker is available to create and maintain containers.

From the host machine, you can initially download the Docker project using Git:

```
git clone https://github.com/dotcloud/docker.git
cd docker
```

Docker is under heavy development and is changing quickly. After initial installation, you can update your version of Docker using Git as well:

```
git pull
```

The Docker project for OS X consists of a Vagrant-managed VirtualBoxVM. To start up and log into the VM hosting Docker:

```
vagrant up
vagrant ssh
```

Once logged in, you can log out of the Vagrant VM at any time by entering exit. From the Vagrant managed box, Docker can be called:

```
sudo docker
```

The ubuntu base image can be downloaded and installed with set of standard Linux utilities available:

```
sudo docker pull ubuntu
sudo docker run ubuntu /bin/echo Docker is running!
```

Docker Help

You can learn a great deal about Docker by using the built-in help. Since the project is changing so rapidly, there is a chance that documentation available online or elsewhere is not applicable to the version you are using. To list available commands, simply type **docker**. Options available for each command can be listed by adding the -help argument:

```
docker
docker build -help
```

Image and Container Maintenance

Once you have been working with Docker for a while, you will amass a number of images and containers. The info command can be used to view a report describing system-wide information, including the total number of containers and images:

```
docker info
```

These comprehensive totals, exited containers, and intermediate images are the subset that is often of immediate interest. Each container after exit remains available until removed. Images tend to accumulate quickly as an image is created during *each step defined in a docker file*. The ps command lists running Docker containers. The images command lists images (excluding intermediate images used to build):

```
docker ps
docker images
```

To list *all* containers or images, include -a. A *.dot* diagram of images that can be viewed using GraphViz (*http://www.graphviz.org*) can be created by specifying the -viz:

```
docker images -viz > docker1.dot
```

Much more detailed information is available on a given container by running docker inspect <container name>. The rm command is used to clean up containers and images. These can be passed as a list to the command:

```
docker rm $(docker ps -a -q)
docker rmi $(docker images -q)
```

Java on Docker

The Docker Git repository included a Vagrantfile used by Vagrant to configure and provision the VM. Docker uses a Dockerfile to configure and provision a container. The FROM instruction indicates the base image for the new machine. There are public repositories of images available, or you can use one of your own. The MAINTAINER indicates the author of the image. The RUN instruction executes commands on the current image and returns the results. The following steps install Oracle's Java 7 SDK and accepts the license as presented. The ADD instruction will copy a file named *Hello.java* to the container where it will be compiled and available for executions:

```
FROM ubuntu:precise
MAINTAINER Casimir Saternos

RUN echo "deb http://ppa.launchpad.net/webupd8team/java/ubuntu precise main"\
| tee -a /etc/apt/sources.list
RUN echo "deb-src http://ppa.launchpad.net/webupd8team/java/ubuntu precise main"\
| tee -a /etc/apt/sources.list
RUN apt-key adv --keyserver hkp://keyserver.ubuntu.com:80 --recv-keys EEA14886
RUN apt-get update

RUN echo oracle-java7-installer shared/accepted-oracle-license-v1-1 select true\
| /usr/bin/debconf-set-selections
RUN apt-get -y install oracle-java7-installer
RUN update-alternatives --display java
RUN echo "JAVA_HOME=/usr/lib/jvm/java-7-oracle" >> /etc/environment
ADD Hello.java Hello.java
RUN javac Hello.java
```

A simple Hello World needs to be created in the directory where the Dockerfile resides:

```
public class Hello{
  public static void main (String args[]){
    System.out.println("hey there from java");
  }
}
```

With the Dockerfile and Java class in place, the container can be built from the image. The -t option specifies a repository name to be applied to the resulting image and identifies it when listing available images:

```
docker build -t cs/jdk7 .
```

In addition, the JDK installed earlier is also installed, and the program that we copied to the Docker container can be run:

```
docker run cs/jdk7 java -version
docker run cs/jdk7 java Hello
```

To be clear, these commands ran within the docker container. Try running them on the Vagrant VM to see a different result (indicating that Java is not installed on the VM):

```
java -version
java Hello
```

A Docker file to run a web application as a WAR on Jetty can be configured by appending to the Dockerfile defined above. The ADD command can be used to copy a file from the Vagrant VM to the Docker container, while the RUN command can use wget or another utility to download a needed file from a referenced URL:[1]

```
ADD rest-jersey-server.war rest-jersey-server.war
RUN wget http://repo2.maven.org/[...see the footnote...]/jetty-runner.jar
```

Copying Files to Vagrant

You might be wondering how *rest-jersey-server.war* ended up on the Vagrant VM, or you might have just cleverly downloaded it using Curl or wget. While downloading is a fine option, it is possible to copy files through a file share or using scp as well.

By default, Vagrant shares the directory with the Vagrantfile to the */vagrant* directory in the VM. In addition, by default, Vagrant forwards SSH (from port 22 to 2222), so files can be copied between the VM and the host machine using scp. For example, from the host machine, *docker.png* can be copied from within the VM to the host machine by running the following command and typing **vagrant** for the password when prompted:

```
scp -P2222 vagrant@localhost:docker.png .
```

The container can then be built from the image and run interactively:

```
docker build -t cas/restwar .

docker run -p 49005:49005 -name restwarcontainer cas/restwar \
java -jar jetty-runner-8.1.9.v20130131.jar \
--port 49005 rest-jersey-server.war
```

Note that with the container running interactively, other vagrant ssh sessions can be opened to run additional commands. If you want to run the web app noninteractively, the command to launch the app server would be included as a final RUN command in the Dockerfile.

By default, Docker invents a name for a newly started container. The -name argument is used above to name the container in a meaningful way, but does introduce the need to take additional manual steps. If you decide to rerun the container with the command

---

1. This URL was too long to fit, and line breaks in URLs are not supported. The actual reference is *http://repo2.maven.org/maven2/org/mortbay/jetty/jetty-runner/8.1.9.v20130131/jetty-runner-8.1.9.v20130131.jar*.

listed above, you must either specify a different container name or delete the one previously created:

```
ID=$(docker ps -a | grep restwar | awk '{print $1}')
docker rm $ID
```

Docker and Vagrant Networking

One of the confusing bits of working with Docker on OS X or Windows is that it involves a physical machine and two levels of virtualization, as depicted in Table 12-2. The physical machine hosts a Vagrant instance providing a fully virtualized VM on which Docker containers are run. There are several different IP addresses visible from different locations and a number of ports which must be open.

Table 12-2. Project servers

Server	Description
Base machine	Includes VirtualBox software maintained using Vagrant
Vagrant instance	A VirtualBox Linux VM with Docker software installed
Docker instance	Hosts a Jersey server running the web application

A port on the base machine needs to be available to Vagrant. This port is opened by configuring the Vagrant file. It is also included in the command used to run the Docker instance. From the outside, it appears that the base machine is simply listening and responding on the port. The networking possibilities are extensive, but this example can be set up in only a few steps.

To start, we will open a port in Vagrant so that your host machine will be able to see things running on it. *Port forwarding* is the practice of specifying ports on the VM to share through a port on the host machine. The specified port is permitted to be the same or different as the one for the host machine. In this example, we will forward port 49005 on the Vagrant VM through to port 49005 on the host machine by modifying the Vagrantfile that comes with Docker:

```
...
Vagrant::Config.run do |config|
  ...
  config.vm.forward_port 49005, 49005
  ...
```

With the single container running the WAR on Jetty as listed above, the ID and IP address of the container can be determined by running a few commands from within the Vagrant VM and the accessed page:

```
ID=$(docker ps | awk '{print $1}' | grep -v CONTAINER)
IP_ADDRESS=$(docker inspect $ID | grep IPAddress | awk -F'"' '{print $4}')
echo $ID
```

```
echo $IP_ADDRESS
curl $IP_ADDRESS
```

The IP address here is meaningful within the Vagrant VM itself. It is not visible to the outside world. This is where the port forwarding specified in the Vagrantfile comes into play. From the host machine, view *http://localhost:49005/* in a browser and you will see the main page from the WAR displayed.

Conclusion

In the 1980s, the term "virtual reality" was popularized by Jaron Lanier. Movies, video games, and sophisticated simulations have benefitted from VR advances since then, but the world of virtualization that has had a larger scale impact among computer professionals is the virtualization of computer hardware itself.

Java's success is largely due to the Java Virtual Machine, an abstraction layer that hides underlying operating system details. Servlet containers and JEE application servers provide an additional level of abstraction. The development of higher levels of abstraction allows a higher degree of specialization by removing entire classes of problems from the immediate problem space. Client-server applications easily run on highly scalable solutions using modern virtualization and can be discretely packaged for easy deployment due to their structured, compartmentalized architecture. There is obviously tremendous benefit to be found in technologies that are in essence the same as—yet not formally equivalent to—some underlying layer of functionality.

It seemed fitting to open a chapter on virtualization with a quote from a fictional character. A compelling character in a movie—no matter how engaging—is distinct from a real person. Even so, virtualization in its many forms imitiates some underlying technology in a way that can make it appear from certain vantage points indistinguishable from the physical representation it emulates.

## CHAPTER 13

Testing and Documentation

Without language, thought is a vague, uncharted nebula.
Nothing is distinct before the appearance of language.

—Saussure

James Lind was an 18th-century Scottish physician. While serving in the Navy, he conducted what today might be described as the first clinical trial. By dividing a dozen sick sailors into groups of two and providing a controlled diet and specific treatments, he was able to determine that oranges and lemons were effective for warding off scurvy. We know today that scurvy is a result of vitamin C deficiency, but it would take a century of similar experiments to eventually lead Casimir Funk to coin the term "vitamin" in 1912.

Clinical trials are an application of the experimental step of the scientific method. The Oxford Dictionary (*http://bit.ly/1dkWsQT*) describes the scientific method as "a method of procedure that has characterized natural science since the 17th century, consisting in systematic observation, measurement, and experiment, and the formulation, testing, and modification of hypotheses." This definition, while accurate, does not capture one of the important outcomes of repeated experimentation, the characterization of phenomena and development of hypotheses that are articulated in clear, unambiguous language. Testing at its best leads to crisp, clear descriptions of the subject being tested that allow subsequent researchers to more clearly communicate.

Software testing finds its roots in this same tradition. It essentially adopts procedures that have been practiced in the natural sciences for the past 400 years. Testing is done to prove or disprove hypotheses. In the case of software testing, this involves an assertion that all or part of a system functions as specified. Software testing can also lead to insights into how an application might be better designed, modularized, and structured. In addition, it can help clarify requirements and identify precise language to describe the system being scrutinized.

Types of Testing

Most software development projects include some claim of being tested, but what precisely is meant by this is not necessarily evident. Testing is a broad subject and can be subdivided based on the outcome of testing, the construction of the tests, the portion of an overall system being tested, or the role of the people involved.

Formal Versus Informal

Ad hoc testing is used when the purpose of testing is not clear and the outcome is expected to be informal and arbitrary. It is analogous to exploratory programming in an REPL. It is a preliminary step to other forms of testing and is a way of kicking the tires of an unfamiliar application. Formalized *acceptance testing* is on the opposite end of the spectrum, as it is structured, organized, defined, and specifically intended to determine whether the customers are going to accept a system. Informal testing is generally a manual endeavor, whereas formalized methods can be highly automated.

Rather than memorizing a laundry list of testing types and methodologies, it is more important to understand the goal of testing and choose an approach that is rigorous enough for the project without adding unnecessary overhead. As shown in Figure 13-1, in the case of test formality, a continuum can be visualized that comprises the range of possible choices. Though the scientific method was cited in this chapter, the selection of applicable test approaches for a given project is more an art than a science.

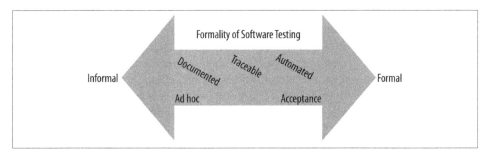

Figure 13-1. Range of test formality

Extent of Testing

The extent of testing can vary a great deal. Simple *smoke tests* (or *sanity tests*) can be carried out to provide minimal assurance of no obvious disruptive defects, whereas *exhaustive testing* is intended to exercise every aspect of a system. The extent to which a system has been tested can be quantifed from different perspectives. *Test coverage analysis* indicates which lines of code are being unit tested. Even in a system that has

100% coverage, every possible permutation of inputs is required to substantiate a claim of exhaustive testing. Few projects can make such a claim, but those that do might only be exercising the functional aspects of the system.

Nonfunctional attributes of a system can be tested as well, including load testing, stress testing, and testing on diverse platforms, browsers, or devices. Cloud deployments have led to innovations in testing that have pushed the boundaries of testing to include intentionally introducing significant system failures to ensure system resilience. For instance, Netflix's Chaos Monkey project (*http://nflx.it/1dkWwjE*) runs within Amazon Web Services and verifies the ability of a system to withstand repeated server failures by seeking out and terminating VM instances in Auto Scaling Groups.

Who Tests What for Whom?

The time, manner, creator, and audience for tests are also significant concerns. Unit tests can be created by developers before code is even written or added when it is all completed. *Black-box* testing generally involves higher-level functional tests written by testers. Unit tests are tied closely to implementation in code, while black-box tests are created without reference to the software's internal structure. Highly isolated tests might evaluate a single tiny aspect of a system, whereas integration testing can ensure defects do not exist in interfaces between related systems.

Testing can also be considered in terms of the people who create the tests and evaluate the results. The audience for test results is initially developers, but later, QA analysts and eventually those authorized to accept a system are viable. Tests can be authored by different parties, including testers and developers. Since tests are created in relation to requirements, there can be significant involvement from business analysts and stakeholders involved in defining requirements. In fact, the definition of tests can contribute to the development of a common, unambiguous language for all parties involved in testing a system.

Testing as an Indicator of Organizational Maturity

In practice, requirements for a software system can reside in many places and exist in many forms. Although documentation is generally assumed to be a primary source, not all projects have formal documentation. Even if a project does have formally defined requirements and a system description, these tend to quickly become outdated in an actively developed system if not automatically generated or intentionally maintained. There are instances where a programmer's memory or comments in code specifically describe expected behavior. In the absence of these, the source code itself might be the only remaining formal description of system functionality. The inaccessiblity of source code is an excellent reason why tests can serve as the most accurate final definition of software requirements outside the system itself.

In fact, sets of well-defined tests can remain in use long after all original code written for a system has been replaced. In this respsect, tests can be a more enduring and valuable artifact than the system under construction itself! They can be an effective means of communication throughout an organization and among stakeholders about the state and functionality of the system.

CMM to Assess Process Uniformity

Conway's Law (*http://bit.ly/1gvq78A*) suggests that "Any organization that designs a system will produce a design whose structure is a copy of the organization's communication structure." It might also be said that software process maturity (the extent to which processes are clearly defined and controlled) is reflected by the state of an organization's software tests. The *Capability Maturity Model* (*http://bit.ly/1nXVQXM*) (CMM) defines a hierarchy of stages describing degrees of structure, process stability, and discipline for an organization reflected in processes for developing and maintaining software. This is shown in Table 13-1.

Table 13-1. Capability maturity model stages

Level	Name	Description	Testing
Level 1	Initial	Inconsistent, disorganized	None, ad hoc
Level 2	Repeatable	Disciplined processes	Some unit testing
Level 3	Defined	Standard, consistent processes	Uniform projects, unit tests run each build
Level 4	Managed	Predictable processes	Continuous integration testing
Level 5	Optimizing	Continuously improving processes	Coverage, code quality, reports

An organization that is highly optimized is less reliant on the heroic effort of a few individuals. It is less prone to missed deadlines, "death marches" (*http://bit.ly/1fhtrlL*), and other symptoms of a project that is out of control. With the focus on *application* scalability, it is possible to lose sight of *organizational* scalability.

Higher CPM is essential if there is an intention to grow an organization over time. Consistent processes and procedures ease the transition of new members to the team. They minimize the amount of time lost having a productive member of the team cease work to teach each new member a set of in-house, undocumented, unenforced practices. They lessen the possibility that actions taken by new members will destabilize the existing application. In the best case, good processes subtly teach employees approaches that will benefit other projects that do not yet have controls in place.

Maven to Promote Uniform Processes

Directly convincing people to adopt a consistent software practice can be difficult. It is much easier to use tools that promote or enforce practices that are in line with organizational goals. For example, Maven introduces a consistent build cycle, which allows extensibility through a plug-in environment without being so flexible as to allow significant deviation from a number of best practices.

One of the objectives of Maven is to provide a uniform build system (*http://bit.ly/1eUV2N6*). Maven might be perceived as inflexibile when compared to Gradle or other build tools. But uniformity implies a degree of rigidity. Rigidity is not simply an evil to be avoided. Decisions must be made to implement structures and tools that provide constraints that will encourage positive uniform processes within an organization. Structured testing processes and reporting are fundamental and applicable to most software projects.

Maven includes two phases for testing by default (test and integration test). These are shown in Figure 13-2 in the midst of the other Maven build life cycle phases. Typically, the Surefire plug-in (*http://bit.ly/1eUV1IQ*) is called during the test phase, and the Failsafe plug-in (*http://bit.ly/1iPUsAV*) is called during the integration test phase. Surefire reports can be presented in an HTML form using the Surefire Report plug-in (*http://bit.ly/1gvqvE7*) while the integration test reports can be rendered in HTML using the Failsafe Report plug-in (*http://bit.ly/1gvqvE7*).

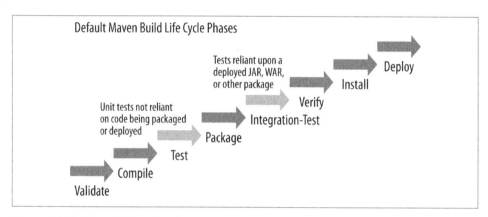

Figure 13-2. Maven life cycle phases

Maven's build life cycle is one of several ways that it promotes project uniformity. Unit testing and integration testing are included phases by default. They occur at a logical point in the process, and produce reports that can be published to a known location (the Maven site). The default phases provide a good basic framework, and Maven can be extended to handle other testing concerns if needed.

Maven can execute an application's unit tests periodically as part of the build process when called by a *continuous integration* (CI) server. There are many such servers available, including the open source Jenkins (*http://jenkins-ci.org*) or commercial products like Team City (*http://www.jetbrains.com/teamcity*) or Bamboo (*https://www.atlassian.com/software/bamboo*). A CI server also tends to promote standard software best practices. CI servers require the use of version control, encourage Maven assets to be properly maintained, and quickly reveal whether the build runs to completion in a reasonable amount of time.

Maven Reports (*http://bit.ly/1omkVJD*) can be published to a designated location by the CI server. These reports provides visibility as to the structure and quality of code. They also make the results of testing evident, including information on the number of tests written, their outcomes, performance, and overall code coverage.

The Goal of 100% Coverage

Once coverage reports begin being used, it is easy to focus on a goal of 100% test coverage to the exclusion of the value of the tests themselves. Coverage tools simply determine which code paths are executed. Some code paths might never be executed in practice; others might identify paths that do not merit testing consideration. Test *coverage* therefore does not indicate test *quality*. Testing by definition can prove only the presence of problems. It cannot prove that none exist. Putting undue emphasis on coverage report percentages can result in programmers making changes that do not benefit the software in any meaningful way.

The makers of JUnit recognize the tension of wanting comprehensive test coverage and also recognize that some code does not require testing. They cite a maxim on their FAQ (*http://bit.ly/NDpHFb*) that, like many highly subjective rules of thumb, rings true:

"Test until fear turns to boredom."

An organization can relatively quickly achieve Level 3 of the Capability Maturity Model in a preliminary way by using Maven with JUnit tests on all projects and adding each project to a CI server. Publishing reports indicating test results can contribute to clear communication beyond the development team about the state of the software and related tests. Although Maven includes capacity for handwritten documentation, it does not include mechanisms out of the box related to requirements or their relationship with the tests that are constructed.

An additional level of project review and process improvement can be accomplished by tracking project statistics *over time*. Data related to code complexity, test coverage, total lines of code, duplicated code, occurences of comments, and coding practice violations are objective measures that can be calculated and stored in a database using a product like SonarQube (*http://www.sonarqube.org*). This helps to identify trends indicating that a code base is improving or deteriorating.

BDD to Promote Uniform Processes

Informal testing is often done with the intention of finding bugs or causing a malfunction. Such tests can be retained and run regularly to ensure that problems are not reintroduced later. The creation of a set of unit tests that run regularly at build time can become an extremely effective safety net in the ongoing support of an application. But tests should not be viewed in isolation. They are integral to other aspects of software development. Consider this statement that appeared in *Code Complete* by Steve McConnell (Microsoft Press) in 1993: "As you're writing the routine, think about how you can test it. This is useful for you when you do unit testing and for the tester who tests your routine independently."

The insight to note is that *testing while designing* results in better, more structured code, better naming, and other benefits. It suggests a greater appreciation of the close connection between testing and other phases of the SDLC. It also anticipates more recent software testing practices.

Test-Driven Development (TDD) takes the idea of thinking about tests while writing code to a logical conclusion where tests are actually written prior to writing associated code. More specifically, TDD follows a cycle of writing an initially failed test case representing a new requirement followed by writing, coding, and refactoring that causes the test to pass.

Behavior-Driven Development (BDD) was subsequently introduced by Dan North to help developers better understand where to start in TDD, what to test, what should be put in a given test, and how to name them. BDD provides a narrative style that bridges the gap between code and human language. TDD is wide open about the style of tests being created, whereas BDD follows a TDD-style workflow but provides a more formal format for behavioral specification.

BDD requires more personal commitment across an organization to be successful but addresses several areas related to attaining higher CMM levels. BDD requires involvement and communication *across* teams. Quality assurance testers, developers, and business analysts must coordinate efforts in order to be effective. The benefit is the construction of relevant test cases directly tied to requirements and expressed in common, unambiguous shared language.

Maven, in conjunction with mature testing frameworks, introduces a coherent organization and structure to developer processes. Including BDD encourages communication and process refinement that extends beyond developers to those involved in testing and requirement-gathering and definition.

Testing Frameworks

Testing approaches tend to be codified in testing packages. JUnit (*http://junit.org*) is used for unit testing in Java, while Jasmine (*http://pivotal.github.io/jasmine*) is used for unit testing in JavaScript. JBehave (*http://jbehave.org*) is a Behavior-Driven Development framework for Java, while Cucumber (*http://cukes.info*) is Ruby-based.

JUnit

JUnit (*http://junit.org*) was originally written by Erich Gamma and Kent Beck. It has grown well beyond its humble beginnings to its rather sophisticated form in JUnit 4. In previous versions, unit tests belonged to specific object hierarchies and followed method-naming conventions in order to be functional. Like many projects in the Java ecosystem, JUnit 4 relies heavily on annotations. For instance, rather than having to explicitly create methods named `setUp()` and `tearDown()`, the `@before` and `@after` annotations are used to run code before and after test execution. The `@beforeClass` and `@afterClass` are also available to run code before and after test class instantiation. The `@Test` annotation replaces the former "test" naming convention for methods, and the `@ignore` directive can be used rather than the distasteful practice of commenting out tests. Since assertions can no longer be found in the object hierarchy, the static import of assertion classes is generally required. Assertions can also be used to specify parameterized tests or test suites.

TestNG

Another Java unit-test framework that has gained attention in the last few years is TestNG (*http://testng.org/doc/index.html*). It has similar functionality to JUnit at this point but included certain features, such as parameterized tests, before they became available in JUnit. It is also better able to manage *groups* of tests. This provides the flexibility required for effective integration testing. Some developers prefer TestNG's conventions and use of annotations over JUnit's as well.

Unit tests are generally written in the same programming language as the main application. There are obvious advantages to this because specific isolated methods or functions of the application can be easily exercised. As use of unit tests gained popularity, they served as a sort of documentation of usage among developers. A common response to the question, "How does this project work?" is, "See the unit tests." Unfortunately, programming languages do not help nonprogrammers clearly understand how a system functions. In many cases, requirements cannnot be derived from tests even by programmers who know the language.

Jasmine and Cucumber are written to provide BDD implementations that in large part support human languages. Jasmine uses JavaScript to specify tests, while Cucumber is basically an interpretter for a little language called Gherkin. Gherkin is a business-readable DSL to describe the behavior of software. The actual programming language code used to test an application is separated into external files.

Jasmine

Jasmine (*http://pivotal.github.io/jasmine*) expresses requirements using JavaScript strings and functions. It is small and lightweight, so it can be included easily in a project and run simply by opening a browser. The basic structure for a test includes a description of a test suite followed by blocks that contain expectations which are essentially assertions that return `true` or `false`. By convention, they reside in a JavaScript file with "Spec" in the name and are called by opening a *SpecRunner.html* that includes the dependent library:

```
describe("Suite Title Here", function() {
  it("Expectation (assertion) Title Here", function() {
    expect(true).toBe(true);
  });
});
```

While certainly closer to human language, the format of a test remains JavaScript, which to the untrained eye appears as human language riddled with a menagerie of symbols. An uninitiated individual might ask, "Why the sad winking emoticons on the last two lines?"

Cucumber

Cucumber relies on a DSL called Gherkin that closely resembles human language. The *login.feature* file, for example, is a structured text document with a few keywords and neat indentation:

```
Feature: Login
  As a user,
  I want to be able to log in with correct credentials

  Scenario: Success login

    Given correct credentials
    When I load the page
    Then I should be able to log in
```

The code implementation corresponding with each step in the feature is maintained separately:

```
...
Given(/^correct credentials$/) do
end
```

```
When(/^I load the page$/) do
  Capybara.visit(VALID_LOGIN_URL)
end

Then(/^I should be able to log in$/) do
  Capybara.page.has_content?('To NOT Do')
end
```

Regular expressions are used to match text in the test specification. Ruby code is used to perform the actual tests. In this example, Capybara is used for browser automation to open a browser, visit a URL, and determine if expected content is present.

From The Cucumber Book (*http://bit.ly/prag-cucumber*)

Cucumber helps facilitate the discovery and use of a ubiquitous language within the team, by giving the two sides of the linguistic divide a place where they can meet. Cucumber tests interact directly with the developers' code, but they're written in a medium and language business stakeholders can understand. By working together to write these tests—*specifying collaboratively*—not only do the team members decide what behavior they need to implement next, but they learn how to describe that behavior in a common language that everyone understands.

Test frameworks can be invoked directly or by build tools. The project in this chapter includes examples of tests run as part of a Maven build.

Project

The project (*http://bit.ly/1iPUKYp*) for this chapter demonstrates how JUnit and Jasmine tests can be integrated into a Maven project build. It also includes Cucumber tests that use Capybara to call Selenium as an example of BDD applied to browser-automated functional testing.

Rather than implementing something so common and mundane as a "TODO list" application, the project will consist of a "To NOT do list" web application, as shown in Figure 13-3. Such an application can be used to list things that one intends to cease doing or avoid. Fascinatingly refreshing and novel, don't you think?

The project will demonstrate how various testing frameworks can be called from Maven throughout the course of a build. The end result is a site that includes reports on tests that have been run, as well as related documentation.

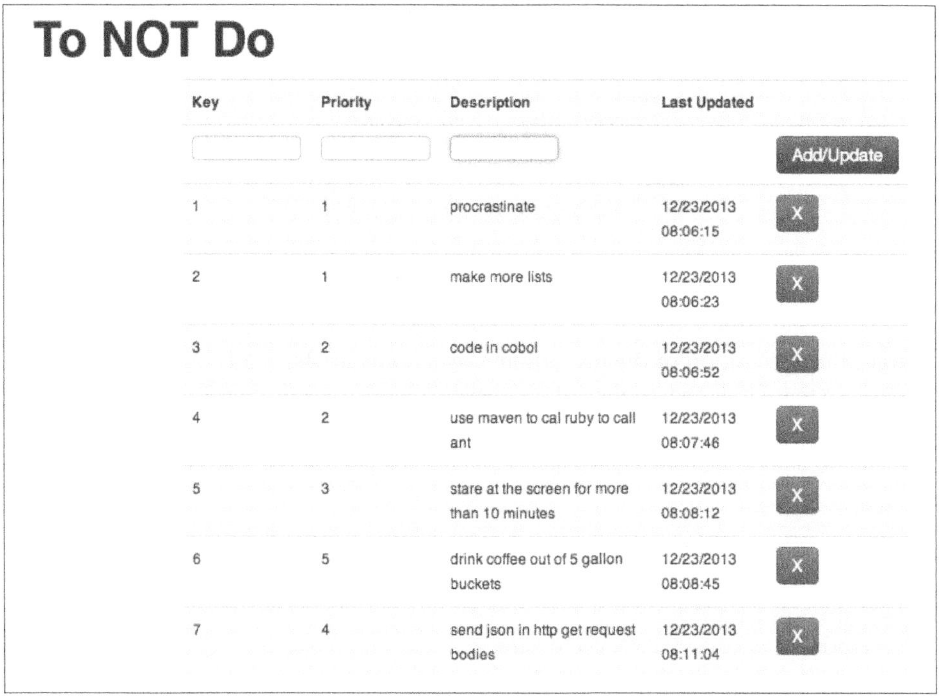

To NOT Do

Key	Priority	Description	Last Updated	
				Add/Update
1	1	procrastinate	12/23/2013 08:06:15	X
2	1	make more lists	12/23/2013 08:06:23	X
3	2	code in cobol	12/23/2013 08:06:52	X
4	2	use maven to cal ruby to call ant	12/23/2013 08:07:46	X
5	3	stare at the screen for more than 10 minutes	12/23/2013 08:08:12	X
6	5	drink coffee out of 5 gallon buckets	12/23/2013 08:08:45	X
7	4	send json in http get request bodies	12/23/2013 08:11:04	X

Figure 13-3. To Not Do web application

JUnit

The starting point for determining project configuration for any Maven project is the *pom.xml*. The dependencies section includes an entry for JUnit that is restricted to test scope:

```
<groupId>junit</groupId>
<artifactId>junit</artifactId>
<version>4.11</version>
<scope>test</scope>
```

Jasmine

In the same way that the JUnit module is added to the *pom.xml* for Java testing, a dependency needs to be added to support JavaScript testing. Justin Searls maintains the Jasmine plug-in used in the project:

```
<groupId>com.github.searls</groupId>
<artifactId>jasmine-maven-plugin</artifactId>
<version>1.3.1.3</version>
```

A sample test included in the project validates the presence and functionality of a dependent library:

```
describe("Validate moment.min.js", function() {

    it("expects moment.min.js to be functional", function() {
            expect(
                moment("20111031", "YYYYMMDD").
                format('MMMM Do YYYY, h:mm:ss a')
            ).toBe(
                    "October 31st 2011, 12:00:00 am"
            );
        });

});
```

Besides the declaration of the preceding Maven coordinates, additional configuration is required to include the JavaScript files used. When correctly configured, the tests will be run when mvn install is executed:

```
...
[INFO]

J A S M I N E    S P E C S

[INFO]
Suite Title Here
  Expectation (assertion) Title Here

Validate moment.min.js
  expects moment.min.js to be functional

Results: 2 specs, 0 failures
...
```

The Jasmine plug-in is a perfect solution in many cases. However, browser-specific code cannot be exercised, which limits its applicability. Browser automation is better suited for testing requirements involving extensive DOM manipulation. A solution like Selenium (*http://docs.seleniumhq.org*) can be used to drive various browsers. Browser automation allows each browser's unique idiosyncrasies to be uncovered. Selenium can be used directly within Java unit tests, but in many cases, automating a browser suggests higher-level functional or integration testing. It is so effective for controlling browsers that higher-level libraries such as Capybara (*http://jnicklas.github.io/capybara*) rely on Selenium as a driver implementation. The following Cucumber example (*http://cukes.info*) uses Capybara in this very manner.

Cucumber

The */ruby* directory contains a Ruby-based version of the Cucumber login test. The Gemfile lists the dependencies, and the *webapp_steps.rb* contains the code to process the specifications defined in the feature files. Start the application in one OS session:

```
mvn jetty:run
```

In a second session, run Cucumber:

```
cd ruby
cucumber
```

The features that have been specified will be run with output that reflects the origin of each step being executed, as shown in Figure 13-4.

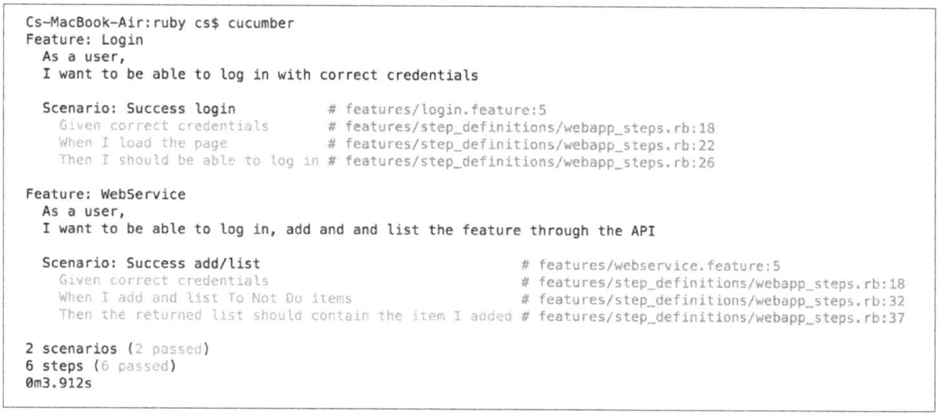

```
Cs-MacBook-Air:ruby cs$ cucumber
Feature: Login
  As a user,
  I want to be able to log in with correct credentials

  Scenario: Success login              # features/login.feature:5
    Given correct credentials          # features/step_definitions/webapp_steps.rb:18
    When I load the page               # features/step_definitions/webapp_steps.rb:22
    Then I should be able to log in    # features/step_definitions/webapp_steps.rb:26

Feature: WebService
  As a user,
  I want to be able to log in, add and and list the feature through the API

  Scenario: Success add/list                                    # features/webservice.feature:5
    Given correct credentials                                   # features/step_definitions/webapp_steps.rb:18
    When I add and list To Not Do items                         # features/step_definitions/webapp_steps.rb:32
    Then the returned list should contain the item I added      # features/step_definitions/webapp_steps.rb:37

2 scenarios (2 passed)
6 steps (6 passed)
0m3.912s
```

Figure 13-4. Cucumber run

Maven Site Reports

The *pom.xml* included in this chapter is quite a bit longer than the ones associated with other projects in this book. Numerous dependencies and plug-ins are not associated with the core application but with testing. In addition, many of the configuration options are used to populate information in a Maven project site.

The Maven Site plug-in is used to generate a site and run it on port 8080:

```
mvn site:site
...
mvn site:run
```

The Maven */site/* directory can contain a variety of resources to customize the site. In Figure 13-5, a *site.xml* has been added to use a custom "skin" to provide a different style to the site.

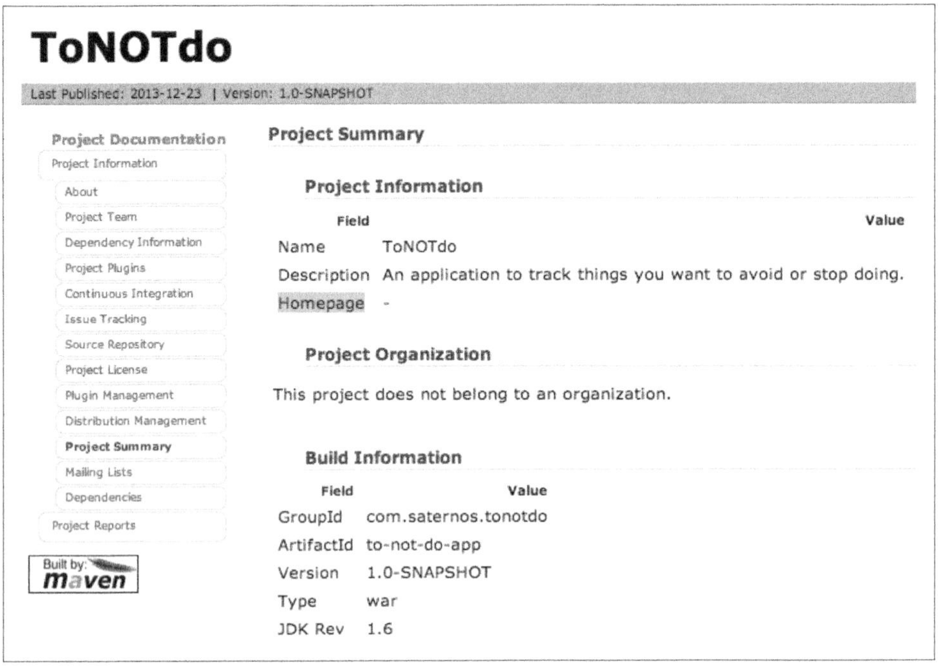

ToNOTdo

Last Published: 2013-12-23 | Version: 1.0-SNAPSHOT

Project Documentation

Project Information

- About
- Project Team
- Dependency Information
- Project Plugins
- Continuous Integration
- Issue Tracking
- Source Repository
- Project License
- Plugin Management
- Distribution Management
- **Project Summary**
- Mailing Lists
- Dependencies

Project Reports

Built by:
maven

Project Summary

Project Information

Field	Value
Name	ToNOTdo
Description	An application to track things you want to avoid or stop doing.
Homepage	-

Project Organization

This project does not belong to an organization.

Build Information

Field	Value
GroupId	com.saternos.tonotdo
ArtifactId	to-not-do-app
Version	1.0-SNAPSHOT
Type	war
JDK Rev	1.6

Figure 13-5. To Not Do Maven site

Conclusion

Scalability in *software* requires well-architected, predictable, performant systems. Testing provides the means of ensuring that such systems are developed. Unit tests, Maven, and systems related to continuous integration promote the creation of such systems by clarifying the development process and making visible the state of an application.

Scalability of an *organization* requires defined processes and clear communication. The same tools listed above, along with an approach like BDD, give testing a definitive social benefit for a team that will tend to feed back into the quality of the software itself.

Software testing provides objective support based on the scientific method and practices that have been refined in the physical sciences. Properly conducted, it also provides immense practical value in demonstrating the quality and performance of an application and encouraging a common understanding of how requirements have been implemented.

## CHAPTER 14

Conclusion

Life is a distributed object system. However, communication among humans is a distributed hypermedia system where the mind's intellect, voice+gestures, eyes+ears, and imagination are all components.

—Roy T. Fielding

It is fascinating to set out to write a book with a general plan in mind and then review the final result. Although different than what I initially envisioned, this book does remain faithful to a theme introduced early on—that of change. The introduction pointed out that there has been tremendous change in the world due to technological innovation and spoke to a few specific areas where this is evident. If anything, the rate of change has been increasing in recent years. It is common for a large-scale project to be considered a legacy application by the time the product is launched.

Extreme reactions like trying to apprehend all of the new innovations or ignoring them altogether are obviously shortsighted and futile. A better response is to identify which shifts are truly significant game changers. The ride through this book highlights some of the areas of software development encountered by Java developers that require a closer look. Two basic sources for insights as to how to react to the seismic shifts that continue to affect web development are the wider development community and the insights of earlier generations.

Community

Other programming communities have significantly different perspectives and can therefore inspire innovations different than those seen among the Java development community. On the whole, Java developers are rather well-established, entrenched, and somewhat corporate. They have much to learn from (and much to offer to) innovative communities that have grown up around JavaScript, Ruby, and Python, among others.

Many great ideas are widely applicable to areas beyond their initial implementation. A novelty in one setting can be a revolutionary idea in another.

History

The second area is to cultivate an awareness of the past. Despite the tendency of modern culture to uncritically adopt whatever is new, it is better to be open to innovation while evaluating it with a broader view. Computer science and software development has a relatively short but rich history. Alan Kay (*http://ubm.io/1eQNBrD*), the computer scientist who coined the phrase "object-oriented" and led development of Smalltalk, has pointed out (*http://bit.ly/1eUUzKE*) the tendency of much of modern computer science and software development to be a manifestation of pop culture (*http://ubm.io/1eQNBrD*), unconcerned with and unaware of what has come before. Many of the most significant and enduring ideas have their origins years or even decades ago. Better to stand on the shoulders of giants and learn from the mistakes of the past whenever possible:

> In the last 25 years or so, we actually got something like a pop culture, similar to what happened when television came on the scene and some of its inventors thought it would be a way of getting Shakespeare to the masses. But they forgot that you have to be more sophisticated and have more perspective to understand Shakespeare. What television was able to do was to capture people as they were.

> So I think the lack of a real computer science today, and the lack of real software engineering today, is partly due to this pop culture.

> — Alan Kay

Coda

I hope you have learned a thing or two from this book. This is an exciting time to be working in software development, as times of change are times of unprecedented opportunity. There is plenty of new technology and no end of problems to which it can be applied. Reading this book and working with the projects can be a step, hopefully the first of many for you, that will be personally rewarding and result in the creation of systems that will make the world better. I will leave you with a thought from the great mathematician and teacher George Pólya who, though an intellectual, recognized the deeply human and personal dimension related to solving problems, which is also applicable to the creative work of software development:

> It would be a mistake to think that solving problems is a purely "intellectual affair"; determination and emotions play an important role. Lukewarm determination and sleepy consent to do a little something may be enough for a routine problem in the classroom. But, to solve a serious scientific problem, will power is needed that can outlast years of toil and bitter disappointment...Teaching to solve problems is education of the will.

> — George Pólya

JRuby IRB and Java API

Human-machine interface styles have varied over time, based on the nature of the device in question as well as somewhat arbitrary trends. Command-Line Interfaces (or CLIs) were the primary means of interacting with operating systems before the 1990s. After that time, they were overshadowed by graphical operating systems and the visually dominated Internet. Despite their relatively humble appearance, CLIs remain popular due to functionality they provide that is not readily available through a GUI.

The pattern of interaction provided by a CLI reflects the functionality of teleprinters (gizmos that evolved from telegraph machines used to send typed messages). A CLI is more reliant on a user's typing ability than a corresponding GUI. This limitation is also an advantage in that CLIs lend themselves to scripting. Most programmers have some experience in a CLI through the command-line shell of whatever operating system they are using. When tasks become more involved, it is simple to bundle a set of commands together into a script. This capability has resulted in many scripting languages, including their own CLIs as an execution environment.

A CLI might also be referred to as a REPL (Read-Eval-Print Loop) or a language shell. Whatever you call them, they are invaluable for exploring language features and getting immediate feedback on the effect of running a given expression or command.

Though Java itself does not include a CLI (Beanshell (*http://www.beanshell.org*) is the closest equivalent), many of the languages supported on the JVM do include (but are not limited to) JRuby, Jython, and Groovy. The close integration of JVM languages with Java makes it possible to interact through CLIs for each of these languages with native Java classes and modules. This is a significantly different style of workflow that can be very helpful when experimenting and debugging. In this chapter, JRuby's IRB (Interactive Ruby shell) is used to execute SQL queries through JDBC connections to a number of Java-based databases.

Why Not IRS?

You might wonder why Ruby does not call its command-line interface IRS (Interactive Ruby Shell). The standard file extension for Ruby programs is *.rb*. Hence "Interactive" plus "RB" results in IRB.

Setup Using Gradle

Gradle will be used to download the set of Java project dependencies used in the following scripts. Note that this is simply a convenience; there is no necessary connection between a build tool like Gradle and a CLI. This Gradle build file was initially generated using `gradle setupBuild`. The resulting *build.gradle* file included comments related to usage. The file was then modified to include the modules needed as well as relevant plug-ins and the repository where they are hosted:

```
apply plugin:'java'
apply plugin:'application'

repositories{mavenCentral()}

dependencies{
    compile 'org.slf4j:slf4j-api:1.7.5'
    compile 'hsqldb:hsqldb:1.8.0.10'
    compile 'com.h2database:h2:1.3.172'
        compile 'net.sf.opencsv:opencsv:2.3'
        compile 'commons-io:commons-io:2.4'
        compile 'org.apache.derby:derby:10.10.1.1'
    testCompile "junit:junit:4.11"
}
```

With the build file defined, the project can be built using `gradle build`. The necessary JARs will be added to your local repository. Again, Gradle is not specifically required for this task. You could instead use Maven, or even manually locate and download each JAR used. Gradle was selected because of its minimal syntax (compared to Maven) and because manually downloading files is error-prone and tedious.

JRuby IRB

Because the following example uses Java classes (the database implementations and JDBC), a Java-based version of Ruby is required. Other implementations will not function. If you are using RVM, install JRuby (if necessary) and select it for use:

```
$ rvm use jruby 1.7.4
```

Install the bundler gem if you have not yet done so (version 1.3.5 was used in this example). When this is available, run `bundle init` to create the Gemfile used by bundle. Add the following three lines:

```
gem 'jdbc-derby', '10.9.1.0'
gem 'jdbc-h2', '1.3.170.1'
gem 'jdbc-hsqldb', '2.2.9.1'
```

These gems wrap the JDBC drivers used by JRuby. Run `bundle` to install these (Ruby) dependencies.

We have seen Java dependencies managed by Gradle, and JRuby dependencies managed by bundler. It is also possible to reference Java JARs directly from JRuby. For convenience, copy the JAR (included in the Gradle init) in a lib directory under our current location. The file will be inside your local Gradle repository:

```
$ find ~/.gradle -name opencsv-2.3.jar

$ mkdir lib

$ cp <path to jar file from find command>opencsv-2.3.jar lib
```

The JAR will be accessed from within JRuby using the `require` keyword (which is generally used for importing Ruby files).

Intro to IRB

Logging in to IRB will bring you to a prompt. The specific prompt will vary depending on the version of Ruby you are using:

```
$ irb
jruby-1.7.4 :001 >
```

From this prompt, you can enter an expression and see its immediate evaluation:

```
2.0.0-p247 :001 > 1 + 4
 => 5
```

You can also inspect objects and find out what functionality they offer. Reflection in Java allows objects to be explored and manipulated but is also verbose and complex. By contrast, Ruby provides straightforward access to dynamically interrogate and alter objects. It is well known for its meta-programming capabilities due to its flexibility in this regard:

```
2.0.0-p247 :002 > "Hello World".class
 => String

2.0.0-p247 :014 > "Hello World".methods.grep(/sp/).sort
 => [:display, :inspect, :respond_to?, :split]

2.0.0-p247 :021 > "Hello World".split
 => ["Hello", "World"]
```

For the remaining examples, the prompt and the result will be omitted. But the feedback provided immediately after running a command is the real value of interacting in irb and is best experienced to be fully appreciated.

In the preceding example, Hello World is a string (but is not assigned to any particular variable). It has a large number of methods available, so the example filters (using grep) and orders the ones that contain sp. Finally, having found a method in this manner, we can actually call it on the object (the Hello World string) and see its effect. This approach is not a substitute for referencing documentation, but does render many of the lookups you do otherwise unnecessary.

Java-Based Relational Databases

Within an irb session, we can now explore the APIs available for several Java-based relational databases. If you have ever written a Java class that uses JDBC, you will undoubtedly recall that there is a fair amount of boilerplate code required. Beyond the standard Java requirements (defining a class with a main method), you need to write a good deal of code related to exception handling (import statements, throws clauses in method declarations, try/catch blocks). Add in the additional syntax required for explicitly typing, a bit of output, and a few comments, and a seemingly simple class can become rather bloated. Fortunately, Ruby's syntax is concise, and the interactive environment makes it easy to test drive the APIs.

The three databases we will look at are H2, HSQLDB, and Derby. They are similar from the outside, differing in specific implementation and storage mechanisms, performance, and open source licensing options. Each is accessible via JDBC, and in an irb session we will test each type of SQL statement available, as shown in Table A-1.

Table A-1. SQL statement types

Type	Example	Description
Query	SELECT	Retrieve data
DDL	CREATE, DROP	Data definition language (create, alter, or replace a database object)
DML	INSERT, UPDATE, DELETE	Data manipulation language (modify data)

As it turns out, there are actually some slight variations between databases that are only evident when you actually interact with them (such as SQL syntax, connection strings, and closing of result sets).

To make these examples a bit more concise, a common code required for each can be added to a file and loaded from within irb. This includes code to make Java available, load up the opencsv JAR (used to quickly render a result set as comma-separated values), and add functions to execute SQL (queries, DML, and DDL) and to display SQL result sets:

```
require 'java'
require 'lib/opencsv-2.3.jar'

TEMP_FILE="temp.csv"

def displayResultSet(r)
                writer = Java.AuComBytecodeOpencsv::CSVWriter.new(
                        java.io.FileWriter.new(TEMP_FILE),
                        java.lang.String.new("\t").charAt(0)
                )
                writer.writeAll(r, true)
                writer.close()
    File.open(TEMP_FILE).readlines.each{|line|puts line}
    `rm #{TEMP_FILE}`
end

def exec(statement, conn)
  puts statement
  conn.createStatement().execute(statement)
end

def execQuery(statement, conn)
  puts statement
  conn.createStatement().executeQuery(statement);
end
```

This file is actually loaded into the environment by running load 'dbutils.rb'.

H2

Thomas Mueller created H2 (*http://h2database.com*) and was also heavily involved in the development of HSQLDB. In the following example, a username of sa with a blank password is used to connect to a database named test where SQL statements are then executed. Also note that no VARCHAR length is specified for the name column when the table is created:

```
load 'dbutils.rb'

require 'jdbc/h2'
Jdbc::H2.load_driver

conn = java.sql.DriverManager.getConnection('jdbc:h2:test', "sa", "")
# VARCHAR does not require a length
exec("CREATE TABLE test (id int, name varchar)", conn)
exec("INSERT INTO test(id, name) VALUES (1, 'a')", conn)
displayResultSet(execQuery('select * from test', conn))
exec("DROP TABLE test", conn)
conn.close()
```

HSQLDB

HSQLDB (*http://hsqldb.org*) is known for its inclusion in open source projects like OpenOffice as well as commercial products like Mathematica. Unlike H2, a username and password are not required when getting the connection, and a VARCHAR length is required in the name column:

```
load 'dbutils.rb'

require 'jdbc/hsqldb'
Jdbc::HSQLDB.load_driver

conn = java.sql.DriverManager.getConnection('jdbc:hsqldb:test')
exec("CREATE TABLE test (id int, name varchar(10))", conn)
exec("INSERT INTO test(id, name) VALUES (1, 'a')", conn)
displayResultSet(execQuery('select * from test', conn))
exec("DROP TABLE test", conn)
conn.close()
```

Derby

Derby (*http://db.apache.org/derby*) is an Apache project whose lineage goes back to the 1990s. It has continued through various incarnations at CloudScape, Informix, and IBM. Since Java 6, Sun (later acquired by Oracle) included Derby in the JDK as Java DB. The `create=true` attribute in the JDBC connection string indicates that a database be created if it does not exist when the connection is requested. In addition, Derby requires a result set to be explicitly closed prior to dropping a table that references it:

```
load 'dbutils.rb'

require 'jdbc/derby'
Jdbc::Derby.load_driver

conn = java.sql.DriverManager.getConnection('jdbc:derby:test;create=true')
exec("CREATE TABLE test (id int, name varchar(10))", conn)
exec("INSERT INTO test(id, name) VALUES (1, 'a')", conn)
r = execQuery('select * from test', conn)
displayResultSet(r)
r.close()
exec("DROP TABLE test", conn)
conn.close()
```

Although relational databases were the focus of the previous example, it should be obvious that *any* Java library can be accessed via a script and explored using a similar process.

Conclusion

The immediate feedback provided by CLIs makes them a particularly effective tool despite the move toward graphical methods. Scripts can be constructed by iterative experiments within a CLI, and this process removes not only the traditional build step but even the need to specifically execute a source file. This type of interaction is well understood by many developers, but those who have focused on Java might have had limited exposure. The JavaScript console available in modern web browsers is a modern implementation of a CLI, and as this chapter illustrates, similar server-side processing is available to Java programmers with just a bit of initial setup.

RESTful Web API Summary

HTTP 1.1 Request Methods

Table B-1 summarizes the HTTP 1.1 request methods (*http://bit.ly/1kCmS4w*).

Table B-1. HTTP 1.1. request methods

HTTP verb	Action to take on a resource	REST action
GET	Retrieve	Like SQL SELECT
HEAD	Retrieve without response body	LIKE SQL SELECT 1
POST	Create (or append)	Like SQL INSERT
PUT	Update (or create) of full resource	Like SQL UPDATE (or INSERT if doesn't exist)
PATCH	Partial update	Like SQL UPDATE (part of a resource)
DELETE	Delete	Like SQL DELETE
TRACE	Echo request	Diagnostic to determine changes made by intermediate servers
OPTIONS	Return supported methods	Determine which HTTP methods are allowed for the resource
CONNECT	Support for HTTP tunneling	Support HTTP tunneling

HTTP 1.1 Response Codes

Tables B-2 through B-6 summarize the HTTP 1.1 status codes (*http://bit.ly/1dkzBVq*).

Table B-2. Informational status codes 1xx

Code	Meaning	Description
100	Continue	Interim response indicating that part of the request has been received (and not yet rejected by the server)
101	Switching Protocols	Server switching to protocols defined by the response Upgrade header

Table B-3. Successful status codes 2xx

Code	Meaning	Description
200	OK	Accepted
201	Created	A new resource is being created
202	Accepted	Accepted, but processing not complete
203	Non-Authoritative Information	Subset or superset of metadata returned in the entity header
204	No Content	No response body included
205	Reset Content	Client should initiate a request to view the resource associated with the initial request
206	Partial Content	Response to a request that included a range header

Table B-4. Redirection status codes 3xx

Code	Meaning	Description
300	Multiple Choices	Resource is available in multiple representations in different locations
301	Moved Permanently	Resource has been assigned a new permanent URI
302	Found	Resource has been assigned a new temporary URI
303	See Other	The response to the request is available under a different URI
304	Not Modified	Response to a conditional GET request where the document has not been modified
305	Use Proxy	Requested resource is accessible through a returned URI of the proxy
306	(Unused)	Not used in current HTTP version
307	Temporary Redirect	The requested resource resides temporarily under a different URI

Table B-5. Client error status codes 4xx

Code	Meaning	Description
400	Bad Request	Request not understood
401	Unauthorized	Request not authorized
402	Payment Required	Reserved for future use
403	Forbidden	Request not allowed (even with additional authorization)
404	Not Found	Resource not found
405	Method Not Allowed	Invalid HTTP method for the specified URL
406	Not Acceptable	Resource can be generated using the content specified in the accept headers
407	Proxy Authentication Required	Request not authorized (authentication required through a proxy)
408	Request Timeout	Client did not make a request in the time specified by the server
409	Conflict	Request not completed due to the current state of the resource (e.g., changing due to a PUT)
410	Gone	Resource is no longer available
411	Length Required	Content-length header required
412	Precondition Failed	A precondition in the request-header fields evaluated to false

Code	Meaning	Description
413	Request Entity Too Large	Request entity is larger than the server-specified threshold
414	Request-URI Too Long	Request URI is longer than the server-specified threshold
415	Unsupported Media Type	Format not supported
416	Requested Range Not Satisfiable	Content range specified in the header could not be processed
417	Expectation Failed	An expectation in the request-header fields not met

Table B-6. Server error status codes 5xx

Code	Meaning	Description
500	Internal Server Error	Unexpected error condition on the server
501	Not Implemented	Functionality not supported
502	Bad Gateway	The server acting as a proxy received an invalid response from an upstream server
503	Service Unavailable	Server unavailable due to a temporary condition
504	Gateway Timeout	The server acting as a proxy did not receive a timely response from an upstream server
505	HTTP Version Not Supported	HTTP protocol version in the request message not supported

Curl for Web APIs

The Curl (*http://curl.haxx.se*) utility can transfer data to or from a server using a variety of different protocols. A small subset of the command-line options are sufficient for most operations related to RESTful web APIs over HTTP, as shown in Table B-7.

Table B-7. Selected HTTP-related Curl options

Option	Short name	Description
-H	Header	Specify an HTTP header
-d	Data	Sends the specified string data to the server
-s	Silent option	Don't show progress meter or error messages
-L	Location	If the server responds with a location header and a 3xx response code, redo the request on the new location (limit the redirects with --max-redirs)
-X	Execute option	Specify the HTTP request method
-A	Agent	Specify the user agent
-b	Cookie	Specify a cookie (easier to remember using --cookie rather than -b)
-o	Output	Output to a file (or -O to write to a file named the same as the remote one requested)

Sample call:

```
curl -s -H "Accept: application/json" \
-H "Content-Type: application/json" \
http://localhost:8080/hello/world \
-X PUT -d '{"hello": "world"}'
```

JSON Syntax

JSON is a simple data exchange format which is a subset of JavaScript.

JSON Types

- Array (ordered, comma-separated values enclosed in square brackets)
- Object (an unordered, comma-separated collection of key:value pairs)
- Number
- String
- Boolean
- Null

Railroad Diagrams

The following railroad diagrams (*http://bottlecaps.de/rr/ui*) give more a formal description of the subset of JavaScript that constitutes the JSON data exchange format.

Object

An JSON object is a set of zero or more pairs of strings with associated values enclosed in brackets. Each string is followed by a colon, followed by its associated value. If there is more than one string-value pair, they are separated by commas. See Figure B-1.

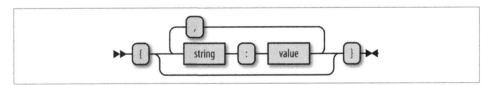

Figure B-1. Object

Array

A JSON array is a comma-separated list of values enclosed in square brackets. See Figure B-2.

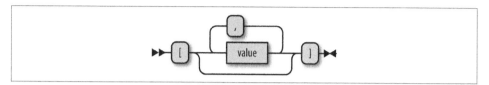

Figure B-2. Array

Value

A value can be a string, number, object, array, true, false, or null. See Figure B-3.

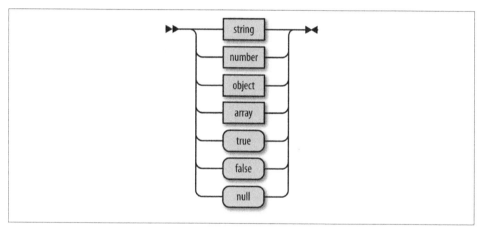

Figure B-3. Value

References

Barrett, Daniel J. *Linux Pocket Guide, Essential Commands*. Sebastopol: O'Reilly Media, 2004.

Burke, Bill. *RESTful Java with JAX-RS*. Sebastopol: O'Reilly Media, 2009.

Crockford, Douglas. *JavaScript: The Good Parts*. Sebastopol: O'Reilly Media, 2008.

Fogus, Michael, and Chris Houser. *The Joy of Clojure*. Stamford: Manning Publications, 2011.

Hashimoto, Mitchell. *Vagrant: Up and Running*. Sebastopol: O'Reilly Media, 2013.

McConnell, Steve. *Code Complete: A Practical Handbook of Software Construction*. Redmond: Microsoft Press, 2004.

Pólya, George. *How to Solve It: A New Aspect of Mathematical Method*. Princeton: Princeton Science Library, 2004.

Resig, John and Bear Bibeault. *Secrets of the JavaScript Ninja*. Stamford: Manning Publications, 2012.

Sonatype Company. *Maven: The Definitive Guide*. Sebastopol: O'Reilly Media, 2008.

Thomas, Dave, with Chad Fowler and Andy Hunt. *Programming Ruby*. The Pragmatic Programmers, LLC, 2004.

Wynne, Matt, and Aslak Hellesøy. *The Cucumber Book: Behaviour-Driven Development for Testers and Developers*. The Pragmatic Programmers, LLC, 2010.

Zakas, Nicholas Z. *Professional JavaScript for Web Developers*. Indianapolis: Wrox Press, 2005.

Index

We'd like to hear your suggestions for improving our indexes. Send email to index@oreilly.com.

BOM (Browser Object Model), 14
Bootstrap, 79
bottom values, 27
browsers
    avoiding refresh, 105
    clearing the cache, 30
    cross-browser compatibility, 143
    for JavaScript development, 29
    in client-side frameworks, 76
    JavaScript compatability libraries, 80
    same origin policy, 45
builders, 186
BuiltWith, 81

C

cacheability, 42
caching, 84
call() method, 22
camel case, 131
Capability Maturity Model (CMM), 200
Capistrano, 180
CDNs (Content Delivery Networks), 53, 84
cfengine, 180, 188
Chaos Monkey, 121, 199
Chef, 187
Chrome, 30
Chrome plug-ins, 105
classes
    JavaScript vs. Java, 23
    nouns as, 127
classical inheritance, 23
CLASSPATH entries, 63
client-server web applications
    advantages of
        application performance, 9
        code organization, 8
        developer productivity, 9, 109
        open-source APIs, 9
        prototyping, 9
        software architecture, 8
    alignment with Web architecture, 5–7
    challenges of, 10
    drawbacks of SOAP for, 38
    forces behind development
        overview of, 1
        software development, 4
        technology, 3
        web users, 2
    history of shift to, 124

technologies related to, 124
    vs. server-driven, 7
client-side frameworks
    Angular, 155
    asset pipelines, 84
    client-side templating, 84
    development workflow, 85, 88
    JavaScript libraries/frameworks
        additional options for, 81
        browser compatibility, 80
        GitHub resources, 82
        most popular, 81
        MV* frameworks, 80
        simplicity of, 79
    jQuery, 140
    overview of, 75
    project example, 86
    Responsive Web Design (RWD)
        components of, 78
        concept of, 78
        HTML5 boilerplate, 79
        Twitter Bootstrap, 79
    starter projects
        application requirements, 76
        browser considerations, 76
        building blocks to consider, 75
        design/flexibility considerations, 76
        GitHub resources, 82
        IDE-generated, 83
        impact of initial choices, 77, 116
        repository download, 82
        starter site download, 83
Clojure, 72, 73
Close, Tyler, 50
closures, 21
cloud-based environment
    JEE deployments and, 170
    maintaining state in, 10
    sophistication of, 118
    testing in, 199
clustering, 180
code compilation, 24, 31, 58, 85
code comprehension, 57
code editors, 120
code on demand, 43
code organization
    file interdependencies, 27
    modular approach to, 8
coding style, in JavaScript, 29

About the Author

Casimir Saternos has been developing software for more than a decade. He has written articles that have appeared in *Java Magazine* and the Oracle Technology Network and has collaborated on several projects for Peepcode screencasts. He spends a good deal of time these days creating web applications using Java, Ruby, and any other technology that happens to apply.

Colophon

The animal on the cover of *Client-Server Web Apps with JavaScript and Java* is a large Indian civet (*Viverra zibetha*). These mammals range throughout grasslands and dense forested areas in southeast Asia, including Myanmar, Thailand, Cambodia, Malaysia, and southern China.

A solitary animal, the large Indian civet is most active at night, when it hunts prey like birds, snakes, frogs, and smaller mammals. It will also eat fruit and roots, but its diet is mainly carnivorous. It sleeps in its burrow (often a hole that has been dug and abandoned by another animal) during the day.

Large Indian civets range from 20-37 inches in length, not including their tails. Their fur is gray-brown, with black stripes on the neck and tail. Females are slightly smaller than males, and breed at any time—generally, they have two litters a year, and raise their offspring alone.

Civet is also the name of the musk these animals excrete to mark their territory. Diluted (and most often collected from the African civet), it has been used as a perfume ingredient for centuries. A synthetic version is used in many modern products, but several species of civet are still illegally trapped for their meat and scent glands.

The cover image is from Lydekker's *Natural History*. The cover fonts are URW Typewriter and Guardian Sans. The text font is Adobe Minion Pro; the heading font is Adobe Myriad Condensed; and the code font is Dalton Maag's Ubuntu Mono.

Have it your way.

O'Reilly eBooks

- Lifetime access to the book when you buy through oreilly.com
- Provided in up to four DRM-free file formats, for use on the devices of your choice: PDF, .epub, Kindle-compatible .mobi, and Android .apk
- Fully searchable, with copy-and-paste and print functionality
- Alerts when files are updated with corrections and additions

oreilly.com/ebooks/

Safari Books Online

- Access the contents and quickly search over 7000 books on technology, business, and certification guides
- Learn from expert video tutorials, and explore thousands of hours of video on technology and design topics
- Download whole books or chapters in PDF format, at no extra cost, to print or read on the go
- Get early access to books as they're being written
- Interact directly with authors of upcoming books
- Save up to 35% on O'Reilly print books

See the complete Safari Library at safari.oreilly.com

O'REILLY®

Spreading the knowledge of innovators.   oreilly.com

©2011 O'Reilly Media, Inc. O'Reilly logo is a registered trademark of O'Reilly Media, Inc. 00000

Get even more for your money.

Join the O'Reilly Community, and register the O'Reilly books you own. It's free, and you'll get:

- $4.99 ebook upgrade offer
- 40% upgrade offer on O'Reilly print books
- Membership discounts on books and events
- Free lifetime updates to ebooks and videos
- Multiple ebook formats, DRM FREE
- Participation in the O'Reilly community
- Newsletters
- Account management
- 100% Satisfaction Guarantee

Signing up is easy:

1. **Go to: oreilly.com/go/register**
2. **Create an O'Reilly login.**
3. **Provide your address.**
4. **Register your books.**

Note: English-language books only

To order books online:
oreilly.com/store

For questions about products or an order:
orders@oreilly.com

To sign up to get topic-specific email announcements and/or news about upcoming books, conferences, special offers, and new technologies:
elists@oreilly.com

For technical questions about book content:
booktech@oreilly.com

To submit new book proposals to our editors:
proposals@oreilly.com

O'Reilly books are available in multiple DRM-free ebook formats. For more information:
oreilly.com/ebooks

O'REILLY®

Spreading the knowledge of innovators

oreilly.com

©2010 O'Reilly Media, Inc. O'Reilly logo is a registered trademark of O'Reilly Media, Inc. 00000

CPSIA information can be obtained at www.ICGtesting.com
Printed in the USA
BVOW10s1037010414

349340BV00005B/7/P

9 781449 369330